ACTA UNIVERSITATIS UPSALIENSIS
Studia Doctrinae Christianae Upsaliensia
22

Sten M. Philipson

A METAPHYSICS FOR THEOLOGY

A Study of some Problems
in the Later Philosophy of

ALFRED NORTH WHITEHEAD

and its Application to Issues
in Contemporary Theology

UPPSALA 1982

Almqvist & Wiksell International
Stockholm – Sweden

Humanities Press
N. J. – U. S. A.

Doctoral Thesis at the University of Uppsala 1982

© 1982 Sten M. Philipson
ISBN 91-554-1246-7
ISSN 0585-508X
ISBN 0-391-02586-6 (in the U. S. A.)

Ƀ
1674
.W354
P47
1982

Philipson, S. M., 1982, A Metaphysics for Theology; A Study of some Problems in the Later Philosophy of Alfred North Whitehead and its Application to Issues in Contemporary Theology. *Studia Doctrinae Christianae Upsaliensis* 22, 173 pp. Uppsala 1982, ISBN 91-554-1246-7. ISSN 0585-508X. ISBN 0-391-02586-6 (in the U. S. A.).

Abstract
Without a satisfactory metaphysics, assertions about God will be unintelligible and impossible to assess. Therefore, the basic question of the present study is: what is an appropriate metaphysics? The author approaches this question by focusing upon Alfred North Whitehead's metaphysical system, hoping thereby to disclose some important problems that must be considered in an attempt to answer the basic question. The first part of the study is a presentation of Whitehead's system, followed by a critical discussion of certain of its features. The author argues that a decisive problem in Whitehead's system is his realism, i. e., the theory that there is a reality existing independently of our consciousness of it. By a critique of Descartes' methodological skepticism, the author then tries to show why such a mode of realism cannot be warranted. Instead, he suggests a modification of it, called *conceptual realism*, i. e., the world we can think of or speak about "coexists" with our conceptualization of reality. However, if this view accepted, our understanding of both the nature of truth and perception is influenced. In the last part of the study, the author applies the theory of conceptual realism to issues in theology. A conceptualist theory of religion is also presented. The study concludes with some suggestions as to the possibility of assessing religious belief-systems.

S. M. Philipson, Department of Theology, University of Uppsala, Box 2006, S-750 02 Uppsala, Sweden.

Printed in Sweden by Infotryck ab, Malmö, 1982

If you can dream, and not make dreams your master,
if you can think, and not make thoughts your aim.

Rudyard Kipling

To my children,
JOHN, EVA, and DANIEL

Contents

Acknowledgements

I wish to express my gratitude to all my friends who made it possible for me to write this book.

I am especially indebted to the Sweden-America Foundation, Stockholm, the American-Scandinavian Foundation, New York, Thanks to Scandinavia, New York, and the Institute for Church and Culture of the Church of Sweden for grants which sustained my study during a year at Harvard (1980–81), the year when much of the research work and writing of the present volume was undertaken. The assistance contributed by Mrs. Margareta Douglas, New York, and Mrs. Suzanne Bonnier, Stockholm, deserves special acknowledgement.

Many people at Harvard made 1980–81 an important year in my life. I owe a debt of gratitude to Brita and Krister Stendahl for their friendship, encouragement and untiring support. They also read and criticized large parts of my manuscript. Professor Gordon D. Kaufman is also to be thanked for suggestions received during the first drafting of the manuscript. Professor Hilary Putnam influenced many of the philosophical positions presented in this volume. The suggestions he contributed during the early stages of writing were of substantial help.

Professor John E. Skinner, Professor Owen C. Thomas (Episcopal Divinity School, Cambridge, Mass.), Professor Peter L. Berger (Boston University), Professor Schubert M. Ogden (Southern Methodist University, Dallas, Texas), and Professor John B. Cobb Jr. (Claremont School of Theology, California) are among the many who contributed in various ways to my work in The United States. I owe them all my gratitude. My thanks also goes to Catherine Keller, Centre for Process Studies, Claremont, who undertook the arduous task of linguistic checking.

Professor Anders Jeffner (University of Uppsala) has been my theology professor and advisor since 1975. He has patiently and unrelentingly examined and encouraged my attempts at theological reflection. My indebtedness to him is great. I also wish to express my appreciation to Professor Hans Hof and Professor Ragnar Holte (University of Uppsala) for many helpful discussions, particularly during the later stages of my work. I am also grateful to Professor Hampus Lyttkens and Assistant Professor Bo Hansson (University of Lund) for their critical examination of an early draft of my manuscript. A discussion with Professor Urban Forell (University of Copenhagen) was also of considerable help. Of all those, however, who took of their time to discuss, suggest and criticize the material presented in this volume, my friend, Assistant Professor Carl-Reinhold Bråkenhielm, deserves special tribute. Even though our views have differed, his criticism served as an invaluable source of inspiration.

I also wish to express my deep gratitude to my wife, Inger, and to my parents, Inga and Berndt, who did the proof-reading.

Finally, the patience of my three children during the writing of this book should not go unmentioned. Even if they never come to share my views, it is my hope that they will some day come to share my love for theological and philosophical reflection. I dedicate this book to them.

S. M. P.

Chapter 1

Introduction

1.1 Metaphysics – a Central Issue for Theology

Ian Barbour points out that theologians inevitably employ metaphysical categories when they speak about God.[1] This is true, he claims, of all the giant figures in the history of Christian theology, such as Augustine (who was indebted to Plato), Thomas Aquinas (who was dependent on Aristotle), and Karl Barth (whose theology was most closely related to Kant's metaphysics, in spite of his rejection of metaphysical speculation).[2]

However, if this is true, must we not understand *all* theology as talk about God, against the background of a metaphysical framework, and must not any individual use of theological language logically involve at least certain metaphysical categories? I believe this is the case, and that to speak of God as personal, individual, transcendent, and the like, apart from a framework provided by some sort of metaphysics, is in fact impossible.

Now some theologians have argued that contemporary Christian theology must articulate its crucial questions in the light of their relation to a certain metaphysical system which they seem to presuppose. For instance, one of America's more prominent process-theologians, Professor Schubert M. Ogden at Southern Methodist University in Dallas, has argued that the main reason so many people today reject traditional Christian theism is that "one can accept it only by affirming the entire classical metaphysical outlook of which it is integrally a part."[3] The understanding of reality expressed in this kind of metaphysics, Ogden claims, is one for which all our distinctive experience and thought as modern secular persons presents negative evidence.

> From its first great formulations by Plato and Aristotle, the chief defining characteristic of classical metaphysics has been its separation of what is given in our experience into two quite different kinds of reality. On the one hand, there is the present world of becoming, of time, change, and real relations, of which each of us is most immediately and obviously a part... On the other hand, there is the wholly other world of timeless, changeless, and unrelated being, which is alone "real" in the full sense of the word and so alone worthy of the epithet "divine." ... Just how these two worlds are to be conceived, especially in relation to one another, has always been a problem for classical metaphysicians...[4]

Ogden claims that insofar as Western men and women have conceived of God at all, they have done so in terms elicited by the ancient Greek metaphysical dualism between "our world" and the "really real world," where the divine resides. The term God, then, is usually employed to refer to a divine reality of some transcendent sort, fundamentally dissociated from this world, in no way dependent upon or conditioned by this world, much as a human creator stands apart from his or her creation. Ogden then goes on to argue that at the base of this metaphysical system there is a conception of our world, with its living creatures as well as its inorganic matter, as something *unreal* and *unimportant*. According to his theory, then, this metaphysical outlook is objectionable sofar as it is presupposed by Christian faith, since it directly contradicts the reality and significance of this world. Our conviction as modern secular men and women is that this world is the locus of meaning and value. We no longer view ourselves as pilgrims passing through a vale of tears on the way to our final, eternal destination.

A similar view about the relation between theology and metaphysics is found among many of the so-called Death of God theologians. One of them, Professor William Hamilton, claims, for instance, that

> in this world . . . there is no need for religion and no need for God. This means that we refuse to consent to that traditional interpretation of the world as a shadow-screen of unreality, masking or concealing the eternal which is the only true reality. . . The world of experience is real, and it is necessary and right to be actively engaged in changing its patterns and structures.[5]

Slightly different is the problem expressed by Professor Gordon D. Kaufman at Harvard.

> A major problem with the concept of "God" arises out of the fundamental metaphysical-cosmological dualism found in the Bible (as well as in traditional metaphysics) and in virtually all Western religious thought. This is the division of reality into "earth" and "heaven" – that which is accessible to us in and through our experience and in some measure under our control, and that beyond our experience and not directly open to our knowledge or manipulation. The latter "world" is, if anything, more real and more significant than the experienced world, since it is God's own abiding place (from whence he directs the affairs of the cosmos) and man's ultimate home.[6]

One may understand these theologians as claiming that the metaphysical system to which Christian theism is related, contradicts important *values* among contemporary men and women. It is this world and what is within it that are important. If, for instance, the concept of salvation in Christian theology is kept in line with what is typical for classical metaphysics, i.e., as salvation *from* this world to a new life in another world, then Christian faith contradicts much of what is considered overwhelmingly important today.

Another way to interpret what these theologians say about the difficulties for Christian theism today is to say that the metaphysics which it seems to presuppose is highly *implausible*, i. e., it is not possible to give sufficient rational reason for its affirmation. It would be, in other words, impossible to believe that Christianity is true, since it is articulated against a metaphysical background which implies a theory about reality that cannot be rightly asserted.

It would be easy to criticize these theologians for giving too schematical a picture of the metaphysics found both in the Bible and in ancient Greek philosophy. For there are, in fact, many metaphysical backgrounds in the Bible, and it is not possible to equate Platonism, Aristotelian philosophy, and Neoplatonism with respect to metaphysics. However, even if one does not agree with their interpretation of Greek philsophy, nor with what they say about the metaphysics in the Bible, it is possible to admit that they have pointed to something important, namely, the relationship between theology and metaphysics. What they seem to say is that it is not possible to deal with the central and specific problems of Christian theology, unless one is also willing to deal with metaphysical issues. If it is true, as these theologians claim, that theology and metaphysics are deeply interconnected, this is an important statement in view of the apparent lack of interest in metaphysics on the part of contemporary theology. This lack is perhaps partly due to the influence of Barth's rejection of metaphysical speculations, and partly to the critique against metaphysics provided by the logical empiricists.[7]

But what does "metaphysics" mean? A rapid survey of the history of philosophy divulges little agreement about what metaphysics is, or how the word should be used. Sometimes philosophers apply the term quite ambiguously. This is the case, for instance, in the writings of Immanuel Kant. In his *An Inquiry into the Distinctions of the Principles of Natural Theology and Morals* he speaks about metaphysics as "nothing else but philosophy about the ultimate principles of our knowledge."[8] But at other times Kant uses the word to mean pretended or illusory knowledge of supersensible realities, of which, he argues in his *Metaphysical First Elements of Natural Science,* it is the task of critical philosophy to expose the hollowness.[9]

If we turn to the philosophy of Aristotle, we find an elaborate discussion about metaphysics. While all men desire knowledge, Aristotle argues in his famous *Metaphysics,* there is a distinction between knowledge as means, which aims at producing something, or securing some effect, and knowledge as an end in itself. The highest wisdom, according to Aristotle, is the search for knowledge about the first principles of reality, i. e., knowledge for its own sake. Metaphysics is this sort of wisdom, and the metaphysician is one who seeks knowledge about the ultimate cause and nature of reality, and who desires this knowledge not for practical reasons, but for its own sake.

In Aristotle's opinion, metaphysics is the most exact of all sciences, "for those which involve fewer principles are more exact than those which involve additional principles, i. e., arithmetic than geometry."[10] Hence metaphysics is the science which concerns itself with being as such. It is the investigation of being *qua* being. The special sciences isolate a particular sphere of being, and consider the attributes of being in that sphere. The metaphysician, on the other hand, does not study being under any particular aspect, trying to discern some particular characteristic of being. He or she is engaged in the investigation of being itself and its essential attributes as being. To say, Aristotle argues, that something is, is to say that it is one. Unity is an essential attribute of being, unity is found in all the same categories as being itself. Elsewhere Aristotle claims that goodness is also one of the transcendental attributes of being applicable in all the categories.

But with which category in particular is metaphysics concerned? With that of *substance* [οὐσία], maintains Aristotle. All things are either substances or attributes of substances, which is the reason why substance is the primary category of being and the focus of the highest of all wisdoms. However, there are many kinds of substances, according to Aristotle, and metaphysics is the study of unchangeable substance, since it concerns itself with being *qua* being, and the true nature of being is disclosed in what is unchangeable and not subject to change and affection. That there is one such unchangeable, stable being which causes change and motion, while remaining itself unmoved, is shown by the impossibility of an infinite series of existent sources of movement. This motionless, changeless substance, comprising the complete nature of being, has a divine character, which is a reason to call first philosophy – or metaphysics – theology. Physics, in Aristotle's system, does not count as a metaphysical science, since it deals with objects that are both inseparable from matter and also subject to motion. Although mathematics deals with theoretical objects, as does metaphysics, these objects are considered in abstraction from matter and thus do not really exist.[11]

Since, as I have already said, there is no clear-cut definition of metaphysics to which all philosophers would agree, I shall now have to stipulate my own. For reasons that will become clear as we continue, I wish to do so in close relationship to the sort of understanding of metaphysics that we found in Aristotle's system. But at the same time, for reasons that shall also become evident in the subsequent discussion, I wish to maintain a relatively open formulation, one that allows for a broad understanding of the character of metaphysical questions. Therefore, I shall use the term *metaphysics* to diesignate a theory in terms of which it is claimed to be possible to describe reality as a whole, or the ultimate characteristics of everything real.[12] I shall distinguish from metaphysical theories, theories that purport to explain, for example, the constitution of matter in physical nature, or the fundamental mechanism of the human body, inasmuch as they do not claim to be able to describe exhaustively *everything* real in terms of the theory; or insofar as they do not claim to tell us whether the conception of matter, or the understanding of what is fundamental to human nature, is a description of the ultimate reality, whose existence is absolute, and to which everything real can be reduced.

It may be pointed out that metaphysical assumptions are often, in fact, inherent also in more limited scientific theories, since beliefs about what there 'is' in reality, or what the ultimate 'nature' of things is, often is the presupposition of particular and limited scientific inquiries. And sometimes scientific theories are assigned metaphysical status, although there is no claim within the theories to a complete description of everything real.

Some philosophers have used the word ontology interchangeably with the word metaphysics, while others, as for instance Kant, have treated ontology as a subdivision of metaphysics. I shall speak about *ontology* as a theory about the fundamental entities in reality, what the world is composed from or "made" of. Hence, ontology is a subdivision of metaphysics, and the reason I wish to conceive of it as such is that the notion of "things" or "entities," and the like, seems to rest on an assumption about the fundamental structure of reality which I want to be able to regard as metaphysical. One example, which plays a certain role in the present study, is the assumption about the existence of a reality "out there" which subsists independently of our consciousness of it. Ontology, thus, is related to metaphysics in the sense that it is a part of a metaphysical system, or in the sense that it is logically connected with certain metaphysical assumptions. In a loose way of speaking, however, it may still be possible to use the words ontology and metaphysics synonymously.

Among all the different ontologies that we may encounter, it is possible to distinguish between three types. Monistic ontologies maintain that everything real consists of one fundamental kind of components. Dualistic ontologies claim that reality is made up from two different kinds of entities. A pluralistic ontology is one which contends that reality consists of a variety of things, and that it is not possible to reduce what is real to one or two kinds of entities. But we may also distinguish between different types of ontologies regarding the character of the components of what is real. Some ontologies claim that reality is of material, some that it is of spiritual character. In a dualistic ontology it is maintained that reality is of both material and spiritual character. Some ontologies, however, contend that reality is of neither material nor spiritual character, but of some neutral stuff. One example of a philosopher who maintained a "neutral monism" is Bertrand Russell. Another example is perhaps Ernst Mach, who in *Die Analyse der Empfindungen* claimed that both bodies and consciousness were of the same ontological sort, namely, sensations. His belief was that "the world consists only of our sensations."[13]

Since metaphysical theories, as I have defined them, are theories about what *is,* they often entail a distinction between facts and fictions. Hence, metaphysics is often related to theories of knowledge or *epistemology.* Such theories are not just concerned with the question of how we are to decide whether we know something or not – or the problem of the criteria for knowledge. They are also concerned with *what* it is that we know – or the extent of our knowledge. The Sophists were among the first to raise the question of objectivity. They asked: How much of our alledged knowledge of nature is really an objective part of it and how much is contributed by the knowing mind? Indeed, do we have any knowledge of nature as it really *is*? These questions are at the centre of many theories of knowledge and it is easy to see that the way they are answered entails metaphysical assumptions about the existence of the external world. But since *theories about perception* are closely related to epistemology, it is natural that also such theories are influenced by metaphysical assumptions. The way they tend to answer the following kind of questions many times seem to presuppose metaphysics: Do our concepts – our conceptualizations of the world – shape or influence what we perceive to be the world and the objects in it? If so, to what extent do concepts determine our experience? By *concept* I mean here that which reveals itself in the kind of expectations seeming to surround the various experiences we have. How do such expectations arise? Are we only passively receiving percepta which emerge from the external world, or are we in some way actively engaged in the process of perception?[14] However, *theories of truth* as well are related to epistemology and its metaphysical presuppositions. Realists maintain that we are somehow able to acquire knowledge about the objective characteristics of nature. Truth, or true statements, are among many realists consequently defined as a *correspondence* between certain states of affairs, on the one hand, and some statements or beliefs, with respect to those states of affairs, that those states of affairs exist, on the other. But the correspondence theory of truth presupposes the assumption that such states of affairs exist, i. e., a metaphysical theory of reality. Also other theories of truth presuppose metaphysics. William James, for instance, in *Essays in Radical Empiricism,* rejected the distinction between thought and things and maintained the theory which is called neutral monism. This, however, had consequences also for the way he conceived of truth. The truth of a belief or assertion, according to James, is its fruitfulness. This is known as the pragmatic theory of truth. John Dewey entertained a similar view and spoke of true knowledge as successful practice. According to him there is no final truth about the world. That the concept of truth and the theory of knowledge also influences what we may call the question of *language and the sociology of knowledge* is not surprising. The way we conceive of the world is usually thought to be, at least to some extent, an intellectual formulation of the human mind. Hence, it is culturally relative. However, to claim that our concept of truth, for instance, or of right and wrong, is relative to our language, is not ineluctably to say that 'anything goes,' or that there is no right or wrong at all. It might be that one entertains a sort of descriptive relativism without becoming a normative relativist. It seems that this choice is dependent on one's metaphysics.

In summary: it seems as if ontology and epistemology are closely connected. If we have a theory about what things really are, then it might be possible to formulate criteria for what is true knowledge and what is not. But on the other hand, if we have available such criteria then we might know the extent of our knowledge.[15] In various empirical theories of knowledge, only what can be corroborated by the evidence of experience, in one fashion or the other, is claimed to be real. Facts, on this view, must be established empirically. However, ontology and epistemology are also interconnected in the sense that they both presuppose certain metaphysical assumptions: for instance, whether there is a real world independent of our opinions about and consciousness of it. Does that about which we have *knowledge* and that of which we *describe* the nature exist on its own?

1.2 The Present Problem

That theology has an instrumental, pragmatic, or existential value, a truth-value if you wish, to many people, seems beyond dispute. But theologians also intend to say something more, something about a reality external to themselves. And they wish to assert something which is true.

A problem, however, is that it is often unclear what the content of such *truth-claims* really is. And further more: it seems often uncertain whether this content has a non-trivial meaning or not. It is not easy to discern whether theology – as talk about God – refers to anything apart from itself. The crucial and interesting question, therefore, is whether God-talk implies ontological assertions of a more wide-reaching nature, besides its mere functional meaning. Does talk about God refer? And in that case, to what? Does it refer to this world or something in it? Does it have to do with some other reality than ours? If so, with which? In what sense is this reality different from, but nevertheless related to our own?[16]

Now the main reason why theology must focus more carefully on metaphysical issues has to do with this problem of the meaning and truth of God-talk. When theologians claim – implicitly or explicitly – that God exists, they do not, of course, mean that the divine exists in the same sense as do material objects. But in what sense then does God exist? To answer this question seems only possible if we know something about the nature of God, i. e., if God's nature is expressed in ontological language. And if theology claims that God, a transcendent being, is related to our world, this seems only possible if it is clear what the world is with respect to *ontology*. Therefore, if theological assertions are claimed to have a non-trivial meaning, the first requirement is that these be intelligible. Since this is something which can be accomplished only if statements about God and the world are expressed in terms of ontological language, dealing with ontology is dealing with the problem of the meaning of God-talk. But ontology is also related to metaphysical assumptions, perhaps even as part of a whole metaphysics:

this dependency would indicate that metaphysics is what gives the ultimate meaning to God-talk. Consequently, if theology wishes to attend to the problem of the *meaning* of statements about God, it must attend to metaphysics.

The problem of theological statements, however, does not only have to do with their claim to assert something meaningful about reality. They also purport to say something which is *true*. If theology, therefore, claims that God is real, that belief in God entails knowledge about reality, and that this knowledge is true, this can only be a justified claim if argued on the ground of a reasonable *epistemology*. The validity of theological assertions about the nature of God and the rest of reality depends on whether it is possible to affirm the theory of knowledge on which it is based. Or in other words: *what* we know about God's nature and relation to this world is dependent on our way of accounting for *how* we know it. But since a theory of knowledge concerning statements about God would imply metaphysical assumptions, this means that a theology which engages itself not only in the problem of the meaning of God-language, but also in the problem of assessing theological truth-claims, has to deal with metaphysics.

In summary: if someone wants to address the problem of the meaning and truth of God-talk, he or she must attend to both ontological and epistemological issues. A theology which devotes itself to the problem of the meaning of God-language, must concern itself not only with ontology, but with the problem of knowledge. On the other hand, dealing with the problem of God's reality is not something one can do fruitfully merely by proceeding from an epistemological point of view. Since both ontology and epistemology imply certain metaphysical assumptions, however, this theological enterprise necessitates dealing with metaphysics.[17] It is in this sense that I have claimed that we must understand *all* theology against a background of metaphysics.

Now this does not mean that the metaphysical presuppositions of theology are explicit, or that all theologians are aware of the metaphysical assumptions to which they are logically committed. On the contrary, the use of metaphysics is often implicit and unconscious. This, however, presents a difficulty, because the lack of an explicit metaphysics creates problems of various kinds, depending on the degree of metaphysical awareness. In theologies without a conscious use of metaphysical categories, statements about God and the divine relationship to the world might be expressed in terms of different, perhaps conflicting or even contradicting, ontological theories.

The next step, then, is to construct a more appropriate ontological theory, perhaps through some sort of revision and integration of present theories, or by elaboration of a new theory. The explication of the metaphysical and ontological presuppositions of such a theology might reveal its inconsistency. It is also, however, possible that even theological systems with a high degree of explicit and consistent use of ontological categories will entail problems with respect to their metaphysical presuppositions. It might be the case that the metaphysics to which the ontological theory is related or connected, is different from, or perhaps contradicts, the metaphysics presupposed by the epistemological theory on which the theological system is based. Or in other words: the theological system may be incoherent with respect to the metaphysics it presupposes. An investigation and a revision of the metaphysical framework is therefore needed also here. The development of a more coherent metaphysics may result in a new theory, or in a decision to establish the theological system on the foundation of one of the two metaphysical theories, while the other is abolished. If such a decision is made, this in turn may have important consequences for the pertaining ontological or epistemological theories.

If it is true, as I have tried to argue, that theology – not in the sense of liturgical or mythical depictions, but in the qualified sense of talk about God – presupposes at least some metaphysical categories, and that a problem for contemporary theism lies partly in its underlying metaphysics, the solution to this problem is not simply an abandonment of the traditional metaphysical system. Instead, theology must revise its metaphysics and try to explore ways of explicating Christian faith in new terms and perhaps against a new metaphysical background. It must seek to show, in terms and categories meaningful to our own time, how it is possible and significant to speak not only of the world, but of God.[18]

This highlights the problem I wish to attend to in the present study, and the main question I want to consider, is this: what would an appropriate theory about reality, a metaphysics, look like? By the word "appropriate" I mean two things. First, an appropriate metaphysics is one which is *rationally acceptable*. Since the concept of rationality is partly related to the requisite metaphysics, it is necessary to develop an understanding of what rationality is alongside the investigation of what an acceptable metaphysics might be. The choice of the word "acceptable" might seem somewhat vague, but this is deliberate, for with it I wish to mark the limits of my ambition, in finding an acceptable metaphysics without necessarily claiming that it is the only reasonable one. To make the distinction clearer, let me suggest that a metaphysics is acceptable if disregarding it is not more reasonable than believing it, and that it is reasonable if believing it is more reasonable than disregarding it.[19] For it is possible to affirm that certain metaphysical positions are acceptable, without thereby claiming that they are all equally reasonable. In this study I shall restrict myself to the attainment of a distinction between rationally acceptable and rationally unacceptable metaphysics.

At this point we may simply note that some theologians contend that metaphysics can never have the same kind of validity as does science, or even common sense, since "its truth is more like the truth of art."[20] Others have expressed stronger theoretical demands for rationality as a condition for accepting a metaphysical position. Some maintain that metaphysical systems can be evaluated by means of criteria not unlike those used in judging scientific theories: i. e., coherence, inclusiveness, and adequacy. Coherence, in that case, refers to consistency, interconnectedness of ideas, conceptual unity, and the reduction of arbitrariness and fragmentation. Inclusiveness refers to scope, generality and ability to integrate diverse specialized language. Adequacy is a matter of relevance and applicability to experience of all kinds.[21]

Secondly, an "appropriate" metaphysics is one which can provide the ground for a conceptual framework which is *suitable for Christian theology*. Furthermore I wish to limit the enterprise to a kind of negative project. I do not wish to deal with the positive question: How is a metaphysical position authorized as appropriate for Christian theological use? I do not intend to discuss which criteria give Christian authority to certain ideas. Rather, I wish to discuss some attempts to formulate criteria according to which certain ideas are claimed to be unchristian. In order to make the distinction clearer, let me suggest that if one can find a position in the history of Christian theology which is similar to the position one is investigating, there is reason not to regard the latter position as unchristian. However, the appeal to one Christian theologian as taking a position in some way similar to that of another does not immediately justify the use of the latter in Christian theology: Christians have claimed a great many things which one might want to repudiate as thoroughly unsatisfactory.

Now it might be argued that Christian faith cannot be authentically expressed at all apart from the sort of metaphysics to which it seems to pertain. Is it perhaps the case, it might be asked, that Christian theism is, and can only be, related to a certain kind of metaphysics? There seems, however, to be no compelling reason to assume that Christian theology must be equated with any particular philosophical system. I shall instead suppose that the claim to any absolute metaphysical synthesis must be avoided, and that – as Ian Barbour has put it – theology must adapt, not adopt, metaphysical categories. It is important to emphasize that all philosophical concepts display an idiosyncratic character, and that the God of the Judaeo-Christian faith traditionally transcends all human concepts.

1.3 Why Choose Whitehead?

When I claim that theology presupposes metaphysics, I do not mean that the metaphysical system must be worked out first, in abstraction, and that when this scheme is complete theology can then proceed with its proper business. I mean that theology presupposes metaphysics, logically, not temporally.

When we wish to investigate what an appropriate metaphysics for theology might be, we need not begin by constructing one. In fact, there are many possible approaches to dealing with this issue. As a method I will suggest that we focus on one deliberate attempt to formulate a metaphysical alternative for our time; the system I have chosen is that of Alfred North Whitehead (1861–1947). The point of departure is not the assumption that Whitehead's system is the only acceptable metaphysics available, but that he tackled some important and crucial issues which contemporary theology must confront. My hope is that a critical assessment of Whitehead's system will help to disclose important problems, problems one must consider in any discussion of what might be an appropriate metaphysics for theology.

There are many reasons why we should choose Whitehead's system, known as process philosophy. One reason is that it is held to be one of the few, indeed perhaps the only, new systematic metaphysics in our century.[22] Professor John B. Cobb, Jr., at Claremont in Southern California, one of the more prominent so-called process theologians in the United States, even claims that Whitehead "ranks with Plato, Aristotle and Kant, as one of the greatest thinkers of all time."[23] In one sense Whitehead embodies a philosophical trend that can be found in the thought of Heraclitus and Buddha in ancient times, and of Hegel and Schelling more recently. In our own time, thinkers such as Henri Bergson and Pierre Teilhard de Chardin carry on this tradition. Yet in many respects Whitehead also represents the starting point of a *new* tradition in philosophy. His special contribution lies in the comprehensiveness of his synthesis of the process point of view, the exactness of his systematic categories, and his application of the resulting vision to a variety of problems in the sciences and humanities. Whitehead's aim at ever-widening application continues in current process thought.

By far the most extensive application of Whiteheadian categories has been within the field of *theology*. Process theology is one of the major alternatives in American theology: this provides another reason for taking a closer look at process thought. The earliest version of process theology came out of the so-called Chicago School of liberal, empirical theism during the late 1920's and 1930's. One of its most prominent voices at that time was Henry Nelson Wieman. Wieman replaced the traditional doctrine of substance metaphysics with the process view that qualitative events are the most real things. Another who employs process thought is Bernard Meland, who is quite critical of Wieman's approach. It is also necessary to mention Charles Hartshorne, who was never formally a student of Whitehead's, but whose viewpoint is strongly influenced by him. The most influential representatives of the second generation of process theologians are John B. Cobb, Jr., and Schubert M. Ogden – both students of Hartshorne's – each of whom has his own distinctive concern.

But Whitehead's thought has exercised influence *outside* theology and philosophy as well. For instance, such biologists as W. E. Agar and L. Charles Birch pursued the implications of process philosophy for their field. Whitehead's philosophy has provided a possible philosophical framework for an ecological understanding of reality. The dualistic philosophy permeating Western modes of thought has drawn a sharp line between human beings and other creatures. Only humans have been granted intrinsic value. Process philosophy stresses the interconnectedness and the mutual dependence of the various levels of actuality. Everything that exists, according to Whitehead, enjoys some degree of experience;

thus humans cannot lay exclusive claim to intrinsic value. We ought therefore not treat non-human nature as mere means for human ends. The importance of pre-conceptual modes of human experience has had a great impact on White-head's understanding of nature. Further, Withehead claims that God is active not only in relation to human beings, but also in relation to nature. In fact, God can be viewed as in a certain sense part of the natural world. Hence, Whitehead's philosophy may be described as a *theology of nature*. It does not present a new "natural theology," in the sense of an argument for the existence of God from evidence in nature. It is an attempt, rather, to view the natural order from the perspective of religious and metaphysical ideas derived primarily from an inter-pretation of human experience. Since this attempt should represent an important feature in contemporary theology, I would argue that we have here one more reason to focus upon process philosophy. For Whitehead's system not only attempts to articulate the notion of God in relation to the world, but to paint a new picture of the world as something utterly valuable and alive.

Another area where process thought has come to play an important role is *feminism*. A theologian who understands herself to be at once a feminist and a process thinker is, for instance, Marjorie Suchocki. But even feminists more distant from process philosophy have expressed appreciation of the vision of reality developed by Whitehead, as offering a metaphysical system based upon an un-derstanding of the self which is supportive of the assertions emerging from women's reflection upon experience. We may here mention Mary Daly as one example.[24] The fact that this side of process thought can be expected to increase in importance, also presents a reason to choose Whitehead's system as the subject of our study.

1.4 The Outline of the Study

The basic question of the present study is: what would an appropriate metaphysics be? The need to find such a metaphysics is related to the problem of the meaning and truth of God-talk. Without a satisfactory metaphysics assertions about God will be unintelligible, and no assessment of them will be possible. The method by which we want to obtain answers to our question is to focus on a conscious at-tempt to formulate a complete metaphysics, with the hope of disclosing fundamental problems to be considered in the effort to answer our basic question. To this end, we have decided to investigate Alfred North Whitehead's philosophy of or-ganism. Some problems in this system will naturally seem more fundamental than others, if viewed in relation to our question. Whitehead's realism and related theories, present such a problem. Therefore this problem deserves to become the subject of a more careful scrutiny. Other problems, although perhaps important and interesting in and of themselves, will be left aside if we can show that they are not of a fundamental or decisive nature with respect to the validity of the whole system. An example of such a problem is the question of whether Whitehead's concept of God is truly Christian. Another concerns his value theory. After having stated which problems are fundamental, the next step will be to see whether there are ways to come to grips with these problems, thereby enabling us to answer the basic question. Naturally, this answer must take the form of a more extensive argument, with a variety of implications.

In a sense Whitehead's system can be taken as a challenge to Christian theology, insofar as it presupposes what he conceives to be an inadequate or inappropriate metaphysics. If God is real, Whitehead claims, the divine cannot be understood as an exception to all other real things. Because God must be both temporal and spatial, Whitehead posits a real relation of God to the world, as well as a real relation of the world to God. God, according to Whitehead, exemplifies the same ontological structure as everything else that is real. If one therefore wishes to consider the more strictly theological issue of God's nature and relation to the world, one has no choice but to come to grips with Whitehead's whole metaphysical system. There is also, however, another reason that this is necessary. Whitehead's is a carefully integrated system, and it is not possible to isolate particular ideas in his scheme to the end of acquiring a full comprehension of them in abstraction from their context. I have therefore found it unavoidable to discuss, albeit quite briefly, Whitehead's complete metaphysics.

My intention, however, is not to deliver a general introduction or an unrelated interpretation of Whitehead's philosophy. The problem I want to focus upon provides a special perspective, which necessarily limits the scope of the study. Nevertheless, this is intentional, for only thus can I hope to accomplish a more comprehensible interpretation of a philosophy generally regarded as complex and not easily accessible. But I will refrain from bringing up any more Whitehead's philosophy than the particular problem requires. At the same time, in the effort to avoid a too elaborate interpretation, I hope not to over-simplify.

Whitehead's philosophy is far from easy to understand. It is abstract and quite elaborate in its intent to be comprehensive. It introduces new and unfamiliar terms and challenges our normal way of trying to come to grips with reality. In Whitehead's largest book on metaphysics, *Process and Reality; An Essay in Cosmology* (1929), all of the basic ideas are presupposed in the discussion of each of them. However, Whitehead's way of presenting his system converges with the content of it. He understands reality as the ultimate unity of an interconnected, pluralistic universe. In this his vision is influenced by William James.[25] For Whitehead, the only way to achieve a full understanding of the world is to find a totally new way of looking at it, i. e., not by sectionalizing or atomizing it, viewing it from the outside as an observer, but through a "unified scheme." *Process and Reality* is perhaps best understood as a way of challenging the conventional mode of apprehending our own existence on the earth, shaped as it is by Greek philosophy and Newtonian physics. This recognition will determine the stance for my effort to interpret Whitehead.[26]

The first part of the study is a presentation of Whitehead's philosophical system, its metaphysical and epistemological theories, in relation to his critique of other systems. Whitehead's metaphysics is a challenge, not only to Christianity, but also to the conceptualization of reality which underlies Newtonian physics – at his time still the prevalent scientific and cosmological outlook. Whitehead attacked the *ontology* of this system, which he took to presuppose a Cartesian dualism between mind and matter. The fundamental ontological entities of reality are not isolated, neutral bits of matter, in no connection with each other, and without intrinsic value. Whitehead, however, also challenged the classical empiricist tradition in *epistemology*. In this empiricism compound sense impressions were understood to resolve into simple discrete units or atoms, distinct and separable from each other. Whitehead presents a clear-cut alternative to this theory, an empiricism closely related to his ontology and entire metaphysics.

The second part of the study focuses on some possible shortcomings of the system. Apart from some minor criticism, my main critique will seize on his realism and his theory of perception. I shall try to show that although Whitehead criticizes the empiricism of the natural sciences of his own time, he nevertheless partakes of the same sort of *realism* as shared by Newton and the natural scientists after him; namely, a realism that is based on the assumption that there is a given world "out there," independent of our conceptualization of it, a world which we discover partly through a special mode of non-sensory experience. I shall argue, first, that Whitehead's theory of perception is not supportive of this form of realism, and, secondly, that it presupposes a metaphysical position which is inconsistent with his ontology. The metaphysical position at issue assumes that we have access to a position outside the world, which enables us to know, and meaningfully speak about, what reality is from a point of view external to reality. I shall refer to this position as "the metaphysical witness." The question is then whether it is possible to modify Whitehead's realism, so that, without using the metaphysical witness, we can still meaningfully claim that God is real and that belief in a divine reality is somehow true.

The third part of the study will begin with a discussion of some implications of the classical mode of realism in science and philosophy. By a critique of Descartes' methodological skepticism I shall then try to show that the idea of something like a metaphysical witness does not warrant such a mode of realism. I shall continue to outline a different view, tentatively calling it *conceptual realism*. Since the acceptance of such a view ineluctably leads to certain consequences regarding theories of truth and the fact – value dichotomy, I must touch upon these issues as well. The next step is then to apply the discussion to the problem of God-language in contemporary theology. I will submit my own understanding of what function the concept of God serves within a person's belief-system, and why it is meaningful to speak about God at all. By relating the theory of religion to metaphysical issues in the closing section, I shall finally discuss certain suggestions for the assessment of religious belief-systems.

Chapter 2

The Philosophy of Alfred North Whitehead

2.1 The Nature of Whitehead's Metaphysical System and his Realism

After having dealt almost exclusively with problems in science and mathematics,[27] Whitehead, in his later years, shifted to a broader, philosophical approach. The problem for him was to investigate the ultimate nature of reality, or expressed in his own words:

> The final problem is to conceive a complete [παντελής] fact. We can only form such a conception in terms of fundamental notions concerning the nature of reality. We are thrown back upon philosophy (AI 158).

By formulating his problem in this way Whitehead placed himself in a line with the philosophical enterprise of Aristotle in the *Metaphysics:*

> And indeed the question which was raised of old and is raised now and always, and is always the subject of doubt, namely, what being is [τί τὸ ὄν], is just the question: what is substance [οὐσία]? For it is this that some assert to be one, others more than one, and that some assert to be limited, others unlimited. And so we also must consider chiefly and primarily and almost exclusively what that is which *is* in this sense.[28]

When Whitehead speaks about "a complete fact" as the focus of his philosophical interest, this seems to be equivalent with what Aristotle spoke about as "that" which "is" in the fullest sense of the word, i. e., being itself.[29] However, Whitehead does not speak about being, but about fact, something particular and concrete which constitutes reality. This is also the *that* which Descartes spoke of as that "which requires nothing but itself in order to exist."[30] But Whitehead does not speak about these facts as substances. He calls them *"actual entities"*. However, we may understand the term as the equivalent of Aristotle's οὐσία. As we shall see, Whitehead also speaks about *"actual occasions"* in place of the term "actual entities." These facts, the most real things that are, have a leading characteristic: they are *actual*. Whitehead says:

> The general Aristotelian principle is maintained that, apart from things that are actual, there is nothing – nothing either in fact or in efficacy (PR 64).

Beyond the actual entities there is nothing that is more real, "because in sepa-ration from actual entities there is nothing, merely nonentity – 'The rest is silence' " (PR 68). In Whitehead's system these entities are viewed as the fundamental pieces of which reality is composed. They are the furniture with which the universe is made.

> The actual world is built up of actual occasions: and by the ontological principle whatever things there are in any sense of 'existence,' are derived by abstraction from actual occasions (PR 113).

This account is certainly too brief to clarify the ambiguous term; but the purpose now is only to make clear in what sense Whitehead develops his system. Partly, Whitehead is concerned with the elaboration of an ontological theory, a theory about the ultimate components of reality. It also seems obvious that it is a *monistic* theory. Whether it is a neutral monism or some other form of monism can be left aside at present, since we have not yet discussed the nature of actual entities. However, the scope of Whitehead's system is wider than merely ontological. White-head's philosophy is a metaphysics, almost in the same sense as Aristotle's "first philosophy": it is an investigation of the true characteristics of everything real; it is a theory in terms of which it is possible to describe reality as a whole.

> By 'metaphysics' I mean the science which seeks to discover the general ideas which are indespensably relevant to the analysis of everything that happens (RM 82n).

Although the term 'metaphysics' occurs in Whitehead's writings, he usually speaks about "speculative philosophy." There is a difference in Whitehead's system between the two terms, but for our purposes, however, it is negligible.

> Speculative Philosophy is the endeavour to frame a coherent, logical, ne-cessary system of general ideas in terms of which every element of our experience can be interpreted (PR 4).

Whitehead's metaphysics, or speculative philosophy, is thus the endeavour to discover such general ideas and fundamental notions as can provide an all-inclusive understanding of reality. It is the study of the most general characteristics of events within the world. Its nature is conceptual synthesis. By imaginative ge-neralizations from immediate experience, Whitehead wants to develop such an inclusive scheme, whose categories will be sufficiently universal to be exemplified by every entity in the world. These categories contain a set of ideas in terms of which the whole range of human experience can be interpreted. Insofar as the endeavour to frame such an all-inclusive system of interpretations is successful, its power lies in its ability to integrate and illuminate a wide range of experiences in science, art, history, ethics, and religion. Therefore, Whitehead emphasizes that any warranted metaphysical scheme must be *applicable to experience,* i. e.,

28

it should be possible to interpret *all* types of experiences and events in terms of the system. Metaphysics must take into account all manner of data; scientific, aesthetic, emotional, physical. Whitehead even claims that religious experiences are among the data that

> contributes its own independent evidence, which metaphysics must take account of in framing its description (RM 76).

Whitehead understood religious concepts to be derived from special experiences, but to have such a universal validity that they are in fact applicable to the ordering of all experience.

> The dogmas of religion are the attempts to formulate in precise terms the truths disclosed in the religious experience of mankind. In exactly the same way the dogmas of physical science are the attempts to formulate in precise terms the truths disclosed in the sense-perception of mankind (RM 57).

Metaphysics, then, takes into consideration facts from all fields of experience. At the same time it lends meaning of the world of experience. What we consider to be fundamental about reality, what we believe to be truly real, determines what we will consider true knowledge, values are, the best way to organize human society is, and so forth. Our *orientation in life* presupposes some sort of conceptual scheme assisting us to interpret reality. At the bottom of the conceptualization of reality, in terms of which we understand our present situation – that is, what to believe and what to do – we usually find metaphysical assumptions, ideas about the fundamental structure of reality, that function as ordering factors in the scheme. And precisely because of its extreme generality, its concern with reality as a whole, metaphysics frequently purports to give a comprehensive understanding of all human knowledge and experience. It is sometimes claimed that a metaphysical scheme can order the great diversity of beliefs that we hold about the nature of the world in an all-embracing unity, such that we may achieve a sort of "Gestalt" of the totality of our knowledge and experience. When a metaphysical system produces such a Gestalt, it purports to present a model of the world as a whole. To elucidate what is meant by "a model of the world" we may turn to the notion of "root metaphor" introduced by Stephen C. Pepper in his *World Hypothesis*.

When people desire to understand the world they look about for a "clue to its comprehension." They then hit upon some area of common-sense fact and try to see if they cannot understand other areas in terms of this one. The original area then provides the basic analogy, or what Pepper calls the *root metaphor*.[31] To develop a root metaphor involves discriminating the characteristics, or the structure, of the original area. A list of such characteristics can then become the basic concepts of explanation or description, in terms of which it becomes possible to study all other areas of knowledge and experience. A *world hypothesis*, in Pepper's terminology, is the development of such a root metaphor.

According to Pepper's theory, it is possible to discern various root metaphors. One he calls "organicism."[32] The "organicist" believes that every actual event in the world is a more or less concealed organic process. He believes that a careful scrutiny of any actual process in the world would exhibit its organic structure. According to the organicist, the facts of the world are not organized from outside; they organize themselves. The connections between the facts are present all the time, working in nature.

If we now think of Whitehead's philosophy as a world hypothesis, the root metaphor in it is precisely that of the organism. The world, as Whitehead conceived of it, is an organism; a dynamic, evolving reality, consisting of interconnected but distinct and autonomous entities or events. And one of the conspicuous features of his system is the perspective in which a sense of universal belonging and unity is kept together with the respect for the integrity of each actual entity.

Whitehead's fundamental criterion of assessment was that the metaphysical scheme must be *coherent*, i. e., its concepts should not only be logically consistent, but also integrated parts of a unified system of interrelated ideas that presuppose each other. Of course, one might argue that in the effort to create a coherent system of this kind, there is the risk of distorting or misinterpreting experience in the attempt to fit it into the all-embracing scheme. Whitehead, however, claimed that coherence, as a requirement for any understanding of reality in which all fields of experience are seen as interrelated is, on the contrary, "the great preservative of rationalistic sanity" (PR 9); it underlies every attempt at a rational view of reality.

> Faith in reason is the trust that the ultimate natures of things lie together in a harmony which excludes mere arbitrariness. It is the faith that at the base of things we shall not find mere arbitrary mystery. The faith in the order of nature which has made possible the growth of science is a particular example of a deeper faith. This faith cannot be justified by any inductive generalisation. It springs from direct inspection of the nature of things as disclosed in our immediate present experience. There is no parting from your own shadow. To experience this faith is to know that in being ourselves we are more than ourselves: to know that our experience, dim and fragmentary as it is, yet sounds the utmost depths of reality: to know that detached details merely in order to be themselves demand that they should find themselves in a system of things: to know that this system includes the harmony of logical rationality, and the harmony of aesthetic achievement (SMW 18).

The idea of coherence as a criterion of assessment in Whitehead's philosophy is, hence, related to this fundamental faith in a *cosmic coherence*, a belief that reality, ontologically speaking, *is* a coherent whole, a unity, and not merely arbitrary.

To apprehend Whitehead's mode of realism, it might be helpful to view it in relation to the movement of twentieth-century realism, connected in England with such thinkers as T. P. Nunn, Bertrand Russell, and G. E. Moore, and in America, William P. Montague, Ralph Barton Perry and William James. In opposition to late nineteenth-century idealism, this movement emphasized the independence of human consciousness and its object, without separating the knower from the known. The hope was to achieve a notion of objective knowledge without falling into the problems of idealism. The central question, especially among American New Realists, was this: how can a real object, an objective thing, be present in consciousness and knowledge, and still be an independent piece of the external world? William James' idea of pure, uncontaminated experience came to play a special rôle here, which also influenced Whitehead. However, the New Realism movement also had an impact on theology. A line of theological reflection and investigation, extending from Paul Tillich, and Reinhold and H. Richard Niebuhr to Whitehead and Henry Nelson Wieman, formed a new frontier of realism, breaking free from the enclosure of mentalism, which was thought to engulf the theological thinking of that time.[33] Decisive here – as over against the idealist influence on theology – was the emphasis upon an *otherness* beyond the human world in assertions about the divine. The aim of the realist movement in theology at this time was to achieve an objective stance in theological inquiry.[34]

Whitehead's mode of realism, his belief that the universe *is* objectively coherent, related and connected, and not just conceptually integrated, dominates the character of his whole metaphysics. But Whitehead's philosophy of organism is based on a certain form of epistemology: at the base of our knowledge of the world we *experience reality as a totality*. This experience is the ground of faith in a rational order of the universe: "It springs from direct inspection of the nature of things as disclosed in our immediate present experience." This basic experience possesses a unity, apprehended integrally by our faculties; and the experience includes an awareness of our mutual interaction with the environment. Only by analysis can we abstract sense-data from the totalities we perceive. Our primitive awareness is that of being in a world, not of constructing or creating one.[35]

2.2 The Theory of Perception

As we have seen, metaphysics in Whitehead's understanding seeks a conceptual scheme that will enable us to interpret all experience. We have noted that the rational enterprise of finding such a scheme, according to Whitehead, is based on a *faith* that the experience of ourselves and the world can be investigated rationally, i. e., that there is a rational *order* in nature, and that everything is ontologically related to everything else. Whitehead seems to think that this faith, in turn, is anchored in the depths of our experience. At the base of the experience of ourselves and of the world is a sort of *perception* of reality as a totality. We perceive a unity in which every entity in the universe is *interconnected* and *interrelated*. Everything is united in the solidarity of one, common world.

> In the world, there are elements of order and disorder, which thereby presuppose an essential interconnectedness of things. For disorder shares with order the common characteristic that they imply many things interconnected (AI 293, old ed.).

According to Whitehead, metaphysics is nothing but an explication of this fundamental experience of the universe as a whole. Thus metaphysics is not simply a speculation without epistemological ground; and as we shall see, the theory of perception is essential to Whitehead's entire system. A discussion of Whitehead's theory of perception, which provides the foundation for his realism, seems therefore to be the natural approach to his metaphysics.

Three concepts constitute the theory: perception in the mode of *causal efficacy;* perception in the mode of *presentational immediacy;* and perception in the mixed mode of *symbolic reference.* Ordinary, conscious human perception, what we usually call sense experience, of, say, a gray stone, is in Whitehead's language "perception in the mixed mode of symbolic reference." To understand this kind of perception we have to consider the two more primitive modes of perception which compose the mixture. These two more elementary modes are causal efficacy and presentational immediacy.

However, the main aspect of Whitehead's theory can be summarized in terms of his rejection of the kind of understanding present among the majority of empiricist philosophers. In the more conventional and traditional theory, perception and experience are thought to take place by means of our *senses.* These accounts of perception often emphasize *visual* perception as especially important. This seems to be the kind of understanding presupposed not only by such empiricists as Locke and Hume, but also by philosophers like Kant as well as by more current thinkers such as Karl Popper and Rudolph Carnap. This understanding has its origin among the ancient Greek philosophers. The Greeks began with perception in its most elaborate form, namely, visual perception. However, the core of this whole understanding of perception as primarily sense-perception is that the only solid *ground for knowledge* lies in assertions that may be directly, or indirectly, verified by appeal to such perceptions.

In classical empiricism, such as Hume's, compound impressions and ideas ultimately resolve into simple impressions and ideas, each of which is distinct and separable from other simple ideas and impressions. It is this view that has been called the 'atomism' in empiricism, for the picture or the paradigm that emerges is one in which all experience is reducible to simple discrete units or atoms, "stubborn bits of matter" or "simple locations." It is basically this understanding of perception and its influence on other fields which Whitehead wants to challenge.

32

The general features of his own empiricism may be readily summarized. Its controlling purpose is to offer a clearcut alternative to "the sensationalist doctrine," which has been prominent in modern philosophy since Descartes. This doctrine can be defined as the belief that

> the primary activity in the act of experience is the bare subjective entertainment of the datum, devoid of any subjective form of perception (PR 239).

This implies that experience is thought of as consisting in the *first* place of a bare consciousness of certain data, especially sense data, so that all emotional and purposive experience must be conceived as derivative from it. Hence, whatever does not count as conscious experience, cannot be called experience at all.

For Whitehead, the primary and essential phases of experience are purposive and emotional (PR 246). Consciousness *presupposes* experience, not experience, consciousness. Consciousness only illuminates the more primitive modes of "prehension." He says:

> The principle that I am adopting is that consciousness presupposes experience, and not experience consciousness. It is a special element in the subjective forms of some feelings. Thus an actual entity may, or may not, be conscious of some part of its experience (PR 83).[36]

It is a mistake, Whitehead argues, to equate experience exhaustively with sense perception, or to assume that sense experience is the only mode of perception. On the contrary, what we call sense perception is derived from a more elemental and nonsensory awareness of ourselves and the circumambient world. This form of nonsensuous perception Whitehead calls perception in the mode of *causal efficacy*. According to his theory the basic mode of experience is an intuitive awareness of our own past mental and bodily states, as they compel conformation to themselves in the present. When we interpret reality, Whitehead claims, the material for the interpretation is not provided by the senses themselves.

> But the evidence on which these interpretations are based is entirely drawn from the vast background and foreground of non-sensuous perception with which sense-perception is fused, and without which it can never be. We can discern no clean-cut sense-perception wholly concerned with present fact (AI 181).

Because this is so, Whitehead argues, the conventional doctrine of the primacy of sense perception has been completely mistaken.

> The whole notion of our massive experience conceived as a reaction to clearly envisaged details is fallacious. The relationship should be inverted. The details are a reaction to the totality. They add definition. . . They are

interpretive and not originative. What is original is the vague totality (MT 109).

Before we can undertake the comparatively high-level discrimination of reality by means of our senses, we are already aware of ourselves and others as causally efficacious powers mutually interacting with one another.

> The discrimination of details is definitely a secondary process, which may or may not assume importance... The primitive stage of discrimination is not primarily qualitative. It is the vague grasp of reality, dissecting it into a threefold scheme, namely, "The Whole," "That Other," and "This-My-Self."
>
> This is primarily a dim division. The sense of totality obscures the analysis into self and others... There is the vague sense of many which are one; and of one which includes the many. Also there are two senses of the one – namely, the sense of one which is all, and the sense of the one among the many (MT 110).

Since the elements in this fundamental experience of the universe as a totality are emotional and appetitive, not in the character of ordinary sense-experience, Whitehead talks about them as "feelings."

There is a feeling of the ego, the other, the totality (MT 110). This 'feeling,' this 'experience,' this perception in the mode of causal efficacy that we are, each of us, one among others and at the same time embraced in the unity of the whole is at the base of Whitehead's entire metaphysical system.

Our primitive sense of identification with our bodies, which is betrayed, for example, by our certainty that we "see *with* our eyes, taste *with* our palates, touch *with* our hands" (PR 258), is not a product, then, of sense perception but is its underlying presupposition. The mode of causal efficacy is, therefore, most evidently exhibited by what Whitehead called the "withness of the body." Whitehead maintains that the empiricists, although they were aware of the fact, "dropped out this withness of the body; and thus confined perception to presentational immediacy" (PR 125). But our clear perception of ourselves as centers of experience, with memories of the past and anticipations of the future, must be traced back to a vague but elementary awareness of ourselves and the surrounding world beyond our bodily life. Hence, human experience is not fundamentally sensory. The world of sense data is a highly organized construct of the mind, based on data that are not physical objects completely external to our bodies.

Now, we must not interpret this in such a way as to suggest that Whitehead denies sensory input. His point is that we must not imagine the world out there as a collection of simple objects for sense perception. When we speak about the world, we do not just report what is there before us, that we have discovered by means of our senses. What we call the *physical* world, consisting of things, objects, atoms, etc., is a highly artificial versions of the world, and not a simple fact.[37]

Sense experience, in our ordinary meaning of the phrase, is then a mixed mode of perception, consisting of two primitive forms of perception. At the basis is a nonsensory form of perception, below the level of consciousness. Perception in the mode of causal efficacy is the basic mode of inheritance of feelings from past data, and the feelings it transmits are vague, massive, inarticulate, and felt as the efficaciousness of the past. This is what Whitehead calls "crude" perception.[38] Presentational immediacy, the conscious sensory discrimination of what is before us, is then best understood as an elaboration upon certain aspects of what is present already in causal efficacy.

> Presentational immediacy is an outgrowth from the complex datum implanted by causal efficacy. But the originative power of the supplemental phase, what was vague, illdefined, and hardly relevant in causal efficacy, becomes distinct, well defined, and importantly relevant in presentational immediacy (PR 262).

> The percepta in the mode of presentational immediacy have the converse characteristics. In comparison, they are distinct, definite, controllable, apt for immediate enjoyment, and with the minimum of reference to past, or the future. We are subject to our percepta in the mode of efficacy, we adjust our percepta in the mode of immediacy (PR 271).

Perception in the mode of presentational immediacy transforms what is there in causal efficacy into sharply focussed qualities. It is the kind of perception in which

> there is clear, distinct consciousness of the 'extensive' relations of the world ... In this 'mode' (of perception) the contemporary world is consciously prehended as a continuum of extensive relations (PR 95).

Presentational immediacy is the objectification of what is there in efficacy into spatial relations of shape and perspective, and into contemporary relations. In this mode of perception the conceptual world is consciously 'prehended' as a nexus of extensive relations.

> The pure mode of presentational immediacy gives no information as to the past or the future. It merely presents an illustrated portion of the present duration. It thereby defines a cross-section of the universe: but it does not in itself define on which side lies the past, and on which side the future. In order to solve such questions we now come to the interplay between the two pure modes. This mixed mode of perception is here named 'symbolic reference' (PR 255).

It is not until perception in the mixed mode is attained that there is the ordinary awareness of, for instance, the persisting gray stone.

When we register in consciousness our visual perception of a grey stone, something more than bare sight is meant. The 'stone' has a reference to its past, when it could have been used as a missile if small enough, or as a seat if large enough. A 'stone' has certainly a history, and probably a future (PR 184f).

The sensa involved in experience are derived from a very primitive form of perception and projected onto a sharply defined contemporary spatial region in the mode of presentational immediacy, so that in the mixed mode of symbolic reference one perceives the stone as clearly located and also as a persisting entity with a past and an efficacy for the future.[39] The symbolic reference is "the interpretive element in human experience" (PR 263). We are subject to our percepta in the mode of efficacy, we adjust our percepta in the mode of immediacy. But, according to Whitehead, our process of self-construction for the achievement of a unified experience produces a new product, in which percepta in one mode, and percepta in the other, are synthesized into one subjective feeling; as, for example, when we perhaps perceive before our eyes a gray stone.

The two modes are unified by a blind symbolic reference by which supplemental feelings derived from the intensive, but vague, mode of efficacy are precipitated upon the distinct regions illustrated in the mode of immediacy. The integration of the two modes in supplemental feeling makes what would have been vague to be distinct, and what would have been shallow to be intense. This is the perception of the grey stone, in the mixed mode of symbolic reference (PR 273).

2.3 The Challenge to the Newtonian Worldview

Until now we have discussed Whitehead's view of the metaphysical enterprise and its epistemological basis. But his system did not develop in a vacuum. The thesis here is that Whitehead's belief that Newtonian cosmology suffered from a serious incompleteness, provided the stance for the entire construction of the philosophy of organism. It is best, therefore, to investigate this philosophy by focusing upon the problems contained within Newtonian physics as they appeared to Whitehead.

In his earlier writings, before approximately 1920, Whitehead chiefly concentrated on what he called "the philosophy of science." From the side of mathematics he focused on the way that mathematical concepts could contribute to the understanding of the actual world. His more important treatises concerning a philosophy of nature are *An Enquiry Concerning the Principles of Natural Knowledge* (1919) and *The Concept of Nature* (1920). During the earlier period his main interest was to develop concepts which were suitable for a scientific investigation of nature.

And it was exactly this attempt that finally forced him to focus upon a much wider range of problems, different from strictly scientific ones.

Previously he had conceived of science as a method for investigation of nature as knowable without inclusion of the investigator, analogous to the way an observer perceives an object. In the nineteen twenties he gradually shifted to a different conception of how we are to understand nature.

> Our datum is the actual world, including ourselves; and this actual world spreads itself for observation in the guise of the topic of our immediate experience. The elucidation of immediate experience is the sole justification for any thought; and the starting-point for thought is the analytic observation of components of this experience (PR 6. Cf. also MT 152).

During this period he shifted to the endeavour to develop a metaphysical cosmology that includes the human knower within the natural world. In *Science and the Modern World* (1925) this new conception in Whitehead's philosophy is evident. In *Religion in the Making* (1926) he discusses God's role in nature. In 1926 Whitehead was invited to give the Gifford Lectures, which he delivered in Edinburgh in 1927–1928. In preparation for this, he wrote what has been considered his magnum opus, *Process and Reality* (1929), in which he gives elaborate articulation to his scientific and philosophical notions combined with ideas about religion, aesthetics, and metaphysics, all within a unified scheme. The book starts off with a compressed, summary statement of the fundamental metaphysical concepts. The rest of the book can in a sense be viewed as an attempt at "rendering this summary intelligible" (PR 27). During 1929 he also published *The Function of Reason*, which is considered to be his most accessible book. In *Adventures of Ideas* (1933) he explains the basic ideas of his philosophy and tries to relate those to the way in which ideas in general tend to influence the shaping of society. Whitehead's last book, *Modes of Thought* (1938), delivers an overall view of some central ideas and is also thought of as one of his least difficult books.[40] Although the issue of science in philosophy still remains important in the books of his later years, the main problem is a new one.

In order to understand Whitehead's metaphysical scheme we have to look at some of the basic concepts in Newtonian physics which Whitehead criticizes. He does not oppose Newtonian mechanics completely. There was, he claims, an area in macroscopic experience where it was applicable. But the problem arises when the understanding of *all* reality is reduced to that macroscopic focus, i. e., when we turn limited scientific ideas and concepts into an all-embracing metaphysical scheme, into metaphysics. This form of critique can be summarized thus: Newtonian physics cannot be brought to bear upon fields *outside* its proper area of application.

Newtonian physics claimed that the ultimate facts of reality were *matter, space,* and *time*. It tried to formulate in exact mathematical terms the relation between these notions. These categories, matter, space, and time, were put into focus originally by Galileo (1564–1642), chiefly because they could be treated mathematically. The truth of nature consisted, he held, of mathematical facts, and what was believed to be real in nature was that which could be measured and quantified. The world was taken to be composed of particles to which were ascribed only two sorts of properties: *mass* and *velocity*. Change, in this conceptualization of reality, no longer meant transition from potentiality to actuality, but rearrangement of particles in time and space. Mass and velocity were, according to Galileo, *primary qualities,* characteristics of the objective world independent of the observer. From these 'primary qualities' Galileo distinguished what he called *secondary qualities,* such as colour, sound, and temperature, which he believed to be purely subjective reactions of the senses to the external world, devoid of objective existence. Secondary qualities were completely mind-dependent, while primary qualities were completely independent of mind.

Descartes (1596–1650) gave a philosophical exposition of this distinction in a radical dualism between *mind* and *matter.* The external world, according to Descartes, was self-sufficient matter extended in space. Even here, mathematical concepts, as being the "clear and distinct ideas" of which one could be cognitively certain, were according to Descartes the keys to understanding nature. Final was to be replaced by efficient causation in explanations of the world. Mind, on the other hand, was unextended "thinking substance" (*res cogitans*), defined in terms totally dissimilar to those of matter, or "extended substance" (*res extensa*), so that a relation between mind and matter could hardly be conceived at all, although both were understood somehow to proceed from God as their source. However, Descartes realized that the dualism could not be pushed too far. So he argued that there was a connection between matter and mind in each individual human being, namely, in the pineal gland. In spite of the detailed discussion about the relation between body and soul in Descartes' treatise entitled *The Passion of the Soul* (1649), the theory is unclear. The move towards the idea of the pineal gland seems somewhat desperate and was, for instance, also ridiculed by Spinoza.

In Greek thought the material world was taken to be permeated by mind. Mind in nature was believed to be the source of order in the world. Since mind was present everywhere in nature, the sharp distinction between mind and matter could not be drawn as was done in Cartesian philosophy. Nature was understood in terms more resembling a living organism than a machine. It could almost be conceived of as a sort of rational animal. But for the thinkers of the Renaissance, this was precisely the view to be challenged. Nature was now viewed as devoid of intelligence and life. Movement and orderliness in the world were understood to be imposed from outside, by an intelligent mind. The divine creator was depicted in analogy with a builder standing apart from his machine. The famous Julien Offray de La Mettrie, for instance, explained that his mechanistic anthropology in *L' Homme machine* was developed on the basis of Descartes' philosophy.

The abyss between the *observing mind* and the *observed world,* set forth by Galileo and developed by Descartes, set the stage for the thinking of Isaac Newton (1642–1727). Galileo never elaborated a purely mechanistic understanding of nature, but some of the key assumptions of such a view were evident in his writings. Newton, however, brought these forth and articulated to fulfilment the scientific outlook of mathematics and experimentations set out by Galileo, though it must be stressed that he was in no way a 'positivist' in the modern sense of the word. Newton, even more than Galileo, emphasized the *descriptive* character of the scientist's task. Science was to observe nature, discover its hidden patterns, and describe them. Scientific *knowledge* was knowledge about the world, but not about the world as it appeared to be. Behind the world of so-called secondary qualities were the real objects of science. Matter itself, the unchanging substance which is perpetually rearranged, is one such object. The other is the set of laws, according to which nature is changed. And even though Newton claimed that scientific concepts were products, not of observation, but of the creative, human imagination, such concepts still came to be viewed as literal representations of the world, reproductions of objective reality as it is in itself. The *truth* of scientific propositions was, naturally enough, understood as a sort of correspondence between these representations, or concepts, of the world, and the world in itself.

Not in the physics itself, but in the philosophical outlook that was implicit in Newtonian cosmology, we can also find the incitement to a view still lingering among us, namely that the basic elements of the world are describable in terminology of science, and that, in principle, everything which is real is *reducible to physics.* Because physics, at least among many non-physicists, is thought to be a theory about the objectively true character of reality. Or to put it more bluntly: physics has been transformed into metaphysics.

Within Newtonian physics there was a stronger impetus towards an all-embracing metaphysics than Newton himself was probably aware of, or would have approved. For his laws of motion and gravity seemed applicable to *all* objects, from the smallest particle to the farthest planet. It suggested a metaphysical image of the world: the quantitative and mechanical nature was the *only* reality. Such a materialistic cosmology was indeed already present in the intellectual world before Newton. And even if Newton rejected the idea that precisely everything real could be reduced to physics, he accepted Galileo's view that nature could be exhaustively described in terms of particles in motion. The properties that could be treated mathematically – mass and velocity – were alone considered to be the true characteristics of the natural world. Other properties were taken purely and simply to be subjective and unreal. This theory of nature was not overcome until the late nineteenth century, with the advent of quantum mechanics.

Whitehead discussed and criticized the transformation of a limited scientific theory into an all-inclusive metaphysical worldview as the *fallacy of misplaced concreteness* (PR 11, SMW 51). This fallacy can most easily be described as the reification of abstract ideas.

The accidental error of mistaking the abstract for the concrete. . . This fallacy is the occasion of great confusion in philosophy. It is not necessary for the intellect to fall into the trap, though in this example there has been a very general tendency to do so (SMW 51).

However, it should be emphasized that Whitehead also criticized Newtonian cosmology on scientific grounds. Newtonian physics, he claimed, was unsatisfactory even *within* its proper area of application. Whitehead held that the whole scheme contained a severe contradiction which made it incoherent and, therefore, unacceptable: it was incapable of explaining *change* in nature.

There is a fatal contradiction inherent in the Newtonian cosmology. Only one mode of the occupancy of space is allowed for – namely, this bit of matter occupying this region at this durationless instant. This occupation of space is the final real fact, without reference to any other instant, or to any other piece of matter, or any other region of space. Now assuming this Newtonian doctrine, we ask – What becomes of velocity, at an instant? Again we ask – What becomes of momentum at an instant? These notions are essential for Newtonian physics, and yet they are without any meaning for it. Velocity and momentum require the concept that the state of things at other times and other places enter into the essential character of the material occupancy of space at any selected instant. But the Newtonian concept allows for not such modification of the relation of occupancy. Thus the cosmological scheme is inherently inconsistent (MT 145f).

In the Newtonian view, nature was static, and all things were presumed to have been created in their present form. Nature was deterministic. Its future was in principle predictable based on knowledge of the present.

Newtonian physics is based upon the independent individuality of each bit of matter. Each stone is conceived as fully describable apart from any reference to any other portion of matter. It might be alone in the Universe, the sole occupant of uniform space. But it would still be that stone which it is. Also the stone could be adequately described without any reference to past and future. It is to be conceived fully and adequately as wholly constituted within the present moment (AI 156).

We must not interpret Whitehead's criticism of Newtonian physics as if he denied the existence of atoms or electrons within a physical view of reality. But he refused to view them as the ultimate components of reality, for the complete facts of which the world is made are not isolated, neutral bits of matter, in no connection with each other.

The ultimate entities, according to Whithead, must not, and cannot, be viewed as Leibnizian 'monads' without windows or doors, totally self-contained and self-sustaining.

It is not suprising then, that Whitehead also rejects the sharp distinction between the observer and the observed. Instead he urges us to look at the world from the viewpoint of the ultimate entity itself, imagining it as an experiencing subject. It makes no sense, in fact it is erroneous, to try to exclude the perceiver from the perceived. A metaphysical system must include the human experiencing being and thus try to understand the world from within. We have no access to – what Iris Murdoch has called – a "God's eye" point of view, by which we can step outside the world.

> There is no holding nature still and looking at it (CN 14f.).

The reason this is the case can be found in Whitehead's theory of perception and metaphysics: we are ourselves integrated *parts* of the reality which we try to understand and investigate. The sense data that we claim to 'observe' are abstractions from the totality we perceive. The raw material of our experience includes an awareness of our mutual interaction with our environment. Concerning philosophies such as Descartes' and the like, Whitehead says:

> The main point of all such philosophies is that they presuppose individual substances, either one or many individual substances, "which requires nothing but itself in order to exist." This persupposition is exactly what is denied in the more Platonic description which has been given in this lecture. There is no entity, not even God, "which requires nothing but itself in order to exist." According to the doctrine of this lecture, every entity is in its essence social and requires the society in order to exist. In fact, the society for each entity, actual or ideal, is the allinclusive universe, including its ideal forms (RM 104).

Thus, we may summarize Whitehead's understanding of reality sofar as an *interacting, unified plurality of entities of experience.*

2.4 A World in Process

Although Whitehead progressively moved away from the strictly scientific enterprise of investigating the structure of nature, his past always influenced the way he presented and elaborated his metaphysics. A scientific understanding of reality was continually in the back of his mind. Science, Whitehead often claimed, should not on the one hand be overestimated as a source of knowledge about the nature of things, because there is much which cannot be exhaustively understood in scientific terms. Science, in Whitehead's opinion, should be seen as dealing with the quantifiable aspects of things, not as *fully* describing their essence or reality (PR 177–179, 364). Therefore, we must adopt a critical attitude toward the tendency of many current scientists to over-estimate themselves and their results.

> A few generations ago the clergy, or to speak more accurately, large sections of the clergy were standing examples of obscurantism. Today their place has been taken by scientists (FR 43f).

But on the other hand, there is no reason to adopt a profligate attitude toward science and hence disregard its validity or relevance for our effort to understand reality in the widest sense of the term, i. e., for framing the description of a cosmology. Scientific knowledge may well be integrated into this wider understanding.

> The cosmology and the schemes of the sciences are mutually critics of each other. The limited morphology of a special science is confessedly incapable of expressing in its own categoreal notions all forms which are illustrated in the world. But it is the business of a cosmology to be adequate. For this reason a cosmology must consider those factors which have not been adequately embraced in some science. It has also to include all the sciences. (FR 77).

Hence, science should not be contradicted by cosmology or metaphysics or religion. But nevertheless one must be aware that science is in a state of continuous development. And as science advances, it might be forced to leave its former positions, since they might suddenly become incapable of accounting for new discoveries or providing successful explanations. In such a case we may be able to employ modern terminology and speak of a "shift in the scientific paradigm." Whitehead thought, I believe, that the new understanding in physics highlighted such a shift in the scientific paradigm of his own time. The Newtonian physics had "broken down" and there were signs of the beginning of a new scientific era. The world could no more be conceived of as ready-made and static. Bertrand Russell has described this change in the following way:

> The theory of relativity, by merging time into space-time, has damaged the traditional notion of substance more than all the arguments of philosophers. Matter, for common sense, is something which persists in time and moves in space. But for modern relativity-physics this view is no longer tenable. A piece of matter has become, not a persistent thing with varying states, but a system of inter-related events. The old solidity is gone, and with it the characteristics that, to the materialist, made matter seem more real than fleeting thoughts. Nothing is permanent, nothing endures; the prejudice that the real is the persistent must be abandoned.[41]

In the view of modern physics nature is a dynamic process of becoming, steadily changing and developing, radically temporal in character. The elements of matter combined in a paradoxical way the properties of particles and waves, so that they could neither be described as particles nor waves in the traditional sense. The word 'event,' which seemed free of the substantial connotations of the word 'element,' would be much more appropriate. This was also consonant with the general dynamic trend in physics. Not only was mass fused with energy but space was merged with time into space-time. Both space-time and mass-energy was fused into a single, though heterogeneous, dynamic entity, or rather process. Nature was now seen, as much less predictable than Newtonian physics had assumed.

To Whitehead this all meant that we need to acquire a new perspective on the world and on reality in general.

> For the modern view process, activity, and change are the matter of fact. At an instant there is nothing. Each instant is only a way of grouping matters of fact. Thus since there are no instants, conceived as simple primary entities, there is no nature at an instant. Thus all the interrelations of matters of fact must involve transition in their essence. All realization involves implication in the creative advance (MT 146).

Since the world, as we experience it in science and in everyday life, is a world of change, of becoming, of growth and decay, Whitehead thought that the most adequate way of imagining it, describing it and talking about it was as a *process of becoming*. To exist, to be real, to be fully actual, is to be in process. However, Whitehead did not argue that everything in the world was in process. There were also some unchanging propositions, notions and facts, like scientific divisions and abstract categories, which were not in a process of change. But such concepts only represent certain abstract aspects of reality derived from the network of process-events influencing each other. Hence, anything which is not in process is purely an abstraction from that process. Therefore, it counts as "misplaced concreteness" to let such abstractions account for the total reality of the temporal process – which occasionally was what happened with the concepts of Newtonian physics as they were increasingly adopted as parts of an all-encompassing, metaphysical system. They had been, and still were, superbly successful in astronomy and mechanics, but totally misplaced as the basic elements of an all-inclusive and absolute cosmology.

When Whitehead talked about 'process' he used the term in two different context, which we must understand as two different aspects of the one and only 'process,' i. e., the actual reality. One aspect of process he calls *transition,* whereby he refers to the temporal process leading from one happening or event to another. This process

> is the fluency whereby the perishing of the process, on the completion of the particular existent, constitutes that existent as an original element

in the constitutions of other particular existents elicited by repetitions of process ... Transition is the vehicle of the efficient cause, which is the immortal past (PR 320).

When Whitehead talked about events in transition he meant those momentary events which perish immediately upon coming into being. The perishing marks the transition to the succeding event. In this sense Whitehead pictured reality as cumulative. When, upon the completion of one event, the process of creation moves on to the next 'birth,' it carries that event with it as an 'object' which all future events are obliged to 'prehend,' to take account of. They will 'feel' it as *efficient cause*, Whitehead said. The end of one event's 'private life' – its perishing – is the beginning of its "public career" (PR 444).

As we have noticed, Whitehead rejected the concept of 'substance' as that which requires no other entity in order to exist. The fundamental, complete "fact" of the universe is not a substance with its qualities. On the contrary, Whitehead thought that every entity in fact requires other entities in order to exist, i. e., to be in process. And the most significant characteristics of the basic entities in reality are their "prehensions," or "feelings." Prehensions are what an actual entity is composed of and the "vehicles" by which it becomes objectified in other actual entities. Whitehead also called this the "principle of relativity," which can be described as the doctrine that all entities are potentials for the becoming of new entities.

There is nothing in the real world which is merely an inert fact. Every reality is there for feeling: it promotes feeling; and it is felt (PR 472).

Therefore, everything in the world is contingent upon everything else and requires all others in order to exist. Or as Whitehead at one point explains:

If you get a general notion of what is meant by perishing, you will have accomplished an apprehension of what you mean by memory and causality, what you mean when you feel that what we are is of infinite importance, because as we perish we are immortal.[42]

Besides the process of transition, which constitutes temporality, there is also another type of process. Whitehead views events or occasions as real individuals and terms them "actual entities," "actual occasions," or "occasions of experience." For Whitehead these events or occasions, of which the temporal process is made up, are in themselves processes. This, as we have already said, is not remote from the way physicists identify the basic entities in reality as dynamic events or processes. In Whitehead's philosophy these ultimate events are the processes of their own momentary becoming. The notion of temporality is not applicable to this aspect of process. However, at a deeper level of understanding they are not 'things' that endure through a tiny bit of time unchanged. They are more to be understood as taking that bit of time to become.[43] This phase of process Whitehead calls *concrescence*, which

> is the fluency inherent in the constitution of the particular existent ... Concrescence moves towards its final cause, which is its subjective aim (PR 320).

It must once again be emphasized that transition and concrescence are not to be affirmed as two different processes, but as two aspects of one. In order to understand this we must say a few words about what Whitehead meant by *creativity*. The principle of creativity enunciates the following relationship between the *many* and the *one:* 1. at any instant the universe constitutes a disjunctively diverse many; 2. "it lies in the nature of things that the many enter into complex unity" (PR 31). Process is then the creative thrust from the many to the one, producing a novel entity that is other than the many that gave rise to it and thus part of a new many in turn productive of new novel entities. This rhythmic alternation between the many and the one is "process."

> There are two species of process, macroscopic process, and microscopic process. The macroscopic process is the transition from attained actuality to actuality in attainment; while the microscopic process is the conversion of conditions which are merely real into determinate actuality (i. e., it is concrescence) (PR 326).

The world, viewed either from a macrocosmic or a microcosmic perspective, is a web of interconnected events and activities. All occasions are interdependent and have essential references to other times and spaces. Every event is constituted by its relationships, and *nothing can exist except by participation.* That is the reason, as has been pointed out before, why Whitehead refuses to take the standpoint of Newton or Galileo and to try to investigate and understand reality from 'outside,' as an observer. We are, he claims, forced to view reality from 'inside,' because we participate in it essentially and lack access to a position external to the world.

Some events are, of course, arbitrary, imposed by the mind from outside. Such events, for instance, historical events, are "only a way of grouping matters of fact." However, there are also real occasions, certain 'given' events, that have their own unity. They are true *individuals*. These events react and respond to other events. Each event is, therefore, a center of spontaneity and self-creation, contributing distinctively to the creation of the world. Thus, reality consists of this interacting plurality of individual events. Whitehead also calls his metaphysics *the philosophy of organism.*[44]

If we briefly consider Whitehead's detailed analysis of how new events arise, we can say that *causality* in his philosophy is a complex process composed of different factors. However, there are three different major strands that together shape and create novelty in the universe. New events are partly determined by *efficient causation,* by which Whitehead means the influence from previous events. Here we may recall the picture of nature as cumulative, where the new event carries its efficient cause with it as an "object," to which it must conform. The efficient cause of an event is constituted by the objectified antecedent data which the event prehends or feels. The "efficient causation expresses the transition from actual entity to actual entity" (PR 228).

There is however, in addition always an element of *self-causation* in the becoming of a new event. Whitehead rejects every kind of determinism and argues that every occasion has its own individual freedom to contribute something of its own in the way that it appropriates the past, relates to the various possibilities and creates a new synthesis. The fact that every novel event in its process of becoming acquires a definite character to the exclusion of other possibilities, other possible characters, is explained by Whitehead as the event's selection of what he calls *eternal objects.* These objects are the

> Pure Potentials for the Specific Determination of Fact *or* Form of Definiteness (PR 32).

To a certain degree the "eternal objects" resemble the Platonic Ideas, but Whitehead does not claim that these "pure potentials" exist in separation from what is actual. The point of this notion is that nothing novel can come into existence "out of nowhere." To some extent actualities are always the realization of something potential. In order to exist, every entity must have some determinate form or character, i. e., some determinant. It requires some "aim" or "form of definiteness," which is already an "ingredient" in the entity at the beginning of the process of becoming. What Whitehead calls the *subjective* aim is then a feeling or prehension of what the process of an entity or event might achieve. In Whitehead's terminology it is a *conceptual prehension* and arises in the primary stage of the becoming, as something that the event "receives" from God. It is the ideal of what might become of an entity, and as such a lure or a call toward realization. Whitehead calls this *initial aim,* which is the pure feeling of divine purpose.

> The lowest form of mental experience is blind urge towards a *form of* experience, that is to say, an urge towards a *form for* realization ... This urge is appetition. It is emotional purpose (FR 32).

Thus, the concrescing process is partly governed by the possibilities for its outcome, what it is as a '*superject,*' which the concrescing occasion receives. But the becoming occasion also prehends or "decides" which possibilities are to be realized. The process of becoming is not determined by God as its only cause. Rather, the "subjective aim" is constituted by a selection of eternal objects, which God brings to the becoming occasion. As "superject," God offers for each actual entity as its initial aim, a vision of what that entity might become. The initial aim becomes as received the subjective aim, which constitutes the ideal for growth on the part of each becoming entity. It is the subject's response to the feeling of divine purpose. The superject is then a "final cause" in the process of becoming. By this is meant that the process of concrescence moves toward its final cause, which is its subjective aim, and which is preceded by the initial aim (PR 320).

My understanding of Whitehead's usage of "eternal objects" is that they enable him to explain process, namely as the realization of selected antecedent potentialities. To many of us, however, this notion might seem too fantastic, since Whitehead actually thought that all events, even those without consciousness, become actual by selecting among different potentialities, i. e., eternal objects. However, Whitehead thought that low-level events in nature inherit habits of selecting and that these habits sometimes are so strong that we may refer to them as "laws of nature."[45] Hence, this creative selection from among alternative potentialities in terms of goals and aims – of which eternal objects are a part – Whitehead calls *final causation*. The resemblance with Platonism is apparent, no doubt.

The initial phase of concrescence is the phase of efficient causation and the succeeding supplemental phases are the phases of novelty and purposive adjustment. But each event has at least some creative freedom for shaping the particular unity of experience into which its past inheritance is woven and integrated. During its moment of becoming it is *autonomous*. Thus, efficient causality characterizes the transition between events, while final causation dominates the momentary internal growth of the event, as it succesively actualizes its own synthesis and embodies a particular pattern of form. This Whitehead called "conceptual prehension."

In summary, let us look at a passage in *Process and Reality,* where Whitehead tries to explain the notion of "self-creation."

> The doctrine of the philosophy of organism is that, however far the sphere of efficient causation be pushed in the determination of components of a concrescence – its data, its emotions, its appreciations, its purposes, its phases of subjective aim – beyond the determination of these components there always remains the final reaction of the self-creative unity of the universe. This final reaction completes the self-creative act by putting the decisive stamp of creative emphasis upon the determinations of efficient cause. Each occasion exhibits its measure of creative emphasis in proportion to its measure of subjective intensity ... But in the temporal world for occasions of relatively slight experient intensity, their decisions of creative emphasis are individually negligible compared to the determined components which they receive and transmit (PR 75).

2.5 The Notion of Actual Entity

In the Newtonian physics final causation was replaced by efficient causation, though the notion of efficient causation was hardly new. All causality in nature was thus assumed to be reducible to forces between atoms and particles. In this system all change could be exhaustively described as the rearrangement of these ultimate bits of matter. Here change did not mean transition from potentiality to actuality, but simply rearrangement of particles in time and space. This was, as we have already said, the view that Whitehead strongly criticized. The world, he argued, did not consist of static particles merely arranged externally. In this context White-head also rejects the idea that had dominated philosophy since the days of Aristotle, namely, that every entity itself consisted of an unchanging 'substance' with changing attributes or qualities. Instead, Whitehead pictures the world as composed of interrelated and contingent events. These events, he thought, are the basic components of reality, the stuff the world is made of.

> 'Actual entities' – also termed 'actual occasions' – are the final real things of which the world is made up. There is no going behind actual entities to find anything more real. They differ among themselves: God is an actual entity, and so is the most trivial puff of existence in far-off empty space. But, though there are gradations of importance, and diversities of function, yet in the principles which actuality exemplifies all are on the same level. The final facts are, all alike, actual entities; and these actual entities are drops of experience, complex and interdependent (PR 27–28).[46]

Since the Newtonian cosmology "has broken down" (AI 156), the fundamental entities of reality are no longer "simple locations" or "stubborn bits of matter," unrelated to each other, but events: *actual entities* or *actual occasions*.[47] They "replace the 'neutral' of certain realistic philosophers," Whitehead claims, and proceeds to formulate what he terms *the ontological principle*.

> Apart from things that are actual, there is nothing – nothing either in fact or in efficacy (PR 64).[48]

Nothing in the actual world can be traced beyond the notion of actual entities (PR 65, 116). The world, in the widest sense of the word, is then to be understood only in reference to beings existing in and for themselves. But on the other hand, we must remember that actual entities are not to be conceived as existing in and for themselves as isolated events. On the contrary, an actual entity by its very nature requires other actual entities as "ingredients" (AI old ed. 231, PR 10, 220.). And this is at the heart of Whitehead's metaphysical system, since his rejection of the Aristotelian concept of substance, which was presupposed by both Galileo, Descartes and Newton, implies the rejection of that which requires nothing but itself in order to exist. Therefore, the most concrete characteristics of an actual entity are its *prehensions,* which primarily are prehensions or feelings of other actual entities. The so-called "qualities" of actual entities are only abstractions from these prehensions (PR 28, 35, 72, 234).

> The essence of an actual entity consists solely in the fact that it is a prehending thing (i. e., a substance whose whole essence or nature is to prehend) (PR 65).

That human beings or even animals have perceptions does not seem surprising to us. But that *all* basic elements in reality have prehensions certainly becomes a stumbling block to many of us. However, there is no reason to get upset about it, since Whitehead's use of words like "prehension" or "feeling" must be understood as technical definitions that bear only a remote resemblance to their everyday meaning. He uses "prehension" to refer to a "taking account of" other things which does not necessarily involve consciousness (PR 83). Hence, prehension can be attributed not only to high-level creatures but also to low-grade actual entities, ordered as "organisms of organism." Atoms and molecules are "organisms of a higher type, which also represent a compact definite unity," and also large numbers of other inorganic objects can be viewed as ordered into "corpuscular societies," such as stones and vegetables. However, such objects are not actual entities or actual occasions in Whitehead's sense, but organizations of entities or occasions. Therefore, one can speak about molecules, for instance, as 'examples' of actual occasions.

> Each actual entity is conceived as an act of experience arising out of data. It is a process of 'feeling' the many data, so as to absorb them into the unity of one individual 'satisfaction'. Here 'feeling' is the term used for the basic generic operation of passing from the objectivity of the data to the subjectivity of the actual entity in question. Feelings are variously specialized operations, effecting a transition into subjectivity (PR 65).

The essence, Whitehead claims, of a present actual entity, is to prehend. The essence of a past actual entity is to be prehended. To enable us to understand this we must recall Whitehead's notion of "transition." A characteristic that can be applied to all beings is that they are potentialities for entering into the becoming of new actual entities. Thus, in process, *all* actual entities are *subjects,* which is the same for Whitehead as to say that they are "experiences," or that they "feel."

> There is nothing in the real world which is merely an inert fact. Every reality is there for feeling: it promotes feeling; and it is felt (PR 472).

An actual entity is not initially something in itself, which then enters into relation with other entities. The *relation* is what comes first, i. e., the prehension. Hence, when Whitehead uses the word "feeling" or "prehension," he wants us to focus upon the 'relation' as something *real,* instead of upon some abstract notion of substance. We must always remember that these terms are used to resemble only slightly what we mean by conscious human feelings, memories and experiences. We must understand that they are abstractions from the deepest level of human experience, even if Whitehead at the same time seems to believe that they refer to something ontologically real. Otherwise we will ourselves commit the "fallacy of misplaced contreteness" (PR 7, SMW 51).

It is important to interpret Whitehead's thought on this point once again against the background of his critical attitude towards Newtonian cosmology. At the bottom of this cosmology was, as we have said, a mind – matter dualism, initiated by Galileo and explicated by Descartes. Mind and matter represented two different substances. Whitehead resented this philosophical construction. What *we* call mental and physical things are just abstractions from our experience of the complex flux of events around us. They are imposed from the outside, or as Witehead would have it: they are a way of "grouping matters of fact." In *reality* there is no such *dualism* between the actual things which are subjects and those which are merely objects, as there was for Descartes. The dichotomy between mind and matter refers to nothing real. On the contrary, it obscures our understanding of reality, and it distorts our attitudes to the world of nature. Instead Whitehead wants us to grasp reality in a unified scheme, by making organic process and relations between experiencing entities primary, thereby rejecting the dualism between thinking and experiencing things and pure material objects (PR 253). In Whitehead's view, all beings on the planet Earth, living creatures as well as inorganic matter, can enjoy some degree of non-conscious experience. Whitehead does, however distinguish between two poles within the actual entity, the "*mental pole*" and the "*physical pole*." An actual entity's process of concrescence begins with a phase in which the entity prehends an antecedent actual entity, which then becomes a part of the creative process. This is what Whitehead calls a simple physical or causal feeling, which is the phase of *receiving* what is purely given. The mental pole on the other hand refers to a later phase in the process where the actual entity responds and thereby contributes to its own creation (PR 380).[49] Whitehead describes this as a "conceptual prehension," which, however, does not mean "that these mental operations involve consciousness" (PR 379).

Although "no actual entity is devoid of either pole, and though their relative importance differs in different actual entities" (PR 366), Whitehead claims that there is an order in nature distinguishing between different actual entities according to a *hierarchy of value.* While every actual entity has some form of prehension, and, therefore, an instrinsic value, we do not need to think of them as having equal value, since they achieve different degrees of prehension or feeling. Briefly, Whitehead's understanding of the order in nature can be summarized in the following way: 1. Although all actual entities have some intrinsic value, they may be differentiated in terms of the values and degrees of values they can attain.

2. The purpose of nature is the attainment of value. 3. Order among actual entities can serve to make higher values possible. 4. God's purpose is to promote the emergence and preservation of entities capable of enjoying greater value.[50] On the basis of the ability to achieve value and self-determination, it is, therefore, possible to differentiate between levels in nature. Thus, molecules are understood as *low-grade entities,* where the element of self-creation is negligible. They are dominated by their "physical pole." On the next stage Whitehead speaks about *corpuscular societies* (PR 52, 141), by which he means inorganic aggregates like stones or rocks. The *living cell* has a higher capacity for novelty and experience, a greater "intensity of experience" and, therefore, can attain much more value than the inorganic society. However, living cells in turn can be organized into two different groups, *living democracies* and *monarchies* (MT 23–28), which may refer, approximately, to our distinction between plants and animals. In this hierarchy of actual entities we may affirm that the society of entities which constitute the human being is even more capable of attaining value. Hence, the superiority of humans within the total organism may be 'justified' Whitehead thinks. But there is no place for human arrogance toward nature. In Whitehead's metaphysical system there is a continuity between all levels of beings. Women and men are not made of some 'stuff' different from other beings. They are organically linked to simpler forms of nature and it is, therefore, "hazardous to draw any sharp distinction between living things and inorganic matter" (FR 5).

2.6 Whitehead's Theory of Value

Our world is an ongoing process of experience, in which each entity has value for itself. An actual entity is first of all something for its own sake, an end in itself. But the actual entity arises out of its prehensions of other entities or occasions. And these prehensions are primarily *feelings* of the value of what is being prehended. The prehended entities or occasions are felt as *those* value-experiences which are contributing *this* value-experience, namely, the becoming of a new actual entity. Hence, the most significant characteristic of an actual entity is that it is a *value-experience.*

Since this part of Whitehead's metaphysical system, which he calls the "principle of relativity," takes its cue from his theory of perception, we must return to the discussion of this theory.

The most fundamental mode of experience is not sense perception, but an *intuitive awareness* of our past mental and bodily existence and of the surrounding environment of past actual entities which have conformed themselves to the present. "What is the dominating insight whereby we presuppose ourselves as actualities within a world of actualities?" Whitehead asks. And how does it happen "that we know ourselves as creatures in a world of creatures?" His answer is that this awareness is not an inference from sense-perception, but a kind of *non-sensuous perception*, which he calls "causal efficacy."

> There is a feeling of the ego, the others, the totality. This is the vague, basic presentation of the differentiation of existence, in its enjoyment of discard and maintenance. We are, each of us, one among others; and all of us are embraced in the unity of the whole (MT 110).

This non-sensuous perception, which is at the basis of all knowledge, is of emotional character. It is a *value-experience.*

> Our enjoyment of actuality is a realization of worth, good or bad. It is a value-experience. Its basic expression is – Have a care, here is something that matters! Yes – that is the best phrase – the primary glimmering of consciousness reveals, something that matters (MT 116).

Everything we know about ourselves and the surrounding world is based on value-experiences. Values, according to Whitehead, are not simply imposed subjectively from without. They are objectively at the basis of the existence of the entire world.

> At the base of our existence is the sense of "worth." Now worth essentially presupposes that which is worthy. Here the notion of worth is not to be construed in a purely eulogistic sense. It is the sense of existence for its own sake, of existence which is its own justification, of existence with its own character (MT 109).

Thus, Whitehead protests "against the exclusion of value from the essence of matter of fact" (SMW old ed. 138). This, too, I believe, may be understood against the background of his repudiation of the reduction of everything real to physical particles or bits of matter. According to the Cartesian dualism, *matter* was seen as something purely objective and as having only external relations to its environment. It was also regarded as devoid of all intrinsic value. Nature was only assigned instrumental value. Only the human being had intrinsic value. *Mind,* as the other pole of this dualism, was in Descartes' terminology "thinking substance," defined as so dissimilar to the substance of matter as to render any interaction between them difficult to imagine. The whole range of life between the poles of mind and matter was relegated to the side of matter. Animals were viewed as complex machines without feelings or intelligence. Even the human body was pictured as a sort of machine. Any amount of exploitation or manipulation of nature was left to human discretion, since human beings possessed free, rational and controlling minds. The concept of value was imagined to be merely contained within the human mind.

The main point now is to realize the scope of Whitehead's rejection of the Newtonian-Cartesian distinction of mind and matter, because the so-called secondary qualities, which belonged solely to the mind here, are precisely those properties which we today regard as valuable, i. e., as having intrinsic value. The primary quantitative forms – on the other hand – which belong to matter, are now seen as devoid of such value. If they have value, it is only instrumental, i. e., they are valuable as means. But, in Newtonian cosmology matter alone was concretely real in nature. Aesthetic values were simply added subjectively or projected from the outside. They were not real. They existed only in the 'head' of the person who valued, and there was nothing objectively real or valid in his or her doing so. However, for Whitehead, on the other hand, colors, sounds, emotions, and purposes are just as real as physical qualities. Nature is not left without instrinsic value, since in his philosophy all beings yield feelings.

In order to understand Whitehead's value theory it might be helpful to view it in relation to a distinction between different metanormative theories of value, viz., what we mean when we speak about 'values,' or what words such as 'good' refer to. We may then distinguish between those who argue that values stand for properties of some sort, and those who deny this. *Cognitivists,* then, argue that values refer to certain properties, or qualities, and that value judgments are descriptive. Values, at least some values, are said to be facts, and value judgments taken to be factual. *Non-cognitivists,* on the other hand, argue that values do not refer to properties of any kind, but that they might have another function than description in a person's use of them.

They might express feelings, attitudes or desires, some non-cognitivists hold, while others argue that they are prescriptions or recommendations of the kind: "I approve of this. Do it!" Some non-cognitivists believe that values or value judgments can be somehow justified: they can be intersubjectively valid conventions, like "What is pleasant is good." Others such as A. J. Ayer and Jean-Paul Sartre, have thought that there is no rationality what so ever to the values we hold, or to the value judgments we make. There is nothing objectively right or wrong in our acts. Our choice of behaviour is completely arbitrary from an ethical point of view.

Now we may understand Whitehead as having a cognitivistic theory of value. He holds that values are properties inherent in things, regardless of whether there is someone appreciating that thing or not. Whitehead believes this because he thinks that all entities are experiencing subjects. They experience and, therefore, they are intrinsically valuable i. e., having value for themselves. Values according to Whitehead are properties belonging to reality, but of a sort that can not be observed in ordinary sense experience. They can only be intuited.

One way to interpret Whitehead is, therefore, to understand him as challenging the old dichotomy between statements of fact and judgments of value. To Whitehead values are *facts* belonging to the objective world. If this is correct, I shall agree with Whitehead, and argue that the fact – value distinction does not quite hold, however heavily institutionalized it has become in our society.[51] The strategy of my argument, which I shall elaborate in a later section, is basically that factual statements, used as they are in scientific theories as well as in everyday life, presuppose values. I shall argue that at least certain values must be *objective*. If the argument proves valid, I shall claim that Whitehead's position may be defended, namely, that we may not exclude "values from the essence of matter of fact." However, I shall criticize certain other implications of his value theory. I shall touch on the matter now, and return to the issue at a later point.

If all actual entities have feelings, and, therefore, intrinsic value, how can we justify ethical priority? How can we eat carrots or beef, or justify the killing of cancer or of malarial mosquitoes? Do we have any right to claim that the human being is qualitatively more valuable than any animal or even than inorganic matter?

Process thinkers try to answer these questions by making the distinction between *ontological dualism* and *organizational duality*.[52] Everything actual has some kind of experience and, therefore, some kind of intrinsic value. But there is an organizational hierarchy of values, so that when a choice must be made, there is "a basis for discriminating value judgments. Destroying the life of some types of actualities is more serious than destroying that of others. Everything else being equal, those with greater intrinsic values are to be preferred, when a choice must be made."[53] John B. Cobb, Jr. claims, for instance, on grounds that all experience has intrinsic value, that "there is every indication that most experiences of dogs are of more value than any of those of bacteria. To kill a considerable number of bacteria to restore the health of a dog is justified."[54] David Griffin argues, on the basis of what he calls "a hierarchy of *capacity* for value," that "animals, especially those with a central nervous system, are capable of experiencing more value than the plants," and, thus, that they are more valuable.

But now, how about *humans?* Is there a difference between people and the rest of nature? Do human beings have the same capacity for experience, and therefore, the same value? John Cobb argues that there is no point in considering how far feelings extend beyond human feelings. His view is that "no line at all can be drawn, that wherever one deals with actual entities one is dealing with feelings."[55] He believes that much of what we find important in human feelings "depends on such a high evolutionary product as consciousness," and he doubts that there is consciousness where there is no central nervous system.

This argument, however, runs into problems, since it seems impossible to avoid a *relativization of the specific value of human beings*. For while one can appreciate Whitehead's and the process theologian's efforts to protect nature by granting it a value for itself, an area still much to be emphasized, many people would feel reluctance for the perspective on humans which is generated by this effort. For in process philosophy, all value is relative to experience, or more correctly: the value of an actual entity is relative to its capacity for richness of experience. In such a philosophy it is no longer possible to think of all humans as equal, since each certainly has a very different "capacity for experience." Many Christians, it seems, will have some problems here, since in their understanding of what humans are, the value of human beings is not relative to anything in the world. It is not relative to capacity for experience, the capacity for work, any capacity what so ever. It is not, in their view, relative to age, race, gender, education, or social position. The irreducable value of all men, women, and children rests on the sole fact that they *are* human beings, at least potentially, and it is related to the belief that they are created in the image of God. Human value is relative only to God. From this point of view, Cobb's view, as representative for process philosophy, is problematic:

> It is not really evident that the advantage of a mongoloid idiot or a human vegetable should count equally with that of a healthy child.

How about old, senile persons, or a human fetus? Is Cobb's criterion for ethical preference applicable here? Do not people in general have very different capacity for experience?

To raise such questions does *not* imply that

a) humans cannot also be valued by others, or that their behaviour cannot be evaluated, or that

b) human beings are the only beings in the world which are really valuable, and that, therefore,

c) humans are completely free to treat nature as they wish.

And, of course, we may many times be in a position where it is necessary to make the kind of decision that Cobb's example suggests. But the problems involved are related to the criterion for ethical preference proposed by process theologians, on the basis of Whitehead's theory of value. This is an issue to which we shall return, but let us here, however, say only that process theology would do well to come to terms with this issue, especially as much ecological philosophy of today – with which process theology seems frequently to be connected – entails a serious and potentially dangerous tendency to relativize the value of human lives.[56]

There is, however, a second line of argument in process thought, implicit in both Cobb's and Griffin's writings, which has not received proper appreciation. Perhaps more emphasis ought to be put here; if this line of argument is developed further it might provide a basis for resolving some of the problems I have dealt with. Cobb says:

> We conceive of the biota of the planet earth not as life viewed by man but as life viewed by a larger, more inclusive perspective. When we do so we attribute a value to the whole that is greatly enriched by all the complex contrasts and interrelations of the parts, man being one of those parts. Is the perspective from which this rich value can be contemplated a real perspective? . . . If, however, reality is such that there *is* an inclusive

perspective in addition to the limited ones which are human, the value of the variety of life is real. And our callous disregard of the values of the whole for the sake of values of the parts is a violation and desecration that has great ethical importance. To believe this is to believe, implicitly if not explicitly, in God.[57]

Also Griffin argues that the primary focus for a "theology of nature" must be that nature is understood to have *ultimate value in relation to God*. In this context Whitehead's assertion that God has a "consequent nature" is most important. This notion may allow for what was not possible in traditional theism, namely, that nature must be seen as having *significance for God*.

The idea of God's consequent nature involves the affirmation that the values which are first experienced by infinite individuals are then experienced by the everlasting divine individual. Greater variety, intensity, and harmony in the experiences of the world contribute to greater richness in the divine experience.[58]

Only when it becomes clear that the world of nature and history is important to God, can nature be considered a matter of ultimate concern. In the process understanding, nature receives its intrinsic value, at least in part, by being prehended – or experienced – by God. What happens to the world is of utmost concern to God and influences the divine. God takes the world into God's own experience.

2.7 The Nature of God

Turning now to a discussion of Whitehead's concept of God, we may first recall Whitehead's critique of Newtonian physics, which in many respects shaped his stance for the elaboration of the entire process metaphysics. In Newton's worldview, nature was static, with all things created in their present form. Nature was deterministic. Change in this conception did not mean transition from potentiality to actuality, but rearrangement of particles in time and space. As we have said before, Whitehead argued that this cosmology contained a severe contradiction: it could not take account of the creative advance into novelty which is essential to our experience of reality.

The creativity is not an external agency with its own ulterior purposes. All actual entities share with God this characteristic of self-causation. For this reason every actual entity also shares with God the characteristic of transcending all other actual entities, including God. The universe is thus a creative advance into novelty. The alternative to this doctrine is a static morphological universe (PR 339f).

In this creative process God can be conceived as the source for both *novelty* and *order*. Whitehead calls this divine function the *primordial nature of God*. Apart from God there could be no novelty in the world and no order. In this respect God can be said to transcend the world. However, God's creative activity does not imply that he determines the process. The creative process is best understood as an interplay between God, as a non-temporal actual entity, and all other temporal entities. The things which are temporal arise by their participation in what is eternal. Creation is, therefore, a transition of eternal potentialities to temporal actuality. In this process God evaluates and chooses certain potentialities for what an actual entity might become, which Whitehead describes as "the relevant eternal object." God's impact on the creative process is felt as a persuasive "lure" toward realization, to which the becoming actual entity has freedom to respond.

> God is the principle of concretion; namely, he is that actual entity from which each temporal concrescence receives that initial aim from which its self-causation starts (PR 374).

We have already mentioned the concept of "subjective aim" as something necessary in every process of self-creation. An actual entity, in order to exist, i. e. to "become" or to "be in process," must have some *determinate form*. Without such a 'determinant' there can be no process. And so nothing would be. The *initial aim* is, therefore, required in order to "direct" the concrescence and to "initiate" it. This aim must already be present at the beginning of the process. It is not created by the becoming actual entity, but "received" by it. In Whitehead's metaphysics God is precisely this "definiteness" received by the actual entity. God is the *provider of subjective aim*. It is in this context that God is said to be the "primordial ground of novelty" in the world.

Since subjective aim, or definiteness, is required for the process of concrescence, or existence if you will, God can be termed as the *Creator*. However, "creator" in this context does not mean that God creates the world 'out of nothing,' *ex nihilo*, at the beginning of time. God is not prior to the becoming of the creation or outside it.

> God is not *before* all creation, but *with* all creation (PR 521).

This conception of creation and the role that God can be said to play in it is accepted by all process theologians. In their book *Process Theology; An Introductory Exposition*, John B. Cobb Jr. and David Ray Griffin state:

> Process theology rejects the notion of *creatio ex nihilo*, if that means creation out of *absolute* nothingness. That doctrine is part and parcel of the doctrine of God as absolute controller. Process theology affirms instead a doctrine of creation out of chaos.[59]

The concept of creation within the Whiteheadian cosmology must be understood as a *continuous process* of everlasting character. Each actual entity is, in one aspect, of temporal character; it will perish although it will still be in continuity with all other actual entities thereafter. In addition to being something only for itself, it becomes something for other actual entities as well. It becomes a "superject," in Whitehead's terminology. It transcends itself. Whitehead speaks about the perishing of an actual entity as the beginning of its "public career" in other actual entities. Every actual entity, according to Whitehead, becomes present in God "objectively," which means not in its own subjective immediacy. It is "felt effectively" in God's experience and thus contributes to the divine satisfaction. God's aim is at maximum *intensity of experience,* according to Whitehead, for God's self as well as for the world. While all actual entities are of limited duration, "occasions" or "events," God is there at all times experiencing the world, integrating the fading actual entities into the eternal nature of God's being. In Whitehead's metaphysics God is one. However, abstractly speaking, this aspect of God's nature is called the *concequent nature of God,* consisting of God's "physical prehensions" of all actual occasions.

Since the philosophy of organism explicitly rejects dualism, it does not conceive of God the Creator as standing 'apart' from creation. As soon as Whitehead speaks about God as "Creator," he warns us that "there is no meaning to 'creativity' apart from its 'creatures'" (PR 344). If we are to talk about the origin of the creation, it is

> the multiplicity of data in the universe, actual entities and eternal objects (PR 343).

In comparison, for instance, with the notion of God as Creator in the theology of Thomas Aquinas in which the world is totally dependent on God for its existence, the concept of God in Whitehead's metaphysics represents radical modification. God does not determine the world, is more of an organizer than a creator, is of the same basic "stuff" as the rest of the creation, and so forth. However, Whitehead does not entertain a pantheistic concept of God. God is not identical to the world, but is a distinct entity in the world who also enjoys greater freedom than any other actual entity. However, God's independence of the world is relative.

In addition to this we might mention that Charles Hartshorne, who was never formally a student of Whitehead's but one of the first philosophers who appreciated and developed Whitehead's way of thinking, has elaborated a form of theism that is more closely related to pantheism than is Whitehead's philosophy of organism. In his book *The Divine Relativity,*[60] Hartshorne develops a view which he calls *panentheism,* asserting that the world exists solely within the nature of God, which at the same time transcends the world. God is greater than the world. Since God in the philosophy of organism does not include the world, there seems to be no reason to characterize Whitehead as a panentheist.[61]

In classical Christian theology God has been understood as something completely separate and different from the rest of reality. God has *aseitas*. Being by and of itself is attributed only to God. All other beings in the world are somehow dependent in their existence upon God as creator. They are *ab alio*. One problem in a theology that emphasizes God's *aseitas* is this: how can God, a completely different being, be *related* to the world? What sort of being is God, if it is entirely different from everything in the world? The dualism between God and the world is resolved in pantheism, since God and the world are not understood as separate beings. However, the notion of God as a distinct being, enjoying freedom and individuality, simultaneously evaporates. It is here that the advantage of Whitehead's cosmology becomes apparent. For in terms of his ontology it becomes possible to maintain some sort of content for the concept of God's *aseitas,* and yet to explain how God is related to the world. Or, in other words: in Whitehead's philosophy of organism it is possible to determine in which way God and the world are connected, without falling into pantheism. God and the world are more intimately related in Whitehead's system than in classical theology. But they are never identified.

In classical theology, it is hard to avoid conceiving of God's *aseitas* on the model of a clock-maker standing apart from his creation. But if we conceive of the world on the model of an organism, as Whitehead urges us to do, it is easier to understand how God, a distinct being, can be related to and influence the rest of the world. God does not act *on* it – as we can act on things – but *in* it. God is an "event" in the world, according to Whitehead, that penetrates and influences other "events." God does not manipulate the world from without, but – as we shall see – lures, or persuades the world from within.

It might be mentioned that God's having *this* sort of relation to the world may express God's own, free decision. Even if Whitehead does not explicitly discuss it, is seems possible to think that God has chosen to relate to the world in precisely this way. This, however, is a question to which I shall return in a later section.

The concept of creation within Whitehead's metaphysical scheme cannot be viewed as an absolute origination of the world but as an *ordering* of "the multiplicity of data in the universe." It is in connection with this that Whitehead talks about God as the *primordial ground of order.* God embodies the order of possibilities or the potential forms for becoming: *eternal objects.* These are the pure potentials, in analogy with Plato's Ideas, for what an entity might become if realized in the actual world. But since they are only pure potentials, "neutral" as Whitehead puts it, and since the ontological principle implies that "everything must be some-where – and here 'somewhere' means 'some actual entity' " – they exist within the primordial mind of God (PR 73). Therefore, the order in creation is closely related to what Whitehead calls the "conceptual order" of eternal objects in God's mind. In order to investigate what Whitehead intended by the phrase "God's primordial nature", let us begin with a more comprehensive passage and then try to interpret its meaning.

The primordial created fact is the unconditioned *conceptual valuation* of the entire multiplicity of eternal objects. This is the 'primordial nature' of God. By reason of this complete valuation, the objectification of God in each derivate actual entity results in a graduation of the *relevance* of eternal objects to the concrescent phases of that derivate occassion. There will be additional ground of relevance for select eternal objects by reason of their ingression into derivate actual entities belonging to the actual world of the concrescent occasion in question. But whether or no this be the case, there is always the definite relevance derived from God (PR 46. My italics).

Every emergent actual entity receives or "prehends" or "feels" or "experiences" its "definiteness," as God's conceptual evaluation of what is the "relevant" eternal object or possibility or potential for the outcome of that actual entity's process of becoming. Among all the possibilities – eternal objects – for what the entity might become, God selects the relevant ones. Evidently God selects different possibilities for different entities. The divine purpose is a maximization of value, though God leaves the concrescing entity a range of various alternatives to respond to. God elicits the self-creative process by endowing the entity with a certain structure of possibilities among which the entity is free to choose. God seeks through the creative process to elicit a world of such a character that God's own prehensions or experiences of the world will result in the greatest possible *intensity* in God's own experience.[62]

The primordial appetitions which jointly constitute God's purpose are seeking intensity, and not preservation. Because they are primordial, there is nothing to preserve. He, in his primordial nature, is unmoved by love for this particular, or that particular; for in this foundational process of creativity, there are no preconstituted particulars. In the foundations of his being, God is indifferent alike to preservation and to novelty. He cares not whether an immediate occasion be old or new, so far as concerns derivation from its ancestry. His aim for it is depth of satisfaction as an intermediate step towards the fulfilment of his own being. His tenderness is directed towards each actual occasion, as it arises. Thus God's purpose in the creative advance is the evocation of intensities (PR 160–61).

The same idea seems to be expressed in *Modes of Thought*.

The notion of the world-process is therefore to be conceived as the notion of the totality of process. The notion of a supreme being must apply to an actuality in process of composition, an actuality not confined to the data of any special epoch in the historic field. Its actuality is founded on the infinitude of its conceptual appetition, and its form of process is derived from the fusion of this appetition with that data received from the world-process. Its function in the world is to sustain the aim at vivid experience. It is the reservoir of potentiality and the coördination of achievement (MT 93f).

To summarize the aim of the process of concrescence: God's purpose is to maximize the value-experience or the value-intensity in the world, that is, the intensity of God's own experience as well as that of the concrescing entity. However, since all actual entities are potentials for entering into other becoming entities, their anticipated value-experiences are also within God's purpose. Contemporary process theology has often applied this conception of the purpose of creation to the theory of evolution. As an example we may cite a few lines from Cobb and Griffin.

> Each stage of the evolutionary process represents an increase in the divinely given possibilities for value that are actualized. The present builds upon the past but advances beyond the past to the degree to which it responds to the divine impulses. This advance is experienced as intrinsically good, and it also provides the condition for an even richer enjoyment of existence in the future.[63]

When the "relevant" eternal object, as it is conceptually evaluated by God, is prehended or experienced by the actual entity, that object becomes the *final causation* in the process of self-creation. God has thus provided the becoming actual entity with an "initial aim." The "subjective aim" is then the personal response, so to speak, of the entity or the subject, to the initial aim. When it is received in conceptual prehension – or "felt," in Whitehead's language – it becomes the subjective aim. The initial aim is in other words the *ideal* of what the entity might become and the subjective aim is the free response to that ideal of the concrescing subject. The entity is free to actualize the initial aim or respond to other possibilities that are opened to it. As we have seen, the process of self-creation is composed of two components besides final causation, namely, "self-causation" and "efficient causation."[64]

Even if God is 'objectively' present within the experience of the actual entity, this experiential dimension in concrescence does not involve any immediate 'intuition' or awareness of God. God as primordial nature is conceived as an alternative to either a mechanical force or a despotic ruler. God's role in the concrescense is probably best viewed as a *personal relationship* in which God *initiates* and *influences* the move toward a definite outcome of the creative development. Or, as Whitehead expresses it: "God is the great companion" (PR 532).

Through the selection of potentialities God at once "urges" the realization of the individual actual entities and the entire creative process. God does not determine or control it from the outside, but conditions creation from the inside, participating in it.

For the kingdom of heaven is with us today ... What is done in the world is transformed into a reality in heaven, and the reality in heaven passes back into the world. By reason of this reciprocal relation, the love in the world passes into the love in heaven, and floods back again into the world. In this sense, God is the great companion – the fellow-sufferer who understands (PR 532).

God acts in the world, therefore, by *being experienced.* "The power of God is the worship he inspires" (SMW 276, old ed.). The evocative response that such worship may elicit is naturally greater among those actual entities that enjoy some degree of conscious experience. Translated into more traditional language it may be said that God's influence is greater among human beings than lower organisms. God influences the world by evoking "appetion," as Whitehead expresses the thought. Whitehead also speaks about this appetition as "a persuasive lure."

In his book *God and the World*, John B. Cobb, Jr. has adjusted and transformed Whitehead's thoughts for more clearly theological purposes. He describes God as "the One Who Calls us forward." We may now let a passage from this book summarize for us:

The total reality out of which each human occasion arises includes not only the adjacent events in the brain and the past human experiences but also God. Like other events, God influences the becoming occasion by being what he is. He entertains a purpose for the new occasion, differing from that entertained by previous human experience. He seeks to lure the new occasion beyond the mere repetition of past purposes and past feelings or new combinations among them. God is thus at once the source of novelty and the lure to finer and richer actualizations embodying that novelty. Thus God is the One Who Calls us beyond all that we have become to what we might be.[65]

To avoid any misunderstanding we may finally add that God, according to Whitehead, does not create the eternal objects. God "valuates," but does not originate them. Rather, they are best conceived as inseparable from the primordial nature. Without them, Whitehead claims, we could not even think the possibility that God exists. Essential to God is the complete conceptual "envisagement" (PR 50) of all eternal objects.

2.8 The Logical Status of Whitehead's Concept of God

Sofar I have discussed what Whitehead believed to be the nature of God, the content, so to speak, of the concept of God. Now let us consider how Whitehead's notion of God is related to the metaphysical system as a whole. Why is God *needed* as a concept in Whitehead's metaphysics? What is its function? How is it related to religion and to religious experience?

Whitehead's metaphysics is an attempt to unfold for us an understanding of the *world*. The fact that there is a world, which exposes itself to our experience provides the main subject of his metaphysics.

> When it comes to the primary metaphysical data, the world of which you are immediately conscious is the whole datum (RM 83).

But the fact that there is a world depends on the awareness of something else, namely, the awareness that there is an *order* in the universe. This awareness is the presupposition for consciousness of the world, since according to Whitehead,

> there is an actual world *because* there is an order in nature. If there were no order, there would be no world. Also, since there is a world, we *know* that there is an order (RM 101).

Our trust in reason, our faith that it is possible to give a rational explanation for the fact that there is an actual and temporal world, is itself grounded in the awareness of this order in the universe.

> Faith in reason is the trust that the ultimate nature of things lie together in a harmony which excludes mere arbitrariness. It is the faith that at the base of things we shall not find mere arbitrary mystery (SMW 18).

But since we can imagine the possibility that the world could have been quite different, with another order (if any at all), we have to conceive of something which is the foundation of the order of our actual and temporal world, something which puts a *limit* to all the infinite possibilities for reality and selects what sorts of potentiality are to be actualized. This is the reason why it is *necessary* to think or conceive "something" as the ground of order and novelty in our universe.

> The ordering entity is a necessary element in the metaphysical situation presented by the actual world (RM 101).

This procedure of positing a "ground of being," is according to Whitehead common to all metaphysics; more strongly: it is a logical necessity. In Aristole's physics, for instance, special causes were "required" to sustain the motion of material objects. But this could only be done, provided that the general cosmic motion could be sustained. So Whitehead argues that Aristotle "found it necessary to complete his metaphysics by the introduction of a Prime Mover – God," in order to make 'the world go 'round.'[66] In this "he had no other motive, except to follow his metaphysical train of thought." This train of thought was, however, enmeshed "in the details of an erroneous physics and an erroneous cosmology," which – according to Whitehead – the term "Prime Mover" also indicates. Today, Whitehead contends, we reject the Aristotelian physics, as well as the cosmology, and in the place of Aristotle's God as Prime Mover, we require God as the Principle of Concretion (SMW 174).[67]

Hence, Whitehead maintains that the notion of God is required for the *completion* of a metaphysical theory about the true character of reality. Without this notion, it would be impossible to give a coherent and rational account of the actual world and its order. God is thus conceived as the inevitable ordering of things in the universe, as well as the ground of novelty in the world.

> Apart from the intervention of God, there could be nothing new in the world, and no order in the world (PR 377).

Here we can also comprehend why Whitehead believes that there is no way to deliver an argument for God's existence exclusive of the understanding of our world. It is the other way around, rather. To be able to achieve a coherent and intelligible interpretation of the world, and of our experience of it as an ordered universe, it becomes necessary to introduce the notion of God. It is when we want to think rationally and consistently about the nature of reality as a whole, that we cannot avoid thinking about God. To ask what God is apart from the world therefore makes no sense. The idea of God belongs to the idea of the world. It is the complete occurence of the world, with its rational order, that demands an explanation. But since God is a part of this explanation, no separate reason for God's existence can be given. God is the ultimate principle of limitation "for which no reason can be given: for all reason flows from it" (SMW 178). It is also in this context that the relevance of the "ontological principle" becomes apparent: "to search for a *reason* is to search for one or more actual entities;" for "actual entities are the only reasons" (PR 37).

> God is the ultimate limitation, and His existence is the ultimate irrationality. For no reason can be given for just that limitation which stands in His nature to impose. God is not concrete, but He is the ground for concrete actuality. No reason can be given for the nature of God, because that nature is the ground of rationality (SMW 178).

Therefore, the justification of religious beliefs can only be given as an interpretation of our *experience* of the world.

> Our datum is the actual world, including ourselves; and this actual world spreads itself for observation in the guise of the topic of our immediate experience. The elucidation of immediate experience is the sole justification for any thought; and the starting-point for thought is the analytic observation of components of this experience (PR 6, see also MT 152).

Our apprehension of the world as a *cosmos,* where "the ultimate natures of things lie together in a harmony," is something which springs from direct inspection of the nature of things as disclosed in our own immediate present experience (SMW 18).

But this *order*, which is present in our immediate experience, and to which God is the explanation – what is it?

> The order of the world is no accident. There is nothing actual which could be actual without some measure of order. The religious insight is the grasp of this truth: That the order of the world, the depth of reality of the world, the value of the world in its whole and in its parts, the beauty of the world, the zest of life, the peace of life, and the mastery of evil, *are all bound together* – not accidentally, but by reason of this truth: that the universe exhibits a creativity with inifite freedom, and a realm of forms with infinite possibilities; but that this creativity and these forms are together impotent to achieve actuality apart from the completed ideal harmony, which is God (RM 115. My italics).

We have already noted that Whitehead's conception of *causal efficacy* provided a ground for his total metaphysical outlook, and for his understanding of nature as something intrinsically valuable. We also saw that his theory of value was consistent with his metaphysical interpretation of reality. Here we shall recognize that even his notion of God is to be found within the same framework, interconnected with his theory of value. For, when Whitehead speaks about the order, or the harmony, of the world, the fact that everything is "bound together," this is something he thinks, that we are experiencing in the mode of causal efficacy.

According to his theory of experience, the basic mode of perception was a kind of intuitive awareness of our own immediate past mental and bodily states as they compel some degree of conformation to themselves here and now. And our present experience of ourselves as members of "a contemporary world throbbing with energetic values" (AI 282, old ed.), is an experience of *worth;* our own worth as well as that of others. At the base of our whole existence is a *value-experience.* The most primitive mode of experience is an awareness at once of being and value. It is our dim sense of reality, as such, as something that matters or has worth or is of intrinsic importance.

However, beyond this non-sensory experience of reality there is something more. It does not just contain an awareness of ourselves and our fellow creatures but also of the *infinite whole,* which embraces us all. At the very foundation of the awareness of ourselves as human beings and of the whole encompassing universe around us, there is the recognition, albeit "dim and vague," of a third factor. Just as we are never aware of our own existence except as related to others, so is the sense of ourselves and the world as 'important' and intrinsically 'valuable' derived from the awareness of something 'More' – to use William James' expression – which is the decisive ground for the existence and the worth of the entire universe.

65

These three divisions are on a level. No one in any sense precedes the other. There is the whole fact containing within itself my fact and the other facts. Also the dim meaning of fact – or actuality – is intrinsic importance for itself, for others, and for the whole (MT 117).

Since we are embraced by this universe as integrated parts, something we are non-sensuously aware of, we are nonetheless denied any basis for an awareness on a conceptual level of the totality. We are always bound to view the totality from inside and we have no access to an external position as observers of the totality.

A complete understanding is a perfect grasp of the universe in its totality. We are finite beings; and such a grasp is denied to us (MT 42).

But we are able to sense the *importance*, because at the ground of all experience is "emotion." We cannot observe, but we can feel.

Importance is primarily monistic in its reference to the universe. Importance, limited to a finite individual occasion, ceases to be important. In some sense or other, importance is derived from the immanence of infinitude in the finite ... Importance passes from the world as one to the world as many (MT 20).

There exists importance beyond the finite importance for the finite actuality (MT 86).

Apart from this sense of transcendent worth, the otherness of reality would not enter into our consciousness. There must be value beyond ourselves. Otherwise everything experienced would be merely a barren detail in our own solipsist mode of existence ... Human experience explicitly relates itself to an external standard. The universe is thus understood as including a source of ideals ... The sense of historic importance is the intuition of the universe as everlasting process, unfading in its deistic unity of ideals (MT 102f).

But the awareness of the importance of the world, of the universe as consisting of ourselves, others, and the whole, is, in fact, *the sense of deity*.

The unity of a transcendent universe, and the multiplicity of realized actualities, both enter into our experience by this sense of deity (MT 102).

Hence, at the bottom of human experience – and Whitehead would say that this experience is shared by everything, i. e., all actual entities – is the awareness of a transcendent reality at the heart of existence, i. e., *God*.

There is a unity in the universe, enjoying value and (by its immanence) sharing value ... This is the intuition of holiness, the intuition of the sacred, which is at the foundation of all religion (MT 119f).

Accordingly, Whitehead would not have us describe the notion of God as an axiom for speculative theology, nor as some entity inferred by general induction, nor as the result of pure, rational reflection. *God is a reality we are intuitively aware of.* God is part of our experience of ourselves and the circumambient world. Without speaking or thinking about God, we cannot really conceive of ourselves. Schubert Ogden says, for instance:

> Given Whitehead's type of empiricism, this assertion is the only way whereby we can do full justice to what each of us actually experiences. Because at the base of whatever we say or do there is our primitive awareness of ourselves and the world as both real and important, all our experience is in its essence religious. It rests in the sense of our own existence and of being generally as embraced everlastingly in the encompassing reality of God.[68]

Whitehead contends that classical theology has made God the result of "inference," and not something that men and women become aware of in personal "intuition." By inference he seems to think of a general induction from experience, but also of the inference from rational reflection, as for instance in the ontological proof of God's existence (RM 69).

> Christian theology has also, in the main, adopted the position that there is no direct intuition of such an ultimate personal substratum for the world. It maintains the doctrine of the existence of a personal God as a truth, but holds that our belief in it is based upon inference. Most theologians hold that this inference is sufficiently obvious to be made by all men upon the basis of their individual experience. But, be this as it may, it is an inference and not a direct intuition (RM 61).

Whitehead was convinced that the notion of God must be intimately related to human experience. God acts, as we have seen, by being experienced. But also all religious doctrines about God are to be viewed as explications, on a conceptual level, of a certain kind of deep, preconceptual experience, i.e., an intuition of God's presence.

> The dogmas of religion are the attempts to formulate in precise terms the truths disclosed in the religious experience of mankind (RM 57).

> When the religious thought of the ancient world from Mesopotamia to Palestine, and from Palestine to Egypt, required terms to express that ultimate unity of direction in the universe, upon which all order depends, and which gives its meaning to importance, they could find no way better to express themselves than by borrowing the characteristics of the touchy, vain, imperious tyrants who ruled the empires of the world (MT 49, see also PR 520).

But Whitehead believes this sort of religious experience to be incomprehensible if not interpreted against the background of metaphysics.

> Religion requires a metaphysical backing; for its authority is endangered by the intensity of the emotions which it generates. Such emotions are evidence of some vivid experience; but they are a very poor guarantee for its correct interpretation ... The foundations of dogma must be laid in a rational metaphysics which criticizes meanings, and endeavours to express the most general concepts adequate for the all-inclusive universe (RM 81).

This consequently means that all 'dogmas' or 'doctrines' about God have to yield to the same sort of criteria for assessment, as does metaphysics itself, i. e., they must be coherent, adequate, applicable to experience, and they must not contradict science.

> In expressing our conception of God, words such as "personal" and "impersonal," "entity," "individuality," "actual," require the closest careful watching, ... But it is impossible to fix the sense of fundamental terms except by reference to some definite metaphysical way of conceiving the most penetrating description of the universe. Thus rational religion must have recourse to metaphysics for a scrutiny of its terms (RM 75f).

We may here notice that Whitehead was displeased with the Judaeo-Christian concept of God (or at least the way theology was handling it), because

> it leaves God completely outside metaphysical rationalization. We know, according to it, that He is such a being as to design and create this universe, and there our knowledge stops (RM 68).

At this point it might be natural to ask how Whitehead is, in fact, able to *identify* a certain sort of experience with the experience of God, that is, the God of religion? How can Whitehead actually tell that what he calls "God" is precisely what religion speaks of as God?

We may first note that in spite of Whitehead's charge that theology was making God the simple result of inference, Whitehead's own conception is not, in fact, a result of immediate experience or intuition. The way he interprets experience is dependent on a theory which, at least partly, was influenced by person like William James and Henri Bergson. It is this theory that enables Whitehead to identify a certain type of experience as experience of God. What I am saying is simply that the interpretation of experience "as," presupposes a theory or a system of some kind. This is, of course, something which Whitehead would affirm.

> In respect to the interpretation of these experiences, mankind have differed profoundly. He (i. e., God) has been named respectively, Jehovah, Allah, Brahma, Father in Heaven, Order of Heaven, First Cause, Supreme Being,

Chance. Each name corresponds to a system of thought derived from the experience of those who have used it (SMW 179).

It, therefore, seems natural to conclude that Whitehead is not, in fact, trying to tell us what all men and women *mean* when they speak or think about God, but which kind of experience there *is* at the very bottom of the way people conceive of God. We may interpret him as trying to answer the question: what might the notion of God apply to? This indicates that Whitehead is trying to tell us what we *ought* to refer to when we speak about God, or about an experience of God. However, this is not a simple form of persuasion on Whitehead's part. There is a reason for this suggestion, Whitehead seems to think. Because, even if his metaphysical system – which entails the theory explaining the relation between human experience and the experience of God – cannot be empirically tested as a whole, it nevertheless has important empirical significance. What Whitehead calls "experience of God" is not purely a stipulation in order to render the system coherent, but is corroborated by its direct applicability to experience, i. e., the way it is able to do justice to the whole range of human experiences. And if people want to speak about God, which, obviously, they do, no other theory – Whitehead thinks – could more accurately explain what the concept of God might apply to, or what God-talk might refer to, than the theory about a perception of the world in the mode of causal efficacy.

Chapter 3

Critique of Whitehead's Philosophy

3.1 Introductory Remarks

What is the meaning and truth of language about God? This is one of the decisive questions in contemporary Christian theology. In order to answer it we must first come to grips with another question, namely: what is an appropriate metaphysics? The reason is that theologyh, in the qualified sense of statements about God, not only of liturgical and mythical depicitions, presupposes at least certain metaphysical categories.

We have aimed to approach the problem of metaphysics by focussing on a single, deliberate attempt to formulate a complete metaphysics; namely, Whitehead's philosophy of organism. The central intent was to disclose some important problems to be considered as a prerequisite of answering the question about metaphysics. It is, of course, inevitable that all theories conceal certain problems. Since we cannot discuss all the problems of Whitehead's philosophy we must try to discern which are fundamental with respect to the validity of his metaphysics. Naturally we are only able to grapple with a limited number of the ideas in Whitehead's system, namely, the ideas that seem to come into conflict with important strands of ideas in classical Christian theology and metaphysics. This is the purpose of the present chapter. The next step will then be to discuss any fundamental problems, if any, arising in Whitehead's system, to see whether there are ways of resolving them.

3.2 Criticism of Whitehead's Concept of God

A common critique against process metaphysics is that Whitehead's God is too limited, and, therefore, not a Christian concept of God. His God is neither absolutely transcendent, nor completely omnipotent. It is sometimes even said that Whitehead's God cannot be the subject of religious worship simply because this God is too powerless. The God of the Christian religion, it is held, must be completely unlimited.[69]

It is fair to say that Whitehead's God is restricted. For instance, God is limited in power to act. Also, God is only one of the causes implicated in the act of creativity. Furthermore, God does not determine, but "lures" the concrescing actual entity, by providing its "initial aim." God "persuades" the entity by being experienced, but the entity itself always remains free to respond or not to respond. Further, Whitehead rejects precisely the concept of God which is sometimes held to be essential in classical Christian theology, namely, that the world is not necessary to God. Whitehead argues that there is no entity, not even God, "which requires nothing but itself in order to exist" (RM 104). This reason for stressing the "principle of relativity," lay, as we have seen, in his effort to do justice to our experience of the world as an organism of interconnected and related events. "Every entity is in its essence social and requires the society in order to exist." Hence, "to be an actual being is to be limited" (RM 144).

The controversial feature of Whitehead's system seems not to be his conception of *how God acts* in the world. The crucial issue is whether it is compatible with Christian theology to conceive of God *without* affirming

a) that God *transcends* the world by standing absolutely apart from it, i. e., that God is of an entirely different nature than the world, and b) that God is completely *omnipotent*, in the sense of possessing an ultimate power to act, i. e., the power to do or determine *anything* in the universe. These questions are critical, for it is clear that Whitehead's God is not transcendent or ominipotent in the traditional sense. The question is: does this aspect of Whitehead's doctrine of God render his whole metaphysics incompatible with a Christian standpoint? I believe the answer is no.

In the first place, there are indeed aspects of God's transcendence which Whitehead affirms. For instance, God transcends the world by virtue of an everlasting nature. And although God is not absolutely independent of the world. God is relatively independent of it. For even if God does not stand completely over and against the world, God and the world are not identical. God is a distinct being. The world is also more dependent on God, than God is on the world.

Secondly, we may ask whether on a Christian view God's transcendence must indeed be, and has indeed always been, absolute. Do not many Christians assert that God is incarnate in the world? God, they claim, created the world, and, consequently, the world reflects what God is. Humanity, for example, is believed to have been created in the image of God. God is also conceived as acting in the world. It is said to be possible to speak and to think about God. Does this not indicate that according to the concept of God held by many Christians, God is not absolutely separate from the world? And if it is true, as so many Christians have claimed it to be, that we can perceive something of God in the *man* Jesus, there cannot be any such absolute abyss between the human and the divine.

Is it not essential for Christian theology, however, to conceive of the world as completely dependent on God for its existence, while God's being is contingent only upon itself? My answer would run something like this: if God chooses to create a world which is characterized by the sort of ontology that Whitehead thinks characterizes *our* world, then God – logically speaking – cannot appear in it as an unmoved mover, as a self-sufficient and self-sustained ruler, "at whose fiat the world came into being, and whose imposed will it obeys" (PR 519). Or, in other words: if it is true that God's world consists of the sort of self-creative beings as we usually conceive ourselves to be, and if God's purpose with the creation is precisely the emerging of such free beings, with potentiality for un-conditioned love and responsiveness to the divine, then this purpose imposes certain necessary conditions upon God's nature. For in order for humans to become such free, self-creative beings, they require a special environment in which they enjoy a certain degree of autonomy, viz., for their existence they cannot be com-pletely dependent on God. Now it seems that Whitehead's cosmology portrays such an environment; and the question is whether Christian theology, insofar as it conceives of humanity and the world in terms of the characterization presented above, does not presuppose an environment similar to Whitehead's. If this is correct, then it does not seem warranted to claim that Whitehead's metaphysical system is incompatible with Christian theology on the sole grounds that it does not attribute complete transcendence to God's being.

But what about God's *omnipotent* nature? Must not God, as understood from within Christian faith, be absolutely unlimited in power to act? If this question is not answered in the affirmative, there seems to be no reason to regard White-head's concept of God as unchristian simply because he does not subscribe to the idea that God is completely unlimited in power.

In the first place, what does it mean to say that God is omnipotent? There seems to be a strong notion of omnipotence, in which God is understood to be able to do *exactly* anything. God is not restricted by anything, not even by what is *logically impossible,* as, for instance, creating circular quadrangles. This stronger notion of omnipotence seems, however, to have been affirmed by very few Chris-tians, simply because it is unintelligible. It is impossible to understand what it means to say that God could create circular quadrangles.

But there is also a weaker notion of omnipotence which we must consider. According to this version God is understood to yield to certain logical constraints. A formulation of this notion has been presented by Professor Alvin Plantinga. He calls it I-omnipotence, a term originally suggested by David Griffin. Plantinga says that God has I-omnipotence if and only if every state of affairs *possible* in the broadly logical sense is such that it is within God's power to cause it to be actual. But Plantinga, who seems clearly to be working within the premises of classical theism, explicitly denies that God has even this weaker form of om-nipotence, i. e., I-omnipotence.

> For while the state of affairs consisting in Eve's freely taking the apple is possible, it is not within God's power to cause it to obtain; if he *causes* it to obtain, then he causes Eve to take the apple, in which case she does

not take it *freely*. *Eve's freely taking the apple* is a possible state of affairs, but it is not possible that God cause it to be actual. Hence, it is not within God's power to cause it to be actual, and God is therefore not I-omnipotent.[70]

So if, Plantinga concludes, "I am a classical theist, then . . . a classical theist need not (*ought* not, I would add) accept I-omnipotence." Plantinga also says that he doubts that most classical theists have in fact accepted I-omnipotence. He believes that Leibniz, for example, affirmed that God was I-omnipotent. Descartes, he thinks, shared it too, or perhaps even a stronger form of omnipotence. Plantinga also points out that Augustine's view on these matters is not clear. In *De Libero Arbitrio* he seems to offer one of the first versions of the Free Will Defence and in some passages seems to suggest that it is not within the power of God to cause it to be the case that someone freely performs an action. In the case of Aquinas the matter is more complex. At first sight he seems to affirm something like I-omnipotence. But in *Summa Theologiae* I, Q.25, a. 4, however, Thomas discusses the question of whether it is possible for God to restore a fallen woman to virginity. Consider Miss X, who is now no longer a virgin: is it now within God's power to bring it about that she is a virgin? The question is not: is it now within God's power to bring it about that Miss X is both now a virgin and formerly a fallen women; that state of affairs is impossible in the broadly logical sense. The question, instead is just this:

> can God now bring it about that Miss X is a virgin – i. e., that she is not now and never has been a fallen women? *That* state of affairs – *Miss X's being now a virgin* – is indeed possible, but Aquinas concludes that it is not within God's power to cause it to be actual. So Aquinas seems to affirm I-omnipotence, but also to deny it.[71]

A conclusion that we may draw here is that the indictment many traditional theists direct against the Whiteheadian concept of God, the belief that traditional theism affirms a more powerful and worshipful God, has been undermined. For both traditional Christians and process thinkers seem to acknowledge that human freedom places necessary limits upon God's power to act. Their notion of God's omnipotence is, in fact, not a decisive point of disagreement between them.

What is then the real point of disagreement? This is not altogether clear. If we return to Plantinga, the disagreement between him and Whitehead seems to be related to their different understanding of *what worlds are possible*. Plantinga says:

> I have no doubt that you and I could have been significantly free but morally impeccable; there is a possible world in which we are free to do wrong but always do what is right. Indeed, for any significantly free creature there is a possible world in which that creature is significantly free but always does what is right . . . What I do think is this: there are many possible

worlds God could not have actualized; and it is *possible* (I know of no reason to think it is *true*) that among these worlds are all the worlds in which there are free creatures who always do only what is right. There are plenty of possible worlds where free creatures do no wrong, but it *could* be that God might not have actualized any of those possible worlds.[72]

Whitehead, or more correctly, someone who wishes to defend Whitehead's concept of God with its rejection of complete transcendence and omnipotence, could argue something like this: The history of human beings on our planet, even as depicted in the myths of Genesis, starts with a *decision*. In distinction from the animals, who are basically compelled by their instincts, human behavior is not entirely determined. Human beings are able to *choose* between alternatives to satisfy their needs. Their relation to the environment alters from mere passive adjustment to active determination. They start to create tools, and learn how to master the surrounding nature. And hereby they separate themselves, progressively, from nature. They become more and more *free,* and more and more *human.* For freedom and humanity are inseparable. Freedom here means freedom from something, namely, the instinctive compulsion in their behaviour. If that freedom was lacking, we would sink back inexorably into the sub-human, where every notion of morality and responsibility loses its meaning. However, human beings *are* free to choose between good and evil – at least free enough to make sense to speak about them as responsible and ethically conscious.

Certainly, the Whiteheadian would emphasize that human beings are closely related to the rest of nature, and that also non-human actual entities are at least partly free to respond to the influence of the environment. However, this is beside the point of the argument, which is to show that freedom and humanity are inseparable.

But is it not possible to visualize a human being who is not subject to any temptations, and thus would not commit any blameworthy or evil acts? However, would such a creature be what we mean by a human being? A creature who is never subject to temptations, and who therefore never commits sin, could, of course, not be charged with being immoral, simply because it would never commit any moral acts *at all.* Such a creature would not *be* a moral being, and therefore not a human being, since by humans we mean precisely beings that are free to make decisions. However, the fact that no one could ever blame this creature also means that no one could ever praise it for being ethically virtuous, viz., morally good. So even if it is logically possible to think of a world in which there are beings who always choose what is right – and it is certainly possible to visualize such a world – this world cannot be a world which surrounds moral beings. For a world which is supposed to contain moral agents cannot be an environment of just any sort. It must be such that it exposes its inhabitants to veridical alternatives. And furthermore, the beings in this world must be morally *autonomous.* To be a truly moral being, in any possible world, requires an environment fulfilling at least these conditions. The question, therefore, remains: is it possible to imagine a world in which there are morally responsible and free persons, who are always able to choose – and in fact would always choose to do what is morally right? Is it in a broadly logical sense possible to envisage a world with a man or a woman who are in a position to make moral decisions, but who never in fact did choose the wrong alternatives? Would it be possible in such a world – if it is imaginable – to make morally right decisions? Would it be possible to attribute what we mean by moral behavior to such persons?

Plantinga obviously believes that it is possible that there is such a world, which is not to say that he believes that it is actual. A philosopher who believes otherwise is, for instance, John Hick. He says:

> To be a person is to be a finite center of freedom, a (relatively) free and self-directing agent responsible for one's own decisions. This involves being free to act wrongly as well as to act rightly. The idea of a person who can be infallibly guaranteed always to act rightly is self-contradictory. There can be no guarantee in advance that a genuinely free moral agent will never choose amiss. Consequently, the possibility of wrongdoing or sin is logically inseparable from the creation of finite persons, and to say that God should not have created beings who might sin amounts to saying that he should not have created people.[73]

If God wanted to create human beings, as the kind of free and responsible beings we usually believe ourselves to be (at least potentially), and not just vegetative animals or virtuous angels, God could not, in a logical sense, have created them otherwise. If God did not want 'puppets on strings,' or pure celestial beings who by definition always love their creator and do the good, but truly *human* beings, God was simply bound to create them not unlike what we are. That these beings might, and in fact would, make wrong decisions, i. e., sin, was something God would have had to take into account. The 'risk of evil' – and by risk here I mean something which is really unpredictable – was, metaphorically speaking, the price God had to pay to be able to create human beings at all. And if God intended our love for and trust in the divine to be just that free response we assume it to be, then there can be no compulsion in this response. It must be a veridical alternative to choose not to respond to God, which implies that God's relation to the world cannot take simply any shape. God's relation to the world must be conditioned by certain limitations on God's part.

This all brings us to the following conclusion, the defender of Whitehead would contend: if God wanted to create a world with morally responsible and self-creative beings, just as we conceive our actual world to be, then this world had to be characterized by the kind of ontology which is asserted in Whitehead's metaphysical system. And in this world God himself could not appear as an exception. Even the divine must yield to the ontological structure of this world. If God wished to create a world with humans in it, it had to be in the form of a gigantic experiment. God's creation was by necessity the creation of a vast pot of possibilities, or potentials, at the outset. And God did not, indeed could not, determine exactly which potentials were to be actualized.

Thus no element of compulsion or determination could be contained in the experiment, because it would then not have been a real experiment, and God would not have been able to create truly human beings. Furthermore, if God decided to relate to this world and somehow contribute to its development, this would be impossible unless the presence of divinity in the world were ontologically on the same level, so to speak, with the rest of reality.

Is this understanding of God in relation to the world, however, so very different from the understanding of more traditional Christians? It is certainly different, but not primarily with respect to the notion of God's power to act, i. e., God's omnipotent nature. It seems that also Plantinga affirms something very much like it. "There are many possible worlds," he says, "God could not have actualized." The difference here is related, rather, to what can be affirmed to be a "possible world" and what cannot be.

Therefore, we must conclude that there is no reason to regard Whitehead's metaphysics as inappropriate for Christian theology simply because it does not affirm I-omnipotence, or an even stronger notion of omnipotence. For not all Christian theologians claim that God is completely unlimited in power to act. As for the objection that God must be absolutely omnipotent, in order to be the subject of religious worship – it seems strange. Can we only worship that which has absolute power *over us*? In that case worship has more to do with respect and fear than with love and adoration. Such an understanding of worship seems remote from that which has been generally accepted in the practice of the Christian religion.

As for the vision of creation as a sort of continuous, evolving interaction between God and the various phenomena within the world, on its way to greater experiential intensity, it may be said that something of this vision is also found in other Christian traditions. I am referrring to the traditions starting with Irenaeus (A. D. 130–202, bishop of Lyon). In his book *Adversus Haereses*,[74] Irenaeus develops a perspective upon the human, as not ready-made from the start, but as constantly growing, gradually evolving toward the final fulfilment. Even the act of salvation in Jesus Christ, on this view, is seen as a step toward the realization of God's purposes with the creation. For Irenaeus, both creation and salvation have the same aim, namely, that humanity reach its ultimate destination of becoming one with God. Irenaeus started with the story of creation in Genesis, where God says: "Let us make man in our image, after our likeness." He interpreted this passage to mean that human beings were created to *become* something in God's "likeness," but that they still were only vague and dissimilar "images" of God, in the sense

77

that God created humans with free will and the ability to make moral decisions. The human being, in the theology of Irenaeus, is viewed on the model of a child, who is born to grow; this growing is God's continuous creation. Irenaeus thought that humanity, through salvation in Jesus Christ, could grow to a fuller likeness to God, as Christ represents it for us. The act of redemption restores human beings to their proper destination and forges them in their complete likeness to God.

There are certainly many differences between the Whiteheadian and the Irenaeian traditions, as there are between Whitehead's theology and many others that we have discussed. The point, however, is that a view very similar to Whitehead's is already at hand within the Christian tradition. It is true that no emphasis has been put on this aspect of creation and salvation in the Western churches, but there has never been any doubt that this tradition is truly Christian. This does not, of course, in itself authorize Whitehead's metaphysics as appropriate for Christian theological use. Nevertheless, it provides a reason, together with what we have argued before, not to accept the charges on the issue of Whitehead's interpretation of God's power as clearly unchristian. It seems, rather, that if there are problems with respect to Whitehead's concept of God, with his rejection of God's complete transcendence and *omnipotence*, they are not of a decisive or fundamental nature in relation the the question of the appropriateness of his whole metaphysics.

3.3 Criticism of Whitehead's Theory of Value

In this section I wish to consider an issue which does not seem to conform with the common critique of Whitehead's metaphysics. I have touched on the matter before, but I would now like to elaborate. The question to which I wish to draw attention is whether Whitehead's theory of value is appropriate in a metaphysics for contemporary theology.

Let us first briefly recapitulate Whitehead's theory of value by saying that he emphasized that every single entity in the world has a value for itself, an 'intrinsic value.' These values, Whitehead claims, are not imposed from outside, as a subject imposes something on an object. The values are *objectively* present in the 'things.' At the heart of Whitehead's value theory is an idea that everyting in the universe is a subject, namely, a subject for itself, and, hence, valuable for itself, not only for others. Nothing is a mere means for someone or something. It is always intrinsically valuable. The ground for the value is the 'experience' which each entity has, because each entity has at least some experiences, prehensions, or feelings.

Whitehead's theory must be understood against the background of his profound critique of the Newtonian worldview, in which matter was completely devoid of such properties as intrinsic value, something which was believed solely to belong to the mind, viz., the human mind. Whitehead protested intensely against "the exclusion of value from the essence of matter of fact." The basis for value is experience, and all actual entities enjoy such experiences, prehensions or feelings, although they need not be conscious.

When I discussed Whitehead's theory of value in an earlier section, the main criticism concerned the fact that this theory results in a relativizing of the specifically value of human beings. However, this criticism is related to a different problem in the theory which is at focus here. The critique now is that the theory is *unsatisfactory as a theory of ethical preference*. In fact, it does not seem to work. I shall try to show this, by seizing upon one significant example from John Cobb, which I believe represents the difficulties involved.

Cobb says, in a passage already quoted earlier, that "it is not really evident that the advantage of a mongoloid idiot or a human vegetable should count equally with that of a healthy child." The question I now wish to raise is this: how does anyone know for sure what a "mongoloid idiot" experiences or feels? I suspect, but I am not sure, that the preference implied in the example is in fact due to something other than a comprehension of what sort of experiences, or feelings, different individuals are presumed to have. I shall try to explain what I mean.

My contact with mongoloid persons is certainly very limited. I have only had close encounters with mongoloid children, partly – I think – because the majority of mongoloid people die early. Few of them reach the age of forty. But my impression, contrary to what seems to be Cobb's, is that they have *more* intense feelings than do other people. They seem to be more emotional, more loving even, than so-called "healthy" children.

The problem to which I am pointing here, has to do with the fact that we often judge other people and their situation from our point of view, while we *think* that we have *their* perspective in mind. When we meet, say, mongoloid persons, we imagine what it would be for us 'healthy people,' to find ourselves suddenly in their position, which we take to be awesome and terrible. But what reason do we have to believe that this is also *their* experience? My impression, for example, of encountering extremely sick people – I have done some of my work in hospitals – bereft of any sense of human dignity and joy in life, has been very painful. I have asked myself, how anyone could wish to continue to live under such circumstances ? Their life, as I have experienced it from 'outside,' has seemed devoid of value. And in fact, these people sometimes really want nothing other than death. But sometimes I have been astounded by the fact that certain of these people, whose lives I have regarded as meaningless and worthless, do not at all share my view. They, perhaps surprisingly, seem to experience a meaning in their life – certainly different from my understanding of meaning – which they do not want to give up at all.

Now, the correct conclusion to draw is not that, say, euthanasia should be prohibited, but that ethical decisions ought not primarily to be made on the basis of so-called 'healthy' people's experience. For there is also a perspective 'from below,' so to speak, which has to be taken into account. I do not oppose euthanasia or abortion under certain circumstances, and to think this is completely to miss the point. But I am somewhat worried about the elitist perspective from which those issues are sometimes viewed and judged in our society.

Another conclusion which I do not want to draw is that we should retreat into some sort of relativism, where all experiences count as equal, or that we should not try to do everything within our power to help and sustain those among us who seem to suffer from *our* point of view. All I claim is that we must be careful about the way we judge, and, thus, to make ethical decisions concerning other people, and that the notion of "capacity for richness of experience" seems unsatisfactory as a criterion for ethical preference.

From an ethical point of view, what was the importance of Whitehead's theory of value? One suggestion is that Whitehead seems to have realized that the Newtonian cosmology, with its annihilation of the intrinsic value in nature, opened up the door to scientific, technological, and industrial exploitation of our environment. Perhaps he even anticipated our present crisis in the human relationship to nature. It must be acknowledged that this was an extremely important observation, and that the emphasis on nature's value 'for itself,' is still most urgently needed in our society. I certainly want to belong to those who criticize the violation of our physical environment, and I do believe that human beings must come down from their pedestals of superiority over nature. I believe this on moral grounds. But it seems to me that the most efficacious strategy – if one only considers that aspect – for creating a new apprehension of the human relationship to the natural environment, is to stress that *we* have something to gain from abstaining from treating nature as we do today. However, and that is perhaps more important, the moral problem today is not that we are *too* human – and therefore need a conceptualization of reality in which we are dehumanized, so to speak – but that we are not human *enough*. For to be human is neither to supercede nature, nor to suppress fellow human beings. It is, at least in part, to seek to balance the inequalities in the world, and to support the weaker. Therefore, we must try to create a new image of what it means to be human in our world. But it is also necessary that we forge for ourselves a new understanding of nature, as valuable beyond its value for us. The question, however, is whether this can be done within the framework of Whitehead's metaphysics, but without the negative side effects of his value theory. If this question can be answered affirmatively, then it seems that we have no reason to regard the problems involved in the present discussion as fundamental to his system.

If we claim that nature is valuable this can imply two things. Partly its value is of *instrumental* character: it is good as means to other ends. Nature provides us with food, clothing, material to build houses and bridges, and so forth. But nature also has *intrinsic* value. The richness and the beauty of nature are valuable in themselves, simply because of the aesthetic qualities innate in nature. The kind of experiences that we may have in and of nature is therefore also of non-pragmatical character. It is valuable just in itself. A problem within our culture, it seems, is that the intrinsic value of nature has not been sufficiently appreciated. It has in fact been subordinated to the instrumental. It has been understood as something highly subjective and private, in distinction from the instrumental, which has been understood as objective and public. It is, therefore, needed that we find a way to amplify the instrinsic value of nature. At the same time, however, we must be able to argue that just because something has instrumental value, this does not entitle humans to treat it arbitrarily or irresponsibly. The fact that something has instrumental value, has value as means to something else, does not immediately imply that it has *less* value than what is understood to have intrinsic value.

One way which is open to us, beside the way Whitehead's value theory represents, is to argue that *nature has a value in relation to God* – something, in fact, Christian theology has always argued. Nature is valued by God. The basic significance of the tenet of creation is precisely this; "And God saw everything that he had made, and behold, it was very good." This means that it is important to God what happens to nature, in fact, to everything in the world, for it is all God's creation. On that ground it also seems possible to argue that humans are responsible for how they behave in nature, how they 'cooperate' with it. They do not 'own' nature as one owns a thing. Nature is not the private property of human beings. We are, according to the Judaeo-Christian faith, on earth, not as rulers, but as caretakers. Nature does not have its sole value in relation to humanity. It has a value also in relation to God.

Now this line of argument seems to be the sort of approach suggested by H. R. Niebuhr in his *Radical Monotheism and Western Culture*. For monotheistic faith, Niebuhr argues, the starting point is with the " transcendent One for whom alone there is an ultimate good and for whom, as the source and end of all things, whatever is, is good."[75] This enables Niebuhr to state that all other valuesystems are relative, tentative, experimental, and no one of them can be erected into an absolute, or even become ordered above the others. The basic idea here, that there are values in relation to God, seems attractive. For a person who is able to affirm it, this may influence his or her whole attitude toward nature. But, to be able to accept such a value theory, one must first find it reasonable and warranted to accept the belief that there is such a God at all. This problem is therefore something we shall return to in the end of the study.

If we now, however, return to process philosophy we will notice, interestingly enough, that a line of argument similar to Niebuhr's is also present among some of the defenders of this philosophy. It is this line that we have referred to as "the second line of argument," and I tried to show its presence in both John Cobb's and David Griffin's works.[76] Beside the reference to Whitehead's theory of value, these theologians understand nature as having ultimate value in relation to God. It seems also that this perspective has not been sufficiently appreciated among process theologians, and that the theory of God's "consequent nature" might provide them with an important and fruitful idea, which can give to theology what traditional theism cannot: a theory that allows for a world which can meaningfully be thought to have *significance for God*. When it becomes clear both that and how the world of nature is important to God, can nature be considered a matter of ultimate concern for humanity.

The problem we have discussed in this section is a serious one. Process theology today purports to be a theology of nature, and many of its defenders apply ideas in Whitehead's metaphysics to issues in current ecological debate. Nevertheless, it seems that the problems we have pointed to can be resolved within the framework of Whitehead's metaphysics. Therefore, the problems involved in the Whiteheadian theory of value seem not to be decisive for the question of the appropriateness of process metaphysics as a whole.

3.4 Criticism of Whitehead's Theory of Perception and his Realism

In the introduction to this study I tried to make it clear how ontology and epistemology are interconnected. The point was in part to say that the validity of theology as assertions about God, depends not only on our knowing *what* God is ontologically speaking, but also on our finding it warranted to affirm the theory of knowledge on which such assertions are based, i. e., on making account of *how* we know what God is, and *why* we are justified in claiming that God is real.

However, since both epistemology and ontology logically presuppose certain metaphysical assumptions, they are also interconnected with respect to metaphysics. The validity of God-language is, therefore, ultimately dependent on whether it presupposes a coherent and acceptable metaphysics. In the present section this is precisely the issue at stake. The question is: are the metaphysical presuppositions of Whitehead's ontological theory consistent with the metaphysical presuppositions of his epistemology, i. e., his theory of perception. If the question cannot be answered affirmatively, how decisive is this for the acceptance of Whitehead's whole system? In case we find problems of fundamental importance in Whitehead's theory, the next step is to see if these can be resolved by some kind of modification or revision.

One of the more conspicuous features of Whitehead's philosophy is what he called "the ontological principle," according to which there is nothing, either in actuality or efficacy, which "floats into the world from nowhere." Everything in the actual world is referable to some actual entity. Hence, the actual entity is the bottom line, so to speak, in reality, beyond which there is no other or more real thing. God is an actual entity, and so is the most trivial puff of existence far off in empty space, Whitehead claims. Reality is a web of interconnected events. Every event is constituted by its relationships to other events, and nothing can exist except by participation. The typical approach in Newtonian physics, namely, to try to observe reality from an objective standpoint outside or apart from that toward which the investigation is directed, is consequently abandoned by Whitehead. We cannot exclude the perceiver from what is perceived. Instead, he suggests, we must try to describe the world from the point of view of the actual entity itself. The world of sense data, the reality in which we can discriminate between subjects and objects, is only an abstraction from the totality we perceive. Such a world is not the real world, in a metaphysical or ultimate sense of the word.

Now this naturally also influences Whitehead's concept of God. God is not understood as an entity standing absolutely apart from our reality. God is not outside the world. God is not a being on which everything else in reality depends for its existence. God is not that than which nothing greater can be conceived. Many of the severe problems in more traditional theology seem, according to Whitehead, to be hereby avoided, since by means of his ontological theory it is possible to explain *how* God is *related* to and *acts* in the world, without running into the sort of trouble that commonly arises in classical theism. God and all else are ontologically related to each other. They share in experience, they mutually exchange experience, and God acts by being experienced. Creation is no longer an absolute origination of the world, a *creatio ex nihilo*. God is not that timeless and changeless being which requires nothing else in order to exist, while determining everything else in reality. However, this does not mean that there is nothing transcendent in God's being. In the first place, God alone is everlasting; a non-temporal actual entity. God is also transcendent in the sense of not being identical with the world, nor does the world exist only within God. There is further a dimension in God's being which is totally unconditioned by any actual world: the primordial nature of God. And God also transcends the limitations of the actual world: the divine experience is perfect in its intensity.

There is, however, also another side to Whitehead's philosophy, which does not at first seem to contradict the important characteristics of Whitehead's ontological theory, as it has here been summarized. And that is his *realism*. Whitehead believes that reality, ontologically speaking, *is* coherent, a whole, a unity. It is not that we conceive of the world *as* this. Whitehead's system exhibits an ontological 'cosmic coherence.' Our experience of the world as integrated and interconnected is not the result of a conscious, mental activity. Our awareness is of being in the world, not of constructing one.

This awareness presents a reason, according to Whitehead, for accepting epistemological realism: at the base of our knowledge of the world as a dynamic, evolving unity, is an *experience* of reality as a totality. The "raw material" of experience already *has* a unity, a structure. Everything in the universe which is actual *is* really related, and 'really' here means *independently of our minds*. It is not independent of us ontologically speaking. It is independent of us in the sense that everything which we receive in experience has a given, ready-made structure, separately from our consciousness. The unity of reality, according to Whitehead, is there before us; it is already at hand in nature. This structure is not a result of a mental construction. On a fundamental level of our experience of the world the contribution from the environment is pervasive. We passively receive what comes to us from outside. It is only on a higher level that we contribute something. It is in this sense that Whitehead believes that all actual entities in the world are real: they obtain independently of our consciousness, of our minds. It is also in this sense that *God* is real.[77]

Whitehead's theory of value is contingent on this mode of realism. In fact, his entire metaphysical system can be seen as an articulation of this basic experience of reality as a unity. The reason thus why a metaphysical system must be coherent is that reality is coherent. The affirmation of this realism is therefore necessary for the acceptance of Whitehead's whole system, and a critical discussion of it is consequently the main purpose of the present section.

Since Whitehead's realism presupposes that we can know what reality is in itself, independent of our consciousness of it, the crucial questions are these: how is Whitehead able to speak of "a consciousness of ourselves as arising out of a rapport, interconnection and participation in processes reaching *beyond* ourselves" (S 65, my italics)? If reality is something given separately from our minds, how can we know this? How can we possibly know what reality is *apart* from our conscious experience of it? How can we know that the structure of the world *is* a whole, a unity, something coherent, independent of our conceptual perception of it? How can we be justified in believing that what we take to be a coherent cosmos, a perfectly arranged and ordered universe, is not only the result of a mental integration of arbitrary fragments of experience? For to know this, i. e., being justified in affirming this ontological realism, it requires the ability to "look behind the scene," viz., *to observe reality as it is in itself, at the same time as one is having an experience of reality*.

In his theory of perception, this is precisely what Whitehead claims that we can do. The following statements, already quoted, clearly display the connection between Whitehead's realism and his theory of perception.

> Faith in reason is the trust that the ultimate natures of things lie together in a harmony which excludes mere arbitrariness. It is the faith that at the base of things we shall not find mere arbitrary mystery. The faith in the order of nature which has made possible the growth of science is a particular example of a deeper faith. This faith cannot be justified by any inductive

generalization. It springs from *direct inspection of the nature of things as disclosed in our own immediate present experience* (SMW 18. My italics).

Our datum is the actual world, including ourselves; and this actual world spreads itself for observation in the guise of the topic of our immediate experience. The elucidation of immediate experience is the sole justification for any thought; and the starting-point for thought is the analytic observation of components of this experience (PR 6).

In an article in *Process Studies,* Robert H. Kimball draws attention to a similar problem in Whitehead's theory.[78] The basic content of his argument, that Whitehead's theory of perception is incoherent, can be readily summarized as follows: what one cannot do is perceive the causal mechanism which is producing the very perception one is currently having. One can only occupy one perspective at a time. One cannot at the same instant have awareness of "this" cause producing "this" perceived effect. There cannot be any direct assurance that "this" perceived *cause* is actually producing "this" very perceptual datum. The hypothesis of the cause producing the perceived datum must, therefore, at least to some extent, be removed from the very same experience. The notion of the cause must be based on *inference,* not direct perception. But this is not what Whitehead's theory of perception affirms. On the contrary, Whitehead argues that an awareness of the *cause* of a perception is *copresent* with the experience of the *effect* of that very cause. We are aware, according to Whitehead's theory, of the causes of our sensations *while* we are experiencing them.

Before we proceed toward a critical assessment of it, let us briefly recall the core of Whitehead's theory. Whitehead acknowledges two modes of perception, "presentational immedicay" and "causal efficacy." Presentational immediacy presents vivid, clearly defined data, but exhibits no significant connections among them; causal efficacy provides causal relationship, but its data are vague. Presentational immediacy discloses nothing about the past or the future; it shows us only the world experienced *now.* It is not to be viewed as identical with the entire content of our present consciousness. The two modes of perception are related by what Whitehead calls "symbolic reference," which is close to what we speak of as our conscious experience. If we take the concept of presentational immediacy as our point of reference, the revolutionary feature of Whitehead's notion of causal efficacy becomes evident. For there is a kind of experiential phenomenon in which all of us can have access to direct awareness of the causes of our perception in the mode of presentational immediacy: the "withness of the body." According to Whitehead, we know that we touch *with* our hands, taste *with* our palates, see *with* our eyes, etc. The revolutionary claim is that Whitehead argues that we do not alternate between the two modes of perception, but *experience both distinctively at the same time.* This, Whitehead seems to argue, is the case with the man who knew the light *caused* him to blink (PR 265).

Why is this so remarkable? The extraordinary thing is the claim that experience on the one hand is a representational phenomena, something mediated and transformed, and at the same time an awareness of that which is behind our experience, that which causes our experience, on the other. Or in other words: we are in effect able to experience the world from the perspective of the ideal scientific observer, "the ultimate competent observer playing the part of the eye of God," whose standpoint is *outside* the world. But at the very same instant we experience the world from our own limited point of view *within* it. On the one hand Whitehead argues that perception is something mediated: we do not perceive things out there as they are in themselves. Yet, on the other hand he still argues that we experience what reality is objectively, that we can have a sort of direct, unmediated awareness of the things in themselves, viz., we can tell *what* it is that has been modified, transformed, mediated in perception. We can know what the world *is* in itself, indepedent of our minds.

But is this a plausible, or even a possible view? Whitehead seems to think so. His argument, in the case of the man who knew the light caused him to blink, is this:

> The man will explain his experience by saying, 'The flash made me blink'; and if his statement be doubted, he will reply, 'I know it, because I felt it' (PR 266).

Whitehead seems to think that in cases such as this, we enjoy direct experience that causes are operating on us in nature.

Kimball, whose interest is more in the field of philosophy of the mind, argues, against this view, that the intermediate link between seeing, hearing, touching, on the one hand, and the eye, ear, and hand, on the other, is not at all something felt. It is something we *infer*.

> Do we know for certain that we feel with our hands, see with our eyes, hear with our ears, etc.? We certainly think we do, but what evidence do we have for believing it? ... Actually, in the act of sight we do not *see* our eyes; they are the one thing we do *not* see. As Wittgenstein says, "Nothing *in the visual field* allows you to infer that it is seen by an eye." The visual field stops somewhere around where our eyes are presumed to be. But the region where the visual field stops is vague: we might with equal warrant say that we see with the whole top half of our faces as that we see just with our eyes. Moreover, physiology tells us that it is the rods and the cones that are efficacious in sight, but if we were ignorant of physiology, we would have no way of knowing this.[79]

Kimball's point seems to be that the reason we *think* that we see with our eyes, hear with our ears, and so forth, is that this is something we have learnt. Logically it is something we infer on the ground of a process of deductive logic.

The reason is not that this is something we are directly experiencing or immediately aware of. He admits that we *think* that we experience this, but he sees no justification for this belief.

Whitehead assumed that reality is coherent and the mind can move beyond the the external world, the world as it *is* independent of us, i. e., not the world as it *appears* to be. But he also believes that this knowledge is based on something which *presents itself*,[80] something which is *directly evident,* not something that we infer or induce. The justification, according to Whitehead, for *thinking* that, for instance, causes in the external world are operating on us is that this is something directly evident, something we *feel.* But clearly, a feeling – however strong or intense – does not take us *beyond* the feeling. For how could experience possibly give us access to objective or direct knowledge about what is *behind* experience? For example, if an apple tastes sour to me, this does not warrant the claim that the apple *is* sour independent of me. And the reason is that such an assertion is flatly unintelligible. For what would it mean to say that something tastes, sounds, or appears in itself, *apart* from what it tastes, sounds, or appears to someone who is experiencing it?

It seems, rather, that Whiteheadian realism presupposes, in the logical sense, certain assumptions, which provide a base for the claim that we, on the ground of experience, know that there are forces in the external world working on us. In his book *Naming the Whirlwind; The Renewal of God-language,* Langdon Gilkey has given utterance to these assumptions:

1. That the mind has the *power to know* reality as it is, to delineate its real and not merely apparent structures in a total system of metaphysical categories. This involves the power of the mind to move by rational implication alone beyond the immediate, given character of experience, beyond the data, and to construct a conceptual picture of (a) the real, the actual, the concrete (to use Whitehead's phrase) substances or entities that make up the process, and (b) to construct a conceptual picture of the structure of their interrelations as a whole system.

2. That there obtains in some form or another an ultimate *identity or correlation* between reality and the structures, requirements, and criteria of thought.

Gilkey points out that Whitehead (as Aristotle) was an empiricist in the sense that he insisted that no thought that was relevant could fail to start with experience; but this empirical base to his (and Aristotle's) metaphysics does not mitigate the fact that he was also a rationalistic philosopher. That is to say, Gilkey claims, Whitehead assumed that reality is coherent and the mind can move beyond the immediate deliverances of experience.

> Thus the mind can move out from experience by recognized metaphysical principles to picture conceptually the "real," "substance," or "concrete actual entity," and can tell us the ultimate intelligible structure of all events everywhere, including that factor called "God."[81]

Now it seems that these two assumptions, which are the presuppositions for Whiteheadian and similar modes of realism, presuppose an even more fundamental assumption, namely, that we somehow have *access to a position outside the world*, which enables us to know, and speak meaningfully about, what reality is from a point of view external to reality. Following Iris Murdoch I have referred to this assumption as *the metaphysical witness*. This assumption has taken the form of various theories in the history of philosphy.[82] Here we shall only present Roderick Chisholm's interpretation of it.

The question Chisholm discusses is how we can be assured that our beliefs are true. If true beliefs are defined as true in terms of what is evident, then, Chisholm says, we could say that, if a man believes, with respect to a certain state of affairs, that that state of affairs exists, then, what he believes is *true,* provided that what he thus believes would be *evident* to a being such that, for every state of affairs, either it is evident to that being that that state of affairs exists, or it is evident to him that that state of affairs does not exist. This definition enables us to say that "if a man believes truly that Socrates is mortal, then Socrates is mortal, then Socrates *is* mortal. Or in other words: we can, given this definition this definition provides no guarantee that if a man believes truly that Socrates is mortal, then Soctrates *is* mortal. Or in other words: we can, given this definition of truth, no longer be *sure that our true beliefs "correspond with the fact."*

It is to obtain such a needed assurance that Chisholm thinks we are tempted to make certain metaphysical assumptions. It is these assumptions that are implicit in Whiteheadian realism, which is the reason to focus on them here. Chisholm says:

> For we could now add a theory about the nature of "the facts" by saying that Socrates *is* mortal provided that, for a being of the sort envisaged in the new definition of "true belief," the belief that Socrates is mortal is one that would be *evident.* That is to say, Socrates *is* mortal provided these conditions hold: Any being such that, for every state of affairs, either it is evident to him that that state of affairs exists, or it is evident to him that that state of affairs does not exist, would be a being for whom it would be evident that Socrates is mortal.[83]

But how are we to assure ourselves that a belief that is evident to *us* is one that would also be evident to a being for whom all truths are evident? Our metaphysician, Chisholm argues, would have us take one more step. We will be asked, namely, to assume "not only that there is such a being, a being for whom all truths are evident, but also, that each of us is identical with that being, and therefore, with each other."[84]

All the implications of Chisholm's argument do not become clear in this presentation. But the point is that his claim that the beleif in the existence of an external world, about which we are able to have true knowledge, presupposes the assumption that we somehow have access to a point of view where all truths are evident, viz., we are capable of knowing what the world *is,* in the objective sense of the word. Or stated otherwise: we are able to say what reality is from God's eye point of view, or from the position of the metaphysical witness. For otherwise we could never assure ourselves that certain states of affairs exist, or do not exist, and that our beliefs and assertions, with respect to some state of affairs, are that that state of affairs exists or does not exist.

Returning now to Whitehead's realism and theory of perception, let us summarize our argument. Whitehead's understanding of the nature of experience is certainly very different from the understanding of this phenomena implicit in many empirical theories of both historical and modern philosophy. Nevertheless Whitehead seems to entertain a sort of realism akin to the realism of many of the philosophers he criticized. In fact, it is fundamental to his entire philosophy that there is an external world obtaining independently of us, viz., independent of consciousness. Whitehead also believes that there exist states of affairs independently of us, which we are immediately aware of in experience. The justification for believing that there is a reality out there that we can have knowledge about, is "the witness of the body," Whitehead thinks. However, this mode of realism presupposes an assumption that the mind has a power to know reality as it *is,* not just as it appears, and the assumption that there is a correlation or a correspondence between reality, and our thought and beliefs about reality. But these assumptions presuppose in turn another, even more fundamental, assumption, namely, that we can somehow conceive the world from a position outside it, which enables us to compare reality as it is in itself, on the one hand, and our conceptualization of reality, on the other, viz., the hypothetical position of the metaphysical witness.

But now we must ask: is this assumption really consistent with the metaphysical assumption innate in Whitehead's theory about reality as a web of ontologically interrelated actual entities, in which nothing, not even God, exists completely on its own? If every event in the universe is constituted by its relationships to other events, and if nothing can obtain except by participation, how could we ever acquire a perspective on the world from God's eye point of view, so to speak? If everything in reality is essentially and deeply interwoven and connected, how could anyone suddenly view reality from outside, or try to speak about it from such a position? In fact, did Whitehead not reject the attempt in Newtonian physics to try to observe reality, and thus give an objective description of the world, from the standpoint of an absolutely competent observer outside reality? And was his argument not precisely that we cannot do this because we are always included in, and parts of, the world we investigate? He said, for instance:

> A complete understanding is a perfect grasp of the universe in its totality. We are finite beings; and such a grasp is denied to us (MT 42).

This inevitably leads us to conclude that Whitehead's philosophy is inconsistent with respect to the sort of metaphysical assumptions it presupposes. But this also leads to the conclusion that, since Whitehead's unwarranted mode of realism is decisive for the acceptance of his whole system, we must proceed with an investigation of what kind of assumptions about reality are acceptable and justifiable in an appropriate metaphysics for theology.

So far I have only claimed that Whitehead's philosophy is inconsistent; his theory of perception and his realism presuppose metaphysical assumptions that are incompatible with the metaphysical assumption implicit in his ontological theory of reality, according to which nothing can exist except by participation. This means that when Whitehead claims that our experience of the universe as a totality, consisting of ourselves, others, and the whole, *is* the "sense of deity," this is something we infer or induce. But if this experience, or intuition, or awareness, does not take us to a knowledge about reality in itself, this inevitably raises certain questions for many people. For how then can we assure ourselves that God is *real*? If the word God only refers to some profound dimension of human experience, how can we know that God exists? Or are we to understand the use of the word God merely as a way of naming certain features of our experience? But then in what way can religion be *true* of something? Or is religion only experientially adequate? And is the truth of religion simply something pragmatic?

Such questions, however, are really questions about the meaning and truth of God-language. If theology, therefore, purports to assert something which is true and meaningful, in a non-trivial sense of the word, the question at stake is whether an appropriate metaphysics for theology *must* affirm a Whiteheadian mode of realism, but try to find ways of rendering it acceptable. Or is it perhaps the case that we can modify such a notion of realism, thereby avoiding many of its serious problems, but all the same retain a meaning for the concept of God's reality? If our subsequent investigation of what might be an appropriate conception of experience, of realism, and of truth, compel us to some kind of revision or modification, what sort of metaphysical assumptions would this commit us to, and what effect would this have for theories of truth and religion?

Chapter 4

The Problem of Realism in a Metaphysics for Theology

4.1 The Strategy

The need for an appropriate metaphysics for theology is related to the problem of the meaning and the truth of God-talk. Without a satisfactory metaphysics assertions about God will remain unintelligible and no assessment of them will be possible. But since the question about the reality of God cannot be addressed without a discussion of what we mean by reality and truth in general, and how we can know anything about them, we must consequently deal with some broad issues in metaphysics and epistemology, and in theories of perception and sociology of knowledge. In order to bring forth some of the problems involved in these issues, I shall take some examples from the history of philosophy. The purpose is not primarily to deliver a detailed analysis, but to clarify certain *types* of philosophical positions which it is necessary to consider in a discussion of a metaphysics for theology. I shall, therefore, focus on some characteristic ideas, while others will be left aside. A similar method is also employed by Stuart C. Brown – an author I am going to discuss – when he seizes upon certain limited aspects of the philosophy of Kant and others. My choice of examples will be partly directed by my investigation of Whitehead's philosophy, since his realism, in fact his whole system, was elaborated in close relationship to the criticism – and appreciation – of philosophers and scientists such as Plato, Aristotle, Newton, Descartes, and Kant.

In the beginning of this part of our study we shall discuss some implications of the classical – Whiteheadian, if you wish – modes of realism in science and philosophy. By a criticism of Descartes' methodological skepticism we shall then proceed with an attempt to show that the idea of something like "the metaphysical witness" cannot warrant such a mode of realism. The next step will be to outline a different view, a modification of classical realism, which will take us into a discussion about experience, about the concept of truth, and about the fact – value dichotomy. I shall then continue by applying the results of our discussion to the problem of God-language in contemporary theology. The strategy of my argument will be to try to show that questions about God's reality have no intelligible *meaning* insofar as they depend upon the classical mode of realism which sometimes seems to be in the background of such questions, as seems to be the case with Whitehead's realism. The realism I am speaking about is the theory that there is an external world independently of our minds that we can meaningfully speak about or refer to. To the extent that this realism is connected with a distinction between the real world, or reality in itself, and our mental representation of it – a distinction which we may call *metaphysical dualism* – I shall claim that it is confusing, and, therefore, untenable. I shall suggest an alternative view, which I shall call *conceptual realism*. If such a view can be accepted, my intention is to try to show how it can be related to a theory of religion, and how we can develop certain criteria by which it might be possible to test the truth-value of religious conceptualizations of the world.

4.2 Scientism and Metaphysical Dualism

What we may call classical realism, the mode of realism we have so far discussed, has its roots in ancient Greek philosophy. Already in this philosophy we are able to see a link between certain metaphysical assumptions and theories of knowledge. Plato assumes, for instance, that true knowledge must be both infallible and of the 'real.' In the *Theaetetus* he argues that neither sense-perception nor true belief, is possessed of these two characteristics. Sense-perception is relative, elusive, and subjective. The object of true knowledge must be stable and abiding, fixed, capable of being grasped in clear definitions. The main point of Plato's theory of Ideas seems to be possible to summarize thus: true universal concepts, or true knowledge, correspond to an objective reality. These concepts have objective reference to a reality of a higher order than sense-perception. True knowledge is directed toward what *is*, whereas false belief is oriented toward what is not. Here, consequently, we have the incitement to what has been called "the correspondence theory of truth."

Aristotle's language in his *Metaphysics*[85] indicates that he entertained a similar view of true knowledge, namely, that it is a correspondence between our beliefs and sensations, and states of affairs outside us. It seems also that Plato's view in both the *Sophist* and the *Theaetetus* had a considerable impact on his thoughts. To perceive an object is to reproduce its form inside ourselves, while its matter remains outside. Therefore, sensations can be said to be a sort of cognition, even if not a perfect cognition. For instance, in hearing a bell we only receive a limited sensation of the entire composition of the bell. But if there existed objects that were not embodied in matter, it would be possible to reproduce the entire object in our mind. Aristotle believed that 'the good' was such an object.

The view we shall focus on, and critically examine now, however, is not in the first place the ancient Greek form of what we may call *metaphysical dualism*, the view, namely, that what goes on in the mind is distinct from, but nevertheless correlated to, what goes on outside the mind in reality. Rather it is the modern form of it, with the alleged gulf between the physical, or material, world, objectively out there, and the mental representation of that world in our minds. In the intellectual community many philosophers have tried to argue that what gives sense to human language, to theories and descriptions of the world, is a special *correspondence* between words, or sets of words, and states of affairs in the world. It has also been thought that a similar correspondence is what makes sense to religious beliefs. Such beliefs are *about* certain states of affairs in reality, i.e., God. However, this view of true knowledge logically presupposes certain metaphysical assumptions, namely, that *states of affairs exist independently of the belief* that these states exist, or do not exist. These *beliefs,* in turn, are assumed to exist as mental representations or concepts in the mind, independent of those states in the real world that they refer to. That *truth* here "consists in some form of correspondence between belief and fact," is a view much entertained, e. g., by the early Bertrand Russell. In *Logic and Knowledge* he claims that "the world contains *facts,* ... and that there are also *beliefs,* which have reference to facts, and by reference to facts are either true or false."[86] In his book *Do Religious Claims Make Sense?* Stuart C. Brown presents a good summary of this common dualism.

> On such a view, reality consists of states of affairs which obtain quite independently of any language in which we might try to describe them. Our simple descriptions of the world will be true if, and only if, they correspond to actual states of affairs. They will be false given only a lack of correspondence between them and states of affairs.[87]

To this sort on ontological realism, a special kind of epistemology is often juxtaposed. Knowledge about the world is something we acquire, basically, through *discovery.* We are presented as observers, standing apart from what we observe. The more we are able to distinguish ourselves from the object of our investigation, from what we observe, not letting our subjectivity influence what we observe or the way we describe our observations, the more fit we become for achieving true knowledge about reality. *Objectivity* on this view is the character of a description of the *real* world – or of items in that world – when the description is not influenced by human subjectivity. It tells us what is the real fact, what is actually happening out there. It is a description of reality as it is independent of and separate from our minds. Of course, pure objectivity is only the ideal. Objectivity in the actual world is only an approximation of this ideal, that toward which we aim. And the chief mark of a scientific theory, or description of reality, is precisely such objectivity: it is a description or a report of discoveries made by observation of the real and objective world out there.

In the empiricist tradition the main emphasis was put on the observational side of science. However, it ought to be mentioned that ontological realism, the theory that there exist states of affairs – facts – in the external world independent of our minds – can also be related to other theories of knowledge. This is the case, for instance, in the philosophy of Descartes', as it was in the case of Plato's. But since empiricism seems to have pervaded modern science, this is the view we shall pay attention to in the subsequent discussion.

Among many scientists in the empiricist tradition it was progressively realized that our sense-organs were not quite as capable of providing us with that purely objective knowledge, the true picture or report of what was assumed to be out there, as was first supposed by thinkers like Galileo, Newton, Hume, Bacon, and Mill. *What* we see, or hear, or sense, what we observe, is heavily affected by the *way* we see, and by the *way* we describe what we observe. There was among the empiricists a wide variety of opinions as to the extent our subjectivity influences empirical science's ability to disclose the objective structure of reality. But there seemed to be little doubt or disagreement among them that there was a homogenous world out there, independent of the observer, and that sense-data, or sense-experience was at least partly something given.

The *logical positivists,* a group of philosophers taken to consist of thinkers such as Rudolf Carnap, Moritz Schlick, Carl Gustaf Hempel, Alfred Ayer, Hans Reichenbach, and others, represent a special branch of empiricism. I shall speak about 'positivism' and 'positivists' referring to the philosophical tradition emerging from Auguste Comte, in which metaphysics and theology are refuted, and which asserts that knowledge about reality is limited to "positive experience," i.e., that which is given in experience. The logical positivists argued that theories or descriptions of contents that were not empirically verifiable, asserted nothing meaningful and had no factual content. The prominent channels of knowledge were believed to be sense-organs, especially the visual sense. Questions about the existence of an external world and the like were, according to the locial positivists, quite meaningless, since there were no empirical methods of verification for such questions. However, it is interesting to note that in spite of the rejection of metaphysics, logical positivism seems to presuppose certain metaphysical assumptions.[88] The idea, for instance, that experience, at least in part, is something *given* implies a sort of metaphysics. We have already mentioned that Ernst Mach developed a form of neutral monism, in which sensations were believed to be the true components of reality.[89] Other logical positivists entertained forms of phenomenalistic metaphysics.

For the positivist the real was the observable. However, for a *realist* this is not the case. The real is that which belongs to the world independent of our observations. Observation is *about* that which belongs to the real world. Science is the method of discovering and exploring what the world is really like. One of those who have most urgently claimed that there is such a method through which we can acquire true knowledge about the real world is Karl Popper.[90] He is often taken to belong to the logical positivists, but in many respects he is clearly distinguishable from this group. However, he emphatically agreed with the positivists in their strong rejection of philosophical speculations, especially of Hegelian metaphysics. The main argument against metaphysics was that while science had continuously progressed since Galileo and Newton, there was no similar development in metaphysics. Popper's concern, which he shared with the positivists, was to find a criterion of what was to count as science in distinction from metaphysical speculations. However, Popper's criterion was different from that of the positivists, and he repeatedly criticized their philosophy of science. It is important to mention that Popper always remained a realist in his own philosophy of science, holding that scientific theories are about the world which exists independently of us. His language also indicates that he entertained a rather optimistic understanding of the possibilities of sense-perception as means to knowledge. He seems to have regarded everything physical as observable on principle.

Popper's entire methodological program aimed at reenforcing the growth of knowledge. One emphasis of the program was to find a criterion of knowledge that would exclude metaphysical statements. But, as in positivism, the transcendental had an eery way of reappearing. For Popper seems to postulate a ready-made world, with a built-in structure, which he expected the true scientific theory to get its lasso around. According to Popper there is one *absolutely* true theory about reality, even if it is not yet discovered, and this is the theory at which science aims. This, at least, is the impression one gets reading his famous *The Open Society and its Enemies*. In a section called "Getting Nearer to the Truth" he says:

> In all this, the idea of the growth of knowledge – of getting nearer to the truth – is decisive. Intuitively, this idea is as clear as the idea of truth itself. A statement is true if it corresponds to the facts. It is nearer to the truth than another statement if it corresponds to the facts more closely than the other statement.[91]

In physics, for instance, Popper argues that Newton's theory was a better approximation than Kepler's – it got nearer to the truth. But this, he says, does not make it *true:* "it can be nearer to the truth and it can, at the same time, be a false theory." But

> what, then, are we to trust? What are we to accept? The answer is: whatever we accept we should trust only tentatively, always remembering that we are in possession, at best, of partial truth (or rightness).[92]

This view has had a pervasive influence on the way people today conceive of notions such as reality and truth. The most accepted apprehension of what *reality* means in our culture seems to be based on the sort of dualistic outlook which finds expression in writings such as Karl Popper's: it assumes a distinction between our present, approximate, picture of reality – the world for us – and reality in itself – the unconceptualized and undescribed world. *Truth,* according to Popper, is clearly a correspondence between statements and facts. Further, there are facts and, thus, truths that have never been thought, asserted, or discovered, but which nevertheless exist.

This view has also influenced the common view about what it means to say that God is real, and that beliefs about God are true. It can be summarized thus: to believe in God is, among other things, to hold certain ideas about God to be true. That they are true means that they correspond to states of affairs in God which are really the case. The word 'really' here does not mean that which is real for us, but objectively real, i.e., mind-independent. Reality here is that which is real in itself. Hence, when someone claims that God is real, or that God exists, and that beliefs about God are true, this means that God exists for God's self. When people say that religious beliefs are true they mean, then, that these beliefs are true because they correspond to states of affairs outside and independent of themselves. William James has given a description of this mode of realism, viz., metaphysical dualism, in his *Essays in Radical Empiricism*.

> This essential dualism of the theistic view has all sorts of collateral con-sequences. Man being an outsider and a mere subject to God, not his intimate partner, a character of externality invades the field. God is not heart of our heart and reason of our reason, but our magistrate, rather; and me-chanically to obey his commands, however strange they may be, remains our only moral duty. Conceptions of criminal law have in fact played a great part in defining our relations with him. Our relations with speculative truth show the same externality. One of our duties is to know truth. . .
>
> The situation here again is radically dualistic. It is not as if the world came to know itself, or God came to know himself, partly through us, as pantheistic idealists have maintained, but *truth exists per se* and absolutely, by God's grace and decree, no matter of who of us knows it or is ignorant, and it would continue to exist unaltered, even though we finite knowers were all annihilated.[93]

The view James characterizes does not seem to have its roots in Christianity itself. Rather it seems plausible to believe that this kind of God-language reflects a set of metaphysical ideas, which have been alive in the minds of men and women in Western society since ancient times, and which are still, for instance, present in the writings of people like Karl Popper.

Popper is of special interest here, however, since he has delivered an apparently influential critique of Whitehead's metaphysical system. In *The Open Society and its Enemies* he begins the discussion of this system with a quotation from *Process and Reality* where Whitehead argues: "Rationalism, it is admitted, is the method by which advance is made within the limits of particular sciences. . . The proper test is not that of finality, but of progress." Now Popper argues against on precisely this ground, that "while physics progresses, metaphysics does not."[94] In physics, there is a "proper test of progress," namely, the test of experiment and of practice. Modern physics, Popper claims, can legitimately be said to be "better" than the physics of the seventeenth century. But this cannot be said of metaphysics, which has not progressed at all, and whose chief mark is its "practical uselessness." Popper then goes on to say that another feature of Whitehead's metaphysics is the lack of rational arguments. He claims, for instance, that Whitehead learned from Hegel how to avoid Kant's criticism that speculative philosophy only supplies new crutches for lame proofs. "This Hegelian method is simple enough. We can easily avoid crutches as long as we avoid proofs and arguments altogether. Hegelian philosophy does not argue; it decrees." One must "take it or leave it," without further discussion. Therefore, Popper's final judgment about *Process and Reality* is that "the method of the book is irrational".[95]

It might seriously be questioned whether Popper gives a fair interpretation of Whitehead's philosophy; in fact, he completely ignores Whitehead's effort to argue rationally for the relevance and acceptability of his system, as we have seen. Yet, it is not easy to judge Popper's critique, since he does not present us with a clear argument. It is perfectly clear that he rejects Whitehead's metaphysics as irrational. But why? One reason seems to be that it is *inconsistent*. It does not yield to its own proper criterion of rationality, namely, the test of progress. Another reason seems to be that Whitehead states his case without appeal to rationality. But we must then ask: what kind of criterion does Popper require in order to find it rational to believe something to be true about reality? Does he admit only the same kind of evidence as in physics or natural science?

Popper thought that the growth of knowledge is correlated to the growth of science, and tried to articulate such a scientific metod. True knowledge about reality is, therefore, the knowledge which can in some sense be corroborated by scientific evidence. But we may ask whether any exhaustive description of rationality as scientific does not yield too narrow a conception of rationality. Does such a conception not in fact defeat itself? For what sort of *scientific* argument could be given for the belief in a general, human rationality? And would this conception not mark many non-scientific human activities, such as politics, ethics, and history, as irrational?

The purpose of Popper's methodological program was, as we have said, to reenforce the growth of knowledge, and to develop a criterion which would help us to distinguish between science and non-science, between what can be asserted to be true knowledge (or perhaps we should say 'truer' knowledge) and false. The positivist's distinction between science and metaphysics has its counterpart in Popper's distinction between rationalism and irrationalism. However, if we are to acquire a sound and humane conception of rationality, it has to be given a broader definition than that of science. It may be that Aristotle's distinction between *practical knowledge* – as the knowledge about human life and happiness entailed in ethics – and *theoretical knowledge* – as in science – is correct and ought to be countenanced in our culture. In a later section I shall even argue that scientific knowledge actually presupposes practical, or non-scientific, knowledge, and that there are no facts or objective realities that do not in some sense imply certain ideas of the good. And this is important because so many people today believe that true knowledge about the real world is given only by science, and that beliefs which cannot be vindicated by scientific evidence are not really worthy of being called knowledge. This form of *scientism,* the belief that science alone is the source of knowledge, is founded on the sort of metaphysical dualism which we saw underlying Popper's epistemology: there is a single truth about the world, and it is for science to discover it. Truth is a correspondence between beliefs about the world and the world as it is in itself.

The corollary that many people draw from this is that there is one true and final theory about the world, in terms of which it is possible to give an exhaustive description of the ultimate appointments of reality, the true characteristics of the world. That such a theory, however, would be nothing but a metaphysics, few people seem to realize. For today we associate our conception of reality and final truth not with metaphysics but with physics. For modern folk, what is real is what can be *reduced to physical discourse.* This is the view I call 'physicalism,' i.e., true knowledge about reality is only that which is confirmed by physics and which can be expressed in physicalistic language. For example, the British philosopher Mary Midgley in *Beast and Man* bemoans this state of affairs while arguing that feelings are more important than thoughts:

> People find it hard to grasp this point because they see it as antiscientific. Must not the *real* account of what is happening, they say, be the physical one? Are we not speaking only indirectly or superficially, if not superstitiously, whenever we describe an event in other terms than as the movement of electrons? Is not everything else in some way *unreal?*[96]

The sort of scientism we are speaking about here, physicalism, or what could also be called metaphysical materialism, differs, though, in many respects from the standpoint of contemporary physics. The fact that the entities which comprise the world on this view more resemble the atoms in Democritus' or Newton's physicalistic picture of reality, than the non-material elements referred to in quantum physics, is perhaps not so decisive. More important, though, is the fact that quantum mechanics completely lacks the pretention of being a theory about the ultimate elements of the world. On the contrary, it emphasizes that the theory is a description of the world as it is *experienced by the observer,* not what the world is in itself. It does not claim to be a metaphysics which investigates what reality is *independently* of us.

Perhaps one might expect that science investigate certain characteristics of the real world and of objects within it. In modern theories of measurement, however, it is claimed that all types of measurement are *only* statements about the relation between the object and the methods by which it is measured. It is not possible to speak about what the object is in itself, as mind-independent, only how it appears when it is exposed to the influence of a method of measurement. A book about nuclear physics, for example, states: "The definition of nuclear radius is somewhat arbitrary, because the result of a measurement depends on the phenomenon used to define the nuclear radius."[97] The most striking form of this observation was given in Werner Heisenberg's "uncertainty relations," which implie that complete and exact knowledge about the measured phenomena can never be attained. This lack of access to absolute knowledge about what the world is in itself might at first seem devastating to science as a means to achieving true knowledge about the world. The reason this is not the case is that the relevant knowledge for human beings is precisely knowledge about the world with which we are in relation. The metaphysical question about what the world is in itself is usually left out in modern physics as being fruitless and meaningless.

We may remind ourselves that what is now granted as a fact in modern physics – that we cannot exclude the observer from the observed, that the methods of investigation affects the result of the investigation – was in part already pioneered by Whitehead in his attempt to criticize Newtonian physics. Whitehead's effort was to develop a metaphysical conceptualization of the world, as it appears from within, so to speak. Whitehead also claimed that everything in reality is ontologically interconnected and that nothing can exist except by participation. He refuted a mind – matter dualism.

The tendency to reduce reality to the physical has been part of our culture since the 17th century. Classical physics was both anti-metaphysical and at the same time understood itself as giving at least an approximate description of the ultimate components of the universe. This is not to say that Newton was a positivist. Rather, in full awareness of his own work's shortcomings – the fact that his principles could not explain, for instance, the elegant structure of the cosmos, where all planets revolve without colliding in the same direction around the sun – he inferred the work of a supreme intelligence outside the world. This was in fact nothing but a sort of scientific argument for the existence of God. Or, in other words: the assumption about the existence of God is part of an explanatory scientific hypothesis, in terms of which the structure of the physical world is interpreted.[98] So here already we can discern the impetus for our contemporary view that we ought to be able to give scientific, and especially physical, evidence for our beliefs about objective reality.

Newton himself actually accepted Galileo's view that nature could be exhaustively described in terms of particles in motion, though he rejected the idea that his own theory of universal gravitation should be read as a description of the ultimate – or metaphysical – facts of our universe. Nevertheless, scientific concepts in the Newtonian era frequenty came to be taken as *literal representations of the real world,* reproductions of the one and only reality. It is therefore not surprising that the world has been understood to consist of a fixed set of material and immaterial objects, which could be truly described in terms of physics. These objects were, or more correctly came to be, understood as the real facts about our reality.People today, however, seem to be aware that these concepts or systems of description are partly creations or constructions of the scientist. Everybody seems to understand that absolute and pure objectivity is denied us. But scientific, and especially physicalistic, language is still believed to be the *best* way to describe reality; namely, reality as it is in itself. As we saw in Popper's work: physics is getting nearer to the truth. Hence, these concepts about what reality is made from, still play the rôle of an all-encompassing metaphysics, in terms of which we seek to interpret what is real and true in general.

In classical physics only those properties of things that could be treated mathematically – mass and velocity – were considered to be true characteristics of the real world. Other properties were regarded as purely subjective, having no existence outside people's minds. Therefore, the more an 'observer' dismissed him or herself from a physical description of reality, the more subjective, or even distorted, the description became. A true description ought to be a report of facts independent of the observer. In our culture history and the social sciences are occasionally regarded with suspicion precisely for this reason. Popper, for example, argues that the point of view from which the historian decides to look at what has happened cannot be rationally justified, and that history, as a theory about the past, can never be true – or false – in the same sense as can physical theories. Historical events cannot be predicted as physical events might be, according to Popper. For a true theory in physics is only that by virtue of which predictions are confirmed by experiments.

> There can be no history of 'the past as it actually did happen'; there can only be historical interpretations, and non of them final.[99]

The more influenced by value judgments a description is, the more subjective it becomes, and the more removed it is from pure knowledge and science. It might still be legitimate to pursue history in this way – as a matter of fact Popper stresses that we are obliged to – but true knowledge and ideal science simply tell the 'facts' as they are.

Another feature, therefore, of the mode of realism we have discussed here, with its roots in dualistic metaphysics, is the absolute dichotomy, so widely assumed in our society, between *value judgments* and *statements of fact*. Value judgments are understood to be expressions or projections of our emotions or attitudes. It is generally held that facts, or factual statements, are 'value neutral.' Some of the logical positivists required that it should be possible to translate all scientific statements into "neutral observation language." Words like "considerate," "good," "love," "selfish," and the like, are regarded as non-scientific and assert nothing true about the world out there. They cannot be properly applied to facts, but express only subjective feelings or acts of evaluation. They are words of praise or blame, and ought therefore to be eliminated from scientific discourse. There is no matter to the fact in value judgments, and ethics is understood as a mere series of articulations of idiosyncrasies. It is perfectly legitimate to speak about "physical properties," but there is no point to talk about "value properties," or "objective values." When Max Weber first introduced the modern fact-value dichotomy, his argument was precisely that it was not possible to establish the truth of value judgments to the satisfaction of every rational being. And 'rationality' for him meant exactly "scientific rationality."[100]

The reason why natural science, especially physics, enjoys such tremendous prestige in our society and has thus had such a great influence on our modes of thoughts, seems to be the practical success it has had – in making true predictions, devising better ways of controlling nature, and so forth. But also its image as a method of discovering reality – the true facts – not just of discussing it (which is what philosophy and theology are all about in many people's minds), that physics has achieved, has certainly helped to increase its respect in our culture.

If, however, we were to look for a more psychological explanation of why so many people believe that everything real can be reduced to physics, the belief could probably be traced back to the old correspondence theory of true knowledge, with its root in ancient Greek philosophy. There is, namely, a certain conspicuous psychological force in the postulate that there is just *one* true picture of the world, that which corresponds to the real states of affairs. Everybody is, of course, aware that our present conceptualization of the world, i.e., our contemporary picture of reality in physics and astrophysics, is nothing but an approximation of this one and only true theory. But there *is* one, if we are to believe, for instance, Karl Popper, which is absolutely and finally true. And science is getting nearer and nearer to attaining knowledge about this ultimately true theory of the world. It might be that nobody actually possesses this knowledge. It might, in fact, be that no one will ever come into possession of it. Certain things are true just in themselves, even if no one actually believes that they are true, or even that they exist. Or as William James characterized this view: "truth exists per se and absolutely, by God's grace and decree, no matter of who of us knows it or is ignorant, and it would continue to exist unaltered, even though we finite knowers were all annihilated."

4.3 Cartesian Scientism and a Critique of Descartes' Skeptical Device

I indicated earlier that some elements in modern scientism probably could be traced back to ancient Greek philosophy and metaphysics, in particular to the idea of true knowledge as a correspondence between beliefs on the one hand

and the real world on the other. To some extent, this idea implied a sort of dualism. However, it did not assume a sharp Cartesian mind – matter dualism. In Greek metaphysics we find no pure, dead matter, and the material world is not understood as devoid of mind. Matter could, with a simplification, be described as the stuff of which everything is made, whereas mind is the principle, or the source, of order and regularity in the world. The world could thus be conceived on the model of an animal, or a living organism, according to Greek philosophy, with mind present always and everywhere, directing the movements and formation of matter.

Many of the features of contemporary *materialism*, therefore, cannot be traced back to Greek philosophy. Nor can they be understood as a result of science, or physics, itself. In fact, it seems that many of the more conspicuous motifs can be found in a philosophy, but in one more recent than the Greek. I mean the Cartesian philosophy; it seems a plausible hypothesis that Descartes' ideas have exercised a pervasive influence on modern modes of thought. Most people, however, believe that what I call scientism, or materialism, or physicalism, is derived from science itself. If this is correct we ought to be able to explain why Descartes' metaphysical system was one of the main targets of Whitehead's attack on a dualistic conception of the world.

To bring forth the basis of some of the motifs that are found in modern materialism and realism, I shall devote this section to Descartes' ideas. But since realism, as, for instance, the Whiteheadian mode of it, presupposes not only a metaphysical dualism but also the assumption of something like "the metaphysical witness," I shall discuss critically Descartes' skeptical hypothesis – the center of his whole philosophical system – that we might be deceived by an evil spirit, who tells us falsely that there is a real world out there. For on my reading Descartes is not an idealist but a sort of *realist*, trying to prove that there is a real world apart from our minds, "extramental" as he says. I shall then try to show, with an argument similar to that by which Whitehead was criticized, that Descartes' methodological doubt is not supportive of his realism since it presupposes an unacceptable metaphysical theory, namely, that we somehow have access to a position outside reality. The core of my argument will be that such a position is unavailable to us and that it makes no sense to speak about what reality is in itself, i.e., as undescribed and unconceptualized.

Following up on Galileo's scientific approach, according to which truth in nature consisted of mathematical facts, entities that were measurable and quantitative, Descartes developed the idea of a *universal science*, mathematical in its form. He believed there is only one kind of knowledge, and ultimately only one science. Accordingly, we finally have only one way of attaining true knowledge, and there is basically only one scientific method. This method is a set of rules which guides the functioning of our minds.

Our minds, according to Descartes, operate in two ways: intuition and deduction.

Intuition is one form through which we acquire knowledge without "the fluctuating assurance of the senses," the "conception, without doubt, of an unclouded and attentive mind, which springs from the light of reason alone."[101] Deduction, on the other hand, is described as "all necessary inference from other facts which are known with certainty." If we follow the lines of this epistemic method, we shall arrive at the awareness of what Descartes calls "simple natures," which come forth, clear and distinct, in our minds. On the one hand there is a group of *material* simple natures that we define as existing only in bodies. On the other hand there is a group of *intellectual* simple natures, such as willing, thinking, and doubting. There is also a group of simple natures that are common to both material and mental entities, such as existence, for instance. These groups of entities, or essences, are the ultimate concepts, or ideas, into which we can analyze the nature of our world. They also provide the point of departure for deductive inference.

Descartes consequently placed metaphysics within the proper sphere of science, in distinction from Aristotle, and later Kant. Physics, according to Descartes, could be deduced from metaphysics. Just by thinking we can discern the universal laws that govern the material world. Sense-experience can only give us particulars. But although the empirical yields no reliable knowledge, no clear and distinct ideas, it is by *means* of the senses that we become aware of the existence of an external world, Descartes thought.

> In our ideas there is nothing which is not innate in the mind or faculty of thinking, except only those circumstances which point to experience; the fact, for example, that we judge that this or that idea, which we now have present to our thought, is to be referred to a certain external thing, not because these external things transmitted the ideas themselves to the mind through the organs of sense, but because they transmitted something which gave it the occasion to form these ideas, by means of an innate faculty, at this time rather than at another.[102]

Although Descartes cannot be described as an empiricist, he is not an idealist who denies the existence of the external world. He seems to believe, in fact, that there is a world outside of and apart from our minds. But we cannot arrive at this conclusion – which seems to be his point – by means of an argument from sense-experience. On the other hand, we cannot prove the existence of the external world only on grounds of deduction and intuition. For we can *doubt* that there is such a world, even if we agree for purely practical reasons to live on the assumption that there is one. Descartes chooses his brand of realism – the belief that there is a real, objective world out there, independent of our minds – on the basis of a sort of theological argument. For God would be a deceiver if he created us with a natural inclination to believe in the existence of an external reality, without having created such a world. How Descartes reaches the conclusion that there is a God, and that this God is not a deceptive being, is something we can leave aside here, only mentioning that he offers a sort of ontological proof of God's existence. But the affirmation of our own existence is logically – not ontologically – prior to the affirmation of God's existence.

That I exist is something which I know intuitively, Descartes claims. His argument runs as follows. In order to know what is absolutely true and certain – Descartes wants to give himself "entirely to the search after truth" – he makes use of his famous methodological doubt. He wishes to subject everything to the test of doubt, in order to find something – hopefully – which is indoubtable. The fact that I can – or even ought – to doubt my sense perceptions is clear in sense perception itself. For sometimes I take my sense impressions to be what experience – by means of the very *same* sense organs – later reveals to be something different. But, Descartes thinks, it is also possible to doubt deductive notions and intuited knowledge. For it might be that "some evil genius, no less powerful than deceitful, has employed his whole energies in deceiving me."[103] But however much I doubt, there is something which I can never doubt, the fact, namely, that I am doubting. *Cogito, ergo sum.* For even if I am deceived, there must be something which is being deceived, namely, the doubting I. If, as in Caldéron's play, life is but a dream, there is at least always a dreamer. Therefore, the only logical conclusion that can be drawn from the skeptical hypothesis, Descartes thinks, is that I must submit my own existence, as a thinking, dreaming, doubting being. That is something I can be *absolutely* certain about.

This certainty of my own existence becomes "the first principle" of Descartes' entire system, and ultimately everything else is derived from it, including the dualistic conception of the world and the so-called two-substance theory. When I affirm my own existence, as a thinking being and as a spiritual creature, I have, at the same time, a clear idea of something from which this 'I' is absolutely distinct: my own body and the external world. The real existence of an extramental reality is not thereby logically proven. But my clear ideas of such a world surely indicate that it has extension; and that since God, whose existence and essence both follow logically from the intuition of my own existence, would not deceive me, "we must allow that corporeal objects exist." But these objects, and hence the entire world out there, must have a completely different substance, or essence, than the mind. Therefore my body does not have the same essence as my mind. Descartes defines a human being as a mind which makes use of a body. The mind is incorporated in the body. He says, for example:

> I have no doubt that the mind begins to think at the same time that it is infused into the body of an infant, and that it is at the same time conscious of its own thought, though afterwards it does not remember it.[104]

Descartes believed, as did Democritus, Galileo, and Newton before him, that our bodies and the whole material world consist of some kind of particles, even if these entities were not precisely like atoms, floating around in empty space. And even if Descartes was no more a positivist than Newton, his mind – matter dualism provided a stance for a new materialism within his own lifetime. The neo-Epicurean Pierre Gassendi (1592–1655), for instance, argued that the measurable and quantifiable properties of nature are the *only* realities, and that mind is not a real entity. He contributed to philosophy, on the basis of Epicurean texts and selected Cartesian conceptions, an atomistic theory of the true nature of things. Later the French philosopher Julien Offray de La Mettrie (1709–1751) developed a mechanistic anthropology in his *L'Homme machine,* on the basis of the same sort of materialistic conception of reality. We mentioned earlier that even if Newton did not himself develop a mechanistic theory of the world, there was that already at hand in his ideas which could lead to such a theory.

Cartesian philosophy, as one of the major systematic alternatives of its own time, was developed – certainly not always in a direction that Descartes would have approved – into a metaphysics which lingers on. Many of its motifs can be discerned in contemporary materialism. The replacement of metaphysics by science in our culture is one piece of evidence. Another is the mechanistic and materialistic conception of reality, viz., the idea that the world out there – today spoken of as the "real" world – consists of dead matter. Non-quantifiable properties, such as values or aesthetic qualities, so important in Whitehead's speculative philosophy, have consequently come to be regarded as subjective and unreal. Factual knowledge belongs purely to the objective world out there. The *realism* we have described as the belief in an external world, independent of our minds, is often related to this view, as is the idea that everything "real" can be reduced to science of physics. The modern faith in a unified science, so dear to the positivists (though rejected by Popper), is at least present in embryo in Descartes' philosophy, though he meant something very different by the idea of a "universal science." But the general idea that there is one path to true knowledge, one trustworthy method, belongs to Cartesian philosophy. The dualism in Descartes' system, the dichotomy between appearance and reality, also suggests a *representation theory of perception,* where what is perceived in the mind is understood as mental representations of what is outside the mind. When the ontological assumptions behind this dichotomy were forgotten, and the trust in the reliability of our sense-organs was secured, it was only natural that *truth,* the truth of our mental representations, our ideas and beliefs, etc., became a sort of correspondence between what is in the mind and what was assumed to be outside in the real world.

If one wishes to move toward a more critical assessment of Descartes' philosophy, it seems reasonable to fasten on the focus of his system, its first principle, the skeptical device in which the evil demon is postulated whose energies are devoted to deceiving us systematically. To begin with, let us turn to a line of thought in Stuart C. Brown's book, *Do Religious Claims Make Sense?,* and in the next section continue to draw some conclusions from this.

Discussing the relation between language and reality, Brown draws attention to some philosophical problems connected with Descartes' hypothetical device. Descartes' problem was this: how can we be sure that our senses do not perpetually deceive us? How can we be sure that the real world which our senses suggest is indeed out there? Descartes did not in fact claim that there is a deceiving creature or that life is a dream, only that the supposition that this could be the case needs to be disproven. Descartes' assumption, Brown explains, was that unless this hypothesis was disproven, the possibility that it is true would remain, i.e., we could never be quite sure that we are not deceived in supposing ourselves to have a body or having experiences of a world which is independent of ourselves.

Brown describes Descartes' problem as that of raising an *external question,* because if this problem of whether there is a real world out there or whether Descartes is just being deceived is to make any sense, it requires "a foothold outside the language of observation."[105] What this means, it seems, is that in order to raise the question of whether there *is* a world independently of our mental representation of it, our descriptions of the world, one *must have access to a position outside* the whole conceptualization of the world. For from whose point of view could it otherwise be raised? "One might express Descartes' position as that of raising an 'external question' about the language of observation itself." But the question as to whether our senses sometimes deceive us is, by contrast, an "internal question," one which must be settled by means provided *within* the language of observation. Descartes thinks, Brown claims, that, if it is *sometimes* shown that the senses are mistaken, it needs to be shown that it is not *always* the case that they are mistaken. And this, Brown argues, might at first seem reasonable enough. "If the buses on a given route are sometimes late, we might well wonder whether they are not always late." [106] It would at lest *make sense* to suppose that they might always be late. But the bus analogy is deceptive, Brown claims. For, whereas we could find out whether the buses are always late by just the means with which we would find out that they are sometimes late, we could not hope to find out that our senses are *always* deceiving us by the means we use to find out that they *sometimes* deceive us. "For to do that we should have to *rely* on our senses. And we would involve ourselves in self-contradiction if we suppose that we could, while relying on the evidence of our senses, discover them to be wholly unreliable."

Brown then develops his argument in relation to what Wittgenstein in his later writings describes as the "mistake of grammar," by which Wittgenstein refers to the observation that whether a sentence makes sense or not depends on whether it is construed "according to the rules of grammar."[107] Here Wittgenstein does not intend to address what we ordinarily mean by 'grammar,' but the fact that the word 'God,' for instance, could be used in many different senses. In some religions, Wittgenstein thought, it could be used so that it would make sense to say that God had three arms. In other religions, however, it might be that it would not make sense to say that God has arms at all. Theology, according to Wittgenstein, could be understood as a kind of "grammar," for "grammar" tells us "what kind of object anything is." So theology tells us what it makes sense to say and what it does not make sense to say about God. Wittgenstein's point, Brown argues, is that "the standards which govern what it makes sense to say within a given field of discourse must be sought *within* that field of discourse. They cannot, that is to say, be imposed upon a field of discourse from the outside. The question 'Can God be mocked?,' for example, is a question about what it makes sense to say about God. It can only be considered within the context of a particular religion."[108]

Brown explains that this means that "it does not make sense for a man to say: 'I know this object has been observed under normal conditions to be red, but I doubt whether it really is so'." He claims that Descartes' hypothesis, viewed as an "internal question," and so as subject to the standards implicit in a language of observation, is false. Understood as an "external question," it is unintelligible. What Descartes, if anything, is able to show with his device, is that the language of observation needs the support of the language of religion. His intention was to show that our conception of the world as something independently real needs to be supported by a religious "conception of reality." But by doing this he begins with the very conception of reality which he sets out to call into question.

4.4 Some Conclusions concerning Metaphysical Assumptions in Realism and their Impact on the Concept of Truth

Descartes' philosophy is famous for its dualistic ontology, founded on the distinction between what the world seems, or appears, to be, and what it really is; in other words: between what reality is to us, subjectively, and what it is in itself, objectively. Descartes' problem was how we could achieve assurance that there was an objective world apart from our subjective apprehension of it. He thought that by means of methodological doubt we could acquire such assurance.

The conclusion, however, we must draw from the previous discussion is that it makes no sense to use the distinction between the world for us and the world in itself. And the reason is this: who could ever tell what reality is *apart* from our understandning or description of it? From whose perspective could it ever be told what the world *is* totally undescribed, completely separate from human conceptualization? For that is precisely what it means to say that we know what the world is independently of our minds.

In our discussion of Whitehead's realism and theory of perception, we saw that his system logically presupposed the assumption of something we called "the metaphysical witness," namely, that we have access to a position outside the world. Only given this assumption could we understand how Whitehead was able to speak about what reality is independently of our consciousness of it. We argued then that this assumption – bracketing the question of whether it is reasonable to accept it or not – was inconsistent with the entire content of Whitehead's ontological theory, namely, that everything real exists only by participation, and that all actual events are constituted by their relations to other events. Whitehead, in fact, emphasized that our understanding of the world, our theory of reality, must *include* ourselves, and that his own cosmology was an attempt to try to describe reality from the point of view of "the ultimate entity" itself, imagining it as an experiencing object.

But now we must ask: is it reasonable to accept the metaphysical theory that somehow we have access to the perspective of a being who is observing what is going on in the world from a position outside the world, at the same time as we experience it from the inside? That this is reasonable to accept, however, is precisely the assumption underlying not only Whiteheadian, but Cartesian realism as well. In *The Sovereignty of Good*, nevertheless, Iris Murdoch warns us against taking this step. She says, for instance:

> Let us exclude from the discussion something which might at this point enter it, which is the eye of God.[109]

The reason we cannot accept this theory is, of course, that we are not in a position where we could tell what reality looks like to the eye of God, i.e., what reality is in itself. And if we actually were deceived by an evil demon, as Descartes' hypothesis suggests to be possible, then we would not at all know of any external position. We would just go on thinking that everything is perfectly normal. And if, *mirabile dictu*, we somehow had access to God's eye (that is, if we were God), we would not be deceived in the first place. Or we would have to assume that we were deceiving ourselves, which seems to lead us into something like an infinite regress, since we would have to assume someone making that assumption, and so on for ever. However, the whole point of Descartes' story was that we might be trapped in an illusion, and that we do not have access to a check-point where we could compare our picture of the world with what the world is really like. Hence, the entire hypothesis seems to collaps in internal self-contradiction.

If we accept that we do not have access to a check-point outside our reality, from which we can compare our beliefs, or our concepts in the mind, with the world in itself, extramentally, then this seriously affects the *concept of truth*. For then truth can no longer be conceived as a correspondence between ideas or beliefs in the mind, on the one hand, and states of affairs in the real world outside the mind, on the other. This is another point which Stuart Brown makes:

> We are not, that is to say, in the position to check whether or not the correspondence holds. To do this we should have to be able to line up things as they are "in reality" on the one side and things as we observe

them to be on the other. If, *per impossibile,* we could do this, we should then be in a position to compare the two to see if they tally. But the basis for such a comparison does not exist... For we have no dealings with things as they really are *unless* they are dealings we have *in* our dealings with what we encounter through observation. Some philosophers, notoriously Kant, have expressed this point by saying that we have only to do with "appearance". But to say this is to accept the correspondence model, albeit sceptically. What we should do, rather, is to reject the correspondence model altogether.[110]

This seems to suggest that Kant maintained the correspondence theory of truth. One philosopher who denies this, however, is Hilary Putnam, professor of philosophy and mathematical logic at Harvard – an author we shall return to in a later section. Putnam admits that according to Kant truth is "the correspondence of a judgment to its object," but thinks that this is a "nominal definition of truth." Putnam believes that it is a grave error, in fact, to identify Kant's conception of truth with that of metaphysical dualism, which presupposes that we can see whether our beliefs in the mind match something metaphysical outside the mind. On Kant's view, Putnam continues, any judgment about external or internal objects, i.e., physical things or mental entities, says that the "noumenal world" as a *whole* is such that this is the description that a rational being, given the information available to a being with our sense organs, would "construct."

> You must *not* think that because there are chairs and horses and sensations in our representation, that there are correspondingly noumenal chairs and noumenal horses and noumenal sensations. *There is not even a one-to-one correspondence between things-for-us and things in themselves.*[111]

But what then is a true judgment, according to Kant? For Kant did believe that we have *objective* knowledge about laws of mathematics, geometry, and physics. And he also thought that we have knowledge about empirical objects, things as they are in relation to us. Putnam offers the following answer, which he thinks we can extract from Kant's writings:

> A piece of knowledge (i.e., a "true statement") is a statement that a rational being would accept on sufficient experience of the kind that it is actually possible for beings with our nature to have. "Truth" in any other sense is inaccessible to us and inconceivable by us. *Truth is ultimate goodness of fit.*

But why should we conclude that the correspondence theory of truth must be given up? Even if we cannot affirm the notion of a similarity between concepts, mental representations, ideas in our minds, and what they refer to, could not there be some form of abstract isomorphism, or "mapping," of concepts onto things in the external world? Could truth not be defined in terms of isomorphism or mapping? Putnam, however, rejects this suggestion as well:

> The trouble with this suggestion is not that correspondence between words or concepts and other entities don't exist, but that *to many* correspondences exist. To pick out *one* correspondence between words or mental signs and mind-independent things we would have to already have referential access to the mind-independent things.

One way to see this, Putnam thinks, is by reference to the fact that sometimes incompatible theories can be intertranslatable. For example, the Maxwell equations, which describe the behavior of electromagnetic fields, are mathematically equivalent to the theory in which there are only action-at-a-distance forces between particles, attracting and repelling according to the inverse square law, travelling not instantaneously but rather at the speed of light ("retarded potentials").

> The Maxwell field theory and the retarded potential theory are incompatible from a metaphysical point of view, since either there are or there aren't causal agencies (the "fields") which mediate the action of separated particles on each other (a realist would say). But the two theories are mathematically intertranslatable. So if there is a "correspondence" to the noumenal things which makes one of them true, then one can define another correspondence which makes the other theory true. If all it takes to make a theory true is abstract correspondence, then incompatible theories can be true.

If, however, as both Brown, Putnam, and others, have suggested, we give up the correspondence theory of truth, then this incompatibility would not turn out to be a problem. For if truth is not a unique correspondence, then a possibility for a certain *pluralism* could be affirmed. But, as we have seen to be the case with realists such as Karl Popper, the decisive idea is the belief that there is *ultimately only one true theory of the world.*

But if we can no longer speak about truth as a correspondence to reality in itself, can we speak about it at all? We may first point out that to argue that the correspondence theory of truth does not hold, is not to argue that there is no valid conception of truth, that there is no better or worse whatsoever, that there is no matter of fact, or that any belief is as good as any other. It just means that truth has to be conceived differently and that there is no simple and clear-cut principle to which we can easily refer in order to distinguish what is true from what is untrue, what is real from what is unreal. For it seems, nevertheless, that it is possible to retain a distinction between what is false and what is true, between "believing" one is right, and actually "being" right, *without* resorting to the theory about a correspondence with reality in itself.

In his book *Ways of Worldmaking,* Nelson Goodman, formerly professor of philosophy at Harvard, argues that truth must be otherwise conceived of than as a correspondence with a "ready-made world." His general thesis is that we do not have notions of the "existence" of things or the "truth" of statements independent of the *versions* of the world that we construct. Goodman thinks that we should not speak about *the* world, since we, in fact, "make" many worlds, or more correctly: many versions of the world. He does not mean that we live in purely fictional worlds, or that they merely exist in our minds, but that the truth of these worlds is relative to the version, or the discourse, we employ. And in this sense, Goodman believes, we live in many worlds, because we speak about the world in various languages. Goodman argues that to think that the rightness of these worlds is relative, that is, relative to language, is not to stress subjectivity. He claims that it is instead the compactness, the comprehensiveness, and the informativeness, which he calls the *organizing power* of the whole system of description, that gives us some understanding of whether the version of the world is true.[112]

What Goodman (as well as Putnam) presents is, in fact, a clear-cut alternative to the correspondence theory of truth, namely, the so-called *coherence theory of truth*. This theory asserts that a statement (or a belief) is true if, and only if, it coheres with a system of other statements (or beliefs). And a statement (or a belief) is false if, and only if, it fails to cohere with the other statements (or beliefs) of a given system. However, we cannot test the truth of a whole system of description, by checking whether it matches with another systems, or with reality in itself. The truth-value of a whole system has to be judged only on the ground of its "organizing power," as Nelson Goodman suggests.

Certain corollaries of the coherence theory of truth follow.

1. Truth is relative to language. The truth of a belief or a statement is not absolute, but depends on the language of description which we use to speak about reality. If the language alters, or if the system of description is somehow revised, this may influence, perhaps even invalidate, a given statement of the system. So what was once a true statement or belief within a particular system of decription may suddenly not be one anymore.

2. Truth is rational acceptability. Many things that were true for Galileo and Newton, for instance, are not true for us, given our language of description. However, what was once believed to be true about the world, but which is not true in our apprehension of reality, was nevertheless once rationally acceptable to believe. Hence, what we speak of as "true knowledge" for us, may turn out to be untrue in a future understanding of reality. However, it may be rational of us to accept certain beliefs as true, although we might not be able to assert that they are absolutely – or metaphysically – true, i.e., true in the sense that they match reality in itself.

3. Truth of a whole language is a matter of approximation. Whether a certain statement or belief is logically consistent with all other statements of a given system of description, is something in principle possible to determine by means of the methods of logic. But whether a whole belief-system or a complete language has the required degree of, say, compactness, comprehensiveness, and informativeness, is not possible to determine by means of the same methods of logic. The question of the "organizing power" of a given system is a question of approximation. We have to find out whether the whole system does justice to, or "fits," our experiences.

4. There are many truths about reality. Since there are many systems of description that we use – and need to use – when we speak about the world, systems that are not always intertranslatable, each of which can be assumed to fulfil required degrees of compactness, comprehensiveness, informativeness, etc., we must consequently allow for a certain form of "pluralism."

These corollaries, however, raise many questions. In relation to the first corollary: does this not imply too simple a conception of languages and systems of descriptions? For do we not make use of various *types* of language, discourse, and system of description, that are not always commensurable? How, for instance, is the language of logic related to the language of common sense? On the other hand, do we not often mix different types of languages and systems of descriptions when we speak about the world; we combine, for instance, the language of science and the language of common sense?

In relation to the second corollary we may ask: if we define truth in terms of rational acceptability, good reasons, warranted assertability, and so forth, does this not in fact differ considerably from what people *mean* when they claim that something is true? If what was at one time taken to be a true piece of knowledge is false, does this not imply that there are no real "facts" in the world? For how could we be sure that what is a fact for us will not turn out to be untrue? How can we then take account of our experience of apparently stable objects like cars and chairs?

Concerning the third corollary: how can such a vague criterion as "organizing power" be clarified?

In relation to the fourth corollary: how can we avoid a complete relativism? Is it not logically possible to have two different but equally comprehensive sets of coherent statements between which there would be, in the coherence theory, no way to decide which is the set of true statements?

In order to come to grips with some of these problems, let us begin to distinguish between three different *types of statement* that can be conceived to belong to a whole set of statements in a language, discourse, or system of description.

1. Analytic statements are statements that can be logically deduced from a system of tenets or doctrines, such as that of mathematics.

2. Metaphysical statements are statements about what reality is in itself. Such statements can be understood to belong to a theory about reality as a whole, or the ultimate characteristics of everything real.

3. Empirical statements are statements about reality as we experience it and as we describe our experiences. Such statements can be conceived to belong to a set of scientific statements, but also to the language of everyday life, i.e., of common sense.

Analytic statements then are true because the meanings of the words in such statements are internally related as they are. Statements such as "All bachelors are unmarried" or "Twice two is half of eight" are true in virtue of the meanings of the words that express them. However, such statements are true only given their relation to the whole system of which they are members. They are not true in themselves, mind-independent, or metaphysically. Coherence, thus, can then be said to be a *criterion of truth* in virtue of which analytic statements are true or false. However, it is also a presentation of the *meaning of truth;* what it means that something is true.

Metaphysical statements about the ultimate structure of the world, of reality in itself, are sometimes understood to have an empirical base. Some philosophers claim that we can proceed from empirical statements to statements about what reality is in itself, by means of the methods of inductive or deductive logic. This was the case, as we saw, in Whitehead's theory of perception. But that such a move cannot be justified was argued in our critical assessment of his theory. This has also been set forth by thinkers like Chisholm, Goodman, Putnam, and Quine.[113] It seems, rather, that metaphysics can be described as a sort of "conceptual synthesis," to use Frederick Ferré's well known phrase in *Language, Logic and God.*[114] The creative power of the mind, he explains, tries to form a coherent scheme of all the facts, a kind of total view of reality. In a discussion about his theory that religious faith is related to the finding of a *Gestalt* of the whole complex of beliefs we hold about the world, Professor Anders Jeffner at the University of Uppsala suggests a similar understanding of the nature of metaphysics.

> Metaphysical systems consist of different sets of ideas or concepts with which we think about the world as a whole.[115]

If we find it reasonable to accept such an understanding of the nature of metaphysics and metaphysical statements, this means that *coherence* becomes a criterion of truth also in respect to metaphysics. However, "truth" here means "rational acceptability," not a correspondence between a metaphysical theory in someone's mind and the ultimate reality as it is in itself. Whitehead in fact affirmed that the fundamental criterion of assessment was that the metaphysical scheme must be coherent: its concepts should be not only logically consistent but also integrated parts of a unified system of interrelated ideas that presuppose each other.[116]

Whitehead, however, also asserted that any warranted metaphysical scheme must be "applicable to experience," i.e., it should be possible to interpret all types of experiences in terms of the system. Metaphysics must take into account all manner of empirical data; scientific, aesthetic, emotional, physical, even religious.

The question is now how we can affirm empirical statements to be true – or untrue. Must we not say that an empirical statement, whether it is a statement in terms of a scientific discourse or a statement in common sense language, is true if, and only if, there is a correspondence between certain situations, events, or objects in the external world, and our experiences of those *situations, events, or objects*, as those experiences are expressed in that given statement?

In order to answer this question we shall turn to Brand Blanshard and his *The Nature of Thought,* where he denies that we can distinguish between the *objects* of experience in the external world and our *experiences* of these objects in our minds. And this distinction is crucial for the acceptance of the correspondence theory of truth. Blanshard argues instead that we would not even understand, much less know the truth or falsity of, a statement about, say, a blue object if 'blue' were

> divorced in our thought from all the colours in the spectrum to which it is related by likeness and difference, all the shades within its own range, and all the definition it possesses in virtue of being thought as a quality rather than as a substance or a relation.[117]

Blanshard's point is that we would *know* neither the meaning nor the truth-value of such a statement independent of its relations to other statements. However, must we not say that we would be unable to *experience* anything as blue, unless we know what blue is, i.e., unless we have a system of description of which the concept of blue is integrally a part, and which provides us with a frame of reference?[118] This, however, is an issue we shall return to in another section of this chapter.

But how about events or situations? Blanshard maintains that the only method available for testing the truth assertions about *historical events* is to see whether such assertions "cohere" with other assertions about the same event, or with other events that are related to the event referred to in the assertion we wish to test. For instance, no one can now compare the assertion that the Battle of Hastings was fought in 1066 or that Caesar crossed the Rubicon in 49 B.C., with anything but other assertions. However, he also claims that we cannot test the truth of statements about *situations in the present* by a simple check-procedure whereby we can see whether our sense-impressions correspond to that which we claim to experience. If someone wants to test a statement such as "There is a cat on the mat," he or she might propose the following method: "I would look and see. If what I saw corresponded to what was asserted, I would call the judgment true." However, such a method presupposes that "there is some solid chunk of fact, directly presented to sense and beyond all question, to which thought must adjust itself."[119] But what is referred to as "a fact" is really "another judgement or set of judgements, and what provides the verification is the coherence between the initial judgement and these." We must consider, says Blanshard, how much of our previous experience and education, our entire conceptualization of the world, influences our perceptions of, say, a cat on a mat. What is claimed to be a perception of a "fact" is really a "judgement." The test of the truth of a judgment that there is a cat on the mat, Blanshard argues, is really a sort of comparison of the original judgment that there is a cat on the mat, with other judgments. In other words: we test statements about empirical phenomena by checking whether they *cohere* with the whole stock of statements which make up our concep- tualization of the world, that is, with the system of description by means of which we speak about our experiences of reality.

Blanshard's point, it seems, is this: what we claim is a perception of objects or situations in our environment is not a straight-forward act of "facts" simply registering themselves through the sense-organs in our minds. Perception is a form of *interpretation* of sense-data. What we perceive to be a cat on the mat could never be identified as a cat on the mat unless we had a language consisting of statements which provide a meaning to what we perceive. Of course, when we assert that we experience a cat on the mat, we certainly *think* that the truth of this assertion is a correspondence between the experience of (or more correctly, the belief or the assertion that there is) a cat on the mat, and the cat on the mat in the external world. But, in fact, this is not what is really going on. For if that is the case we must then have access to a position *outside* our experience (of the cat on the mat) from which we can judge whether the experience of the cat on the mat, and thus the assertion or the belief that there is a cat on the mat, corresponds to the *real* cat on the mat, i.e., the cat in itself, or the metaphysical cat. But such a belief cannot be justified. It does not even make sense.

Since we have already said that it does not seem reasonable to assume that we are in a position where we could tell what reality looks like from a God's eye point of view, we may grant Blanshard the point that we cannot check whether our statements, assertions, or beliefs correspond to an undescribed or an uncon- ceptualized reality. Nevertheless, Blanshard omits the important distinction be- tween speaking about reality *metaphysically* and speaking about it *empirically*. It is true that we are not able to speak about what the world is in itself, and, hence, to appeal to the correspondence theory of truth for the justification of metaphysical statements. But there is after all a certain meaning of correspondence as a criterion of the truth of empirical statements. For such a statement can be said to be true if there is a *correspondence* between the beliefs that are expressed in terms of a given system of description, and our experiences, as they are themselves represented and described within that system. This is what we mean when we claim that our statement that we see a cat on the mat is true, because what we see, in fact, is a cat on the mat. But what we then speak about is the empirical, not the metaphysical reality. We speak about the cat as we experience it, what the cat is in relation to us. We do not speak about what the cat is in itself, independent of our experience of it.

We can therefore say that it is legitimate to speak about truth as a correspondence with reality *within* a specific conceptualization of what reality is, a conceptualization in terms of which we can describe it meaningfully. However, if we wish to test the truth of a whole language, or of an entire system of description, we cannot check whether it corresponds to reality undescribed or unconceptualized, reality in itself. But we can investigate whether the various beliefs within the system correspond with each other. When such a correspondence is at hand, we speak about a system as *coherent*, by which we mean logical consistency, interconnectedness of ideas, conceptual unity and reduction of arbitrariness and fragmentation within the system. If we say that there is a correspondence between our beliefs of a given system and our experiences, as expressed in terms of the system, we speak about correspondence as *adequacy*, referring to it as a matter of the relevance and applicability of the system to our experiences. We might also include the degree of *inclusiveness* that a system discloses, referring to its scope, generality, and ability to integrate various thoughts and ideas. But what we cannot do is to raise the "external question" about the whole language of observation or the entire system of empirical description, if we intend to settle it by means of an *empirical* investigation. For that would require a foothold *outside* the language or the system at the same time as we speak from within it. The external question is a sort of metaphysical inquiry, not an empirical issue. What we must realize, therefore, is that "the standards which govern what it makes sense to say within a given field of discourse must be sought *within* the field of discourse itself," as Stuart Brown has put it.[120] This means that we have a chance to determine whether what appears to be a true empirical statement is in fact true, if we can determine whether it is consistent with respect to its relationships to the system of other statements of which it is a part and on which its meaning depends. In practice, this is often a matter of degree, since it is not always possible to determine the exact content of a system of statements to which a given statement belongs. Of course, the question of the truth of a particular statement is different from the question of the truth of a whole language or system of description. This is a question therefore to which we shall return. However, if a certain statement within a given system turns out to be inconsistent with respect to other statements of the system, this might render questionable the truth of more than the particular statement. A discovery that what is conceived to be a true system of description is, in fact, incoherent with respect to the relation between its statements, assertions, or beliefs, may jeopardize the truth-value of the entire system, and thus require its revision, or perhaps its complete abrogation.

Now someone might object that a statement can be perfectly true in itself even

116

though it would not have been true unless it had been connected with other true statements; and it can be perfectly true whether we know this or not. Or more strongly: something can be perfectly true without anyone's knowing it to be true.[121] It is certainly correct that we can use a true statement without knowing all its implications, or everything asserted by other statements of the system to which it belongs. But the fact that a given statement may be used *empirically* correct by someone who is ignorant about all its implications or its relations to the group of other statements which gives it meaning, does not imply that the truth of this statement is *logically* independent of those other statements. For it is often the case that we use terms and words belonging to a complete language with which we are not acquainted. But logically speaking, the meaning of a statement – which is the presupposition for a correct use of it – depends on the *context* of other statements of which it is a part. In a sense, of course, "2 + 2 = 4" is true in itself. It is true in all worlds. Nevertheless, its truth is bound up with the meaning and truth of all other statements in the arithmetical system. So if "2 + 2 = 4" is true in all worlds, it is not true in the sense that it is true in all worlds *independent* of the system of arithmetic. For what would that mean? And we have no reason to believe that this does not apply also to other types of statements. Truth is logically *relative* to language. To say, therefore, that something can be true without anyone's knowing it is simply empty, if it means that certain things are absolutely or metaphysically true, not true in relation to a language but in relation to an undescribed and unconceptualized world. If it simply means that it might be true that there are people somewhere in the world with names which we do not *know,* then this is a purely trivial remark. And it does certainly not show that events, situations, and objects, obtain independently of any language.[122]

This, however, highlights a real problem, because the fact that we sometimes use a statement without properly specifying its logical context many times creates uncertainty about the *meaning* of the statement, or the belief expressed in the statement. Furthermore, if the meaning of such a statement is unclear we cannot develop a proper method for *testing* its truth-claims. Or we may apply a method by means of which it is only possible to test truth-claims belonging to a completely different set of statements. Hence, we must know to what system of description, scientific, religious, aesthetic, etc., a given statement belongs, before we can truly justify or deny it. If it is asserted, for instance, that certain states of affairs "exist," this is something we cannot – perhaps we should say ought not – try to test the truth of, unless we know which state of affairs is actuelly referred to, that is, unless we know the ontological status of the state of affaris asserted. This was a point we made earlier in the introduction to our study. And this was also Nelson Goodman's point when he claimed that we do not have notions of the existence of things or the truth of statements independent of the "versions" of the world which we construct. Goodman therefore argued that we ought not to speak about *the* world, since we "make" many versions of the world and speak about it in terms of many languages that are not intertranslatable.

Now it might be objected that we are neglecting the distinctions between analytic and empirical statements, because empirical statements purport to give information about characteristics of events, situations, and objects, in the external world, the abiding realities of experience, in a sense in which analytic statements do not. In other words: how can we take account of our perceptions of such stable things as cars and chairs, if they are only relative to the "version" of the world that we construct? These are consequently the issues to which we must now direct our attention.

4.5 An Outline of a Conceptualist Theory of Perception

To discuss theories of perception is to touch upon a wide area of psychological and philosophical problems and controversies. Philosophers, though, have generally approached the issue from an epistemological point of view. How far, if at all, can perception give knowledge about the material or physical world and what is in it? The answer to this question has resulted in a number of distinct, but nevertheless often closely related, theories, such as direct or naive realism, critical realism, the common-sense theory, and so fórth. Since the issue in this section is generated by problems related to our discussion of theories of truth, we shall direct our interest to *epistemological realism,* i.e., the view connected with the correspondence theory of truth. This theory asserts that the objects of knowledge enjoy an existence independent of and external to the knowing mind. A recurrent feature of epistemological realism is the distinction it makes between the object envisaged by an act of knowledge, sometimes called the epistemological object, the mental object, or the object of mind, in contrast to the ontological object, which is the real thing corresponding to the object in the mind. Realist theories of perception purport to explain *how* something outside the mind is related to something inside the mind. Does the mind have a special power to reach out and grasp what is outside? This is what some realists believe. Others give affirmative answers to this question: does that which is outside in the external world cause that which is inside the mind?

Those, however, who reject the dualism between what goes on in the mind and what is outside the mind, those who reject a realist position altogether – as some of the authors we have previously discussed – and instead entertain the coherence theory of truth, must deal with another problem. For instance, how can we account for the fact that we experience a world of material objects, if we may not think about it as obtaining independently of our minds? One way to come to grips with this problem is to adopt a mode of an *epistemological idealism* which argues, often from the standpoint of rationalism, that there can be no "object" without a "subject." Sometimes it derives *metaphysical idealism* from the identification of objects with ideas. Pure idealism, also called immaterialism, identifies ontological reality exclusively with the ideal, i.e., Mind, Spirit, Soul, Archetypical Ideas, Thought, and so forth. Subjective Idealism maintains that Nature is merely a projection of the finite mind, and has no external or real existence. George Berkeley was, at least according to Kant, a representative of this position, and, in fact, he gave the name "immaterialism" to the central thesis of his philosophy. Objective Idealism identifies an externally real Nature with the activity or the thought of the World Mind or the Absolute Mind. The most prominent exponent of this view is perhaps Friedrich Hegel.

Epistemological idealism, however, is not necessarily connected with metaphysical idealism. In fact, the coherence theory of truth is sometimes even connected with a sort of metaphysical realism. Some supporters of this theory insist that a statement cannot properly be called true unless it fits into one comprehensive account of the universe or of reality, which itself forms a coherent system. This, for instance, seems to be Whitehead's view. But it is also possible to oppose the mode of realism which asserts that there exist material things independently of the knowing or perceiving mind, without asserting that everything real is in the head. This seems to be the view that Nelson Goodman suggests, denying that we live in "purely fictional worlds" and that statements about reality are only expressions of subjective opinions. The question then is this: given some version of epistemological idealism, how can we take account of the *empirical* world, i.e., how are we to understand statements about the realities of experience?

Often we speak about the world as something ready-made, as an object which we perceive through the sense-organs. But on reflection we must admit that we do not conceive of the world as an object of perception. Since the concept of the world is important, we must return to this notion. Here, however, it is more fruitful to begin a discussion about perception with an investigation of statements about the objects of which the world seems to consist.

Without denying that there is sensory input to what we take to be knowledge about reality, the thesis here is that the appointments of reality, the real objects, or the facts, do not exist completely independently of our minds, i.e., of our conceptualization of the world.

Perceiving is not a straightforward matter of physical objects registering themselves upon our retina. Perception is far more complex, for sensory experience is largely shaped by our concepts. Without concepts, a system of description, a language, we would not have a conscious experience of, say, a cat on the mat. For how could we know that what we see is a cat, if we did not know what a cat actually looked like? No more than anything else is a cat a self-presenting object. In terms of our conceptualization we experience reality, which means that our *description* of what we sense entails a large amount of interpretation of our experiences. That is to say: our conceptualization of reality, the system of description we use, *influences* not only the way we describe our experiences, but also *what* we experience. This point is made by Nelson Goodman and many others. He says, for instance:

> The overwhelming case against perception without conception, the pure given, absolutely immediacy, the innocent eye, substance as substratum, has been so fully and frequently set forth – by Berkeley, Kant, Cassirer, Gombrich, Bruner, and many others – as to need no restatement here. Talk of unstructured content or an unconceptualized given or a substratum without properties is self-defeating; for the talk imposes structure, conceptualizes, ascribes properties. Although conception without perception is merely *empty,* perception without conception is *blind* (totally in operative).[123]

Our sensations are contaminated by our concepts. To see a tree or a lake means applying the concept 'tree' or 'lake' to *all* that is in our visual field. But when we describe our experiences we use a language with certain *constraints*. This is what Goodman means by saying that "talk imposes structure, conceptualizes, ascribes properties." And this means not only that the way we conceive of reality influences what we experience. It also means that what we perceive to be a tree or a lake, could actually have been perceived differently given another conceptualization of reality. For example, the perception of what *we* now call a tree, i.e., an object which consists of leaves on branches attached to a trunk, but separate from the ground, could have been described as, say, a conglomerate of green things separate – essentially – from the trunk. For that a tree is exactly what we take it to be is not *given* in experience itself. And that a lake is not only a strange glittring surface, circumscribed by millions of small brown stones, but, say, a cavity in the ground filled with a liquid which chemistry defines as H_2O, and separate from the shore, is not something we merely *discover* by means of our sense-organs.[124]

In the previous section we made a distinction between different types of statements; analytic, metaphysical, and empirical. We then said that empirical statements were assertions about reality as we experience it, whether we think about statements in a scientific discourse or in the language of common sense. We may now make a distinction between empirical statements that are claimed to have a distinguishable material referent, which it is, at least in principle, possible to perceive, and statements that are not claimed to have such a referent. In respect to the second group of statements we may think of such assertions that entails theoretical terms which we use to describe reality, but which are not claimed to have a clearly distinguishable referent. We may here think about such terms as "social class" or "electron," keeping in the mind that it is an open question in physics whether terms like this really have such a referent. Concerning the first group of statements, those which are claimed to have a distinguishable material referent, we may now make a distinction between *artifacts* (like, for instance, cars and cameras) and *natural objects* (like, for instance cats, and cabbage). For though it might be acknowledged that artifacts do not obtain independently of the minds which have constructed them, it may still be argued that, at least, some natural objects are not conceptually contaminated. Hence, they exist independently of our minds. They belong to what we may call the ready-made world.

But we must then ask: which ones? It is certainly not true, for instance, that what we call the universe could be such an object, since our pictures of it are constantly changing. But how about the concept of the human being? That, if anything, must be an example of something given, for have not human beings always been human beings? I believe we must argue that this is not the case. It was not long ago – and it might still be the case in certain places on the earth – that women and children were not regarded and, therefore, not treated as human beings. So the concept must be understood to have changed. Then someone might argue that women and children in any case *were* human beings (in our sense of the word) all along. But that does not work, since it only shows how *we* use the concept 'human being' today. We may nevertheless think that ours is a much better conception. But 'better' from whose point of view? From ours, of course. But this only underlines the fact that 'humans' were picked out differently, say, two hundred years ago.

How about "water?" Has not water always been water? In the first place, what is water? The most natural answer seems to be: H_2O. But, that water is H_2O is a fairly late discovery, and water seems to have been in existence long before chemistry. And even if the understanding of water as H_2O is not a purely stipulated device, it was certainly not simply something "discovered." It is heavily dependent on human concepts and discourse, i.e., on chemistry. And it does not help to argue that water is that "thing" we drink, because we drink many kinds of liquid. And we cannot claim that water is what lakes consist of, because lakes are made from various 'stuffs,' that both taste, smell, and look differently. And the attempt to argue that water is a liquid which boils at $100°$ C is not successful, because, in the first place, this is only true of water at sea level but not at high altitudes. And secondly, it only shows that our concept of water is relative to language, namely, in this case Anders Celsius' system of description.

No more than anything else does water come to us with a clear-cut label. For there are no self-identifying objects, existing completely on their own. As already pointed out: in order to experience something (as something), we must know what it is; we must be able to apply concepts. Furthermore, rather than pointing *at* things, we point things *out*. Immanuel Kant was among those who saw this, and he consequently claimed that experience is to some extent a *construction* of our minds. We are aware of what experiences we have, because we are aware of what objects we experience. On the basis of our conceptualization we *know*

121

what reality is. However, it must be emphasized that this is not to say that there is no sensory input to our knowledge of the world.

Logically, our world can therefore be said to be as much taken as given. In order to see, say, a 'lark' or a 'birch,' we must know that what we see there 'up' in the air or 'down' there in the forest *is* actually a lark or a birch. But how do we know that? It is certainly not something we simply discover. When we say that we see a 'lark' or a 'birch' it is not something we simply *report*. Partly it is something we experience, by means of our sense-organs, partly it is something we stipulate. Of course, it is not stipulated by us in the empirical, but in the logical sense of the word. It might be that we as individuals have not originated but learned to use these concepts. Nevertheless, they are, logically speaking, constructions of human intelligence and creativity. And what we experience is, therefore, at least partly, determined by the prevalent concepts in our culture. However, concepts do change and develop, which, hence, also influences our experience.

Thus, what there is in our experience, what we 'take in' via our sense-organs, is a mess of fragments and disparate data, among which there is no clear-cut sensation of internal relations between these fragments and data. It is all an undifferentiated totality; or, as Whitehead said:

> The details are a reaction to the totality. They add definition... They are interpretive and not originative. What is original is the vague totality (MT 109).

However, this does not exclude the possibility that perception entails some portion of cognitive information. But it is to say that even our perceptions of so-called natural objects, the process of 'taking in' what is there before us, is partly determined by the conceptual scheme we use to describe and interpret what we see, hear, smell, and sense. We organize our perceptions in such a way as to differentiate between the various items in our sensations. We single out and combine what is there, in a way that lends meaning and significance to our sensations. This is a process already happening on a very elementary level of experience. However, this process in everyday life is something unconscious, or at least something we are not aware of. Yet, on higher levels of experience, the process of combining, contextualizing, discerning patterns among our perceptions, etc., is something we are relatively aware of. Therefore, it seems legitimate to claim that the world in which we live is to a large extent our own creation.[125] The vague, undifferentiated totality is not what we would describe as 'our world.' Our world has meaning and significance. It is not a blurred 'something.'

4.6 A Metaphysical Assumption and the Notion of Conceptual Realism

Although what we call the world, or reality, is surely not something purely given, this does not imply that it is *entirely* a mental construction. Perhaps this should be said once more: I do not wish to claim that there is no sensory input to our knowledge of reality, or that the world is just in our heads. What I wish to say is that perception is such a complex process that it is, in fact, impossible to distinguish between what is *given* from the outside, so to speak, and what is the result of the creative mind. And since this is so, we cannot possibly discriminate between what is a contribution from the environment, i.e., that which we call sensory input, and what is not. I have only argued that what we in everyday life speak of as the 'things' or the 'objects' in our world, that which we claim to have knowledge about by means of our sense-organs, *coexist* with the experiencing and knowing mind. This is the view I wish to call *conceptual realism*. The point is that we cannot split up the experiencer and the experienced, the knower and the known. This seems also to be a relevant point to draw from what Kant says in *Opus Postumum*, where he claims that experience is nothing simply given, but a sort of mental construction. It is the "absolute unity of the knowledge of the objects of the senses," he says.[126]

But to speak about "contribution of the environment" or "sensory input to knowledge," to speak about *realism* on the whole, actually implies a sort of metaphysical assumption, namely, that there is something "given," something *beyond* experience, something we do not construct in our minds, something we may regard as the metaphysical "base" for our experience of reality, something which is not contingent on our conceptual framework. But is such an assumption, we must ask, not inconsistent with what we have said sofar? Can such an assumption be justified?

Let us first say that, even if we were to find it reasonable to reject Whitehead's (and similar modes of) realism, we must admit that he was onto something profound in his analysis of experience and perception. For it seems that there is a sort of *transcendental dimension* within our mediated experience of the circumambient world. There is always *in* our experience that which withdraws *from* experience, something 'more,' which we are aware of but cannot meaningfully speak about or refer to. To acknowledge the enigmatic character of experience, however, is not the same as entertaining the eclipse of "reality in itself," or "the world in itself." It might be, as Kant thought, that we cannot help thinking that there is something "behind" the phenomenal world, but to try to speak about it makes no sense. For if we were to speak about what is not described (and even impossible to describe), or conceived within some (read 'any') model of human discourse, this would simply leave us speechless, since we are bound to use words and concepts in order to speak at all.

However, the step from the *affirmation* of the presence of what we can call a 'transcendental dimension' in our experience to the metaphysical interpretation of it demands the most careful attention, since we cannot form any clear conception of what it is. It represents, rather, a kind of limit for our thoughts – what Kant called a "Limiting concept" (Grenzbegriff) in his *Critique of Pure Reason* – which our rationality, our intellectual reflection, cannot go beyond.

What we can say from within our understanding of reality, though, is that reality must be *greater* than we can comprehend. And at least it *makes sense* to utter such a statement. The justification for such a metaphysical assumption as that which is implied in our notion of realism, however, is that without it we cannot believe otherwise than that reality is all in our heads, that it is *all* a construction of our minds. And such a belief would contradict the awareness of reality as something greater than we can understand.

4.7 An Outline of a Conceptualist Theory of Religion

In his *Systematic Theology* Paul Tillich has pointed to a phenomenon in human experience, which is similar to what we have described here as a 'transcendental dimension' in our experience of the world. What he does, however, is connect the awareness of something transcendent in experience with the awareness of God. He says, for instance:

> The question of God is possible because an awareness of God is present in the question of God. This awareness precedes the question. It is not the result of the argument but its presupposition. This certainly means that the "argument" is no argument at all. The so-called ontological argument points to the ontological structure of finitude. It shows that *an awareness of the infinite is included in man's awarenesses of finitude.* Man knows that he is finite, that he is excluded from infinity which nevertheless belongs to him. He is aware of his potential infinity while being aware of his actual finitude.[127]

It seems plausible to assume that this idea also has influenced Tillich's well-known theory of symbols, which asserts that we can only speak about God symbolically. For if we find it reasonable to believe that God belongs to a completely different order than ours, then God must be truly transcendent. If we wish to speak about the Divine, the Being which is of the infinite, we can do this only within the realms of our own finite reality, namely, in the form of symbolic language. Of course, we are free to create such symbolic images, and they certainly serve an important function in many people's religious lives. But it must be made clear that these symbols are in no way descriptions of that being which we speak of as God. We may not allow them to become reified. What God *is,* is completely beyond human comprehension.[128]

The purpose of this section, however, is not to discuss Tillich's theory of symbols and the problems it creates. Instead we shall direct our attention to a theory about what function the concept of God serves in a person's belief system, a theory which is more closely related to conceptual realism than Tillich's theory is.

In the *Opus Postumum* Kant speaks about *God* and *the world* as the ideas that form our "universe," which is the "totality of being."[129] But in spite of the fact that we posit both God and the world as *objects,* they are not objects of experience, not even in principle. We mentioned earlier that it must be admitted that the world is not something we really conceive of as an object of perception.[130] However, Kant's point is that not only the world but also God "lack substance outside my ideas but (represents) the thinking whereby we make for ourselves objects through synthetic *a priori* cognitions and are, subjectively, self-creators of the objects we think."[131]

Now even if I like to think that there is something 'Kantian' about the concepts I am developing, I do not wish to adopt Kant's system wholesale. However, I believe he was correct in asserting that treating the world as something *apart* from our concepts and understanding of the world creates insoluble problems. The world is not an object for immediate inspection, but a concept which conscious beings use to make sense of their experiences. It is the concept by which we *hold together* in our mind the whole fabric of theoretical ideas, sense-impressions, and beliefs which we have acquired through our life.

As this study is oriented to the specific problem of what might be an appropriate metaphysics for theology, we must now apply some of our results to a theory of religion. And the point of departure will be precisely Kant's thesis that not only the concept of the world but also the concept of God are a sort of mental construction.

During our life we obtain a variety of beliefs about our evolutionary past and our relation to the nature from which we have emerged, about our position in the universe, on the earth, and in society. We learn something about our history and we may know something about the future. We hold opinions on what is right and wrong, beautiful and ugly, valuable and worthless, just and unjust, meaningful and meaningless. Some of these ideas are intimately connected with our actions and behavior. They are 'directive beliefs,' and as such are derived from other beliefs about the characteristics and the causal powers of so-called external things, and about our own characteristics and powers. Other beliefs and ideas are immediately related to our experiences, to how and what we experience. Some of these beliefs, concepts, and ideas are rooted, logically speaking, in scientific theories, some in art, politics, religion, and the cultural life of our society, some in personal experience. The intimate relationship between the causes and contents of the various elements in our conceptualization of reality, is immensely complex but need not concern us here. What I want to focus on, rather, is the circumstance that there seems to be no *a priori* connection between the abundance of ideas, concepts, and beliefs, apart from the fact that they are kept together in a person's mind.

When someone tries, then, to create a system or a systematic order of his or her beliefs and ideas, tries to see whether some 'pattern' is applicable to all the fragmentary data within the mind, the outcome of such a process is an achievement I shall refer to as that person's *notional world* – a term recently introduced by Professor Daniel Dennett at Tufts.[132] This term can in a way be said to resemble Husserl's "bracketing" when he wanted to speak about what went on in someone's head without making any assumptions about the existence, or nature, of actual things referred to by the thoughts. The notional world is the idea of a model – but not necessarily of the actual, real, or true model – of one's internal representations. The notional world, in Dennett's sense, is the totality of a thinker's bracketed beliefs. He consequently also speaks about it as "pure Brentano." The notional world, in my use of the term, however, is as a sort of heuristic device, by which a person creates a *unity* of the whole multiplicity of beliefs, ideas, and concepts in the mind. Partly, the notional world is a construct of our own imaginative capability, the product of our intellectual faculties. Partly it is something we acquire from our cultural environment, something we 'pick up,' or learn. Illustrations of such notional worlds are, for instance, Helen Keller's *The World I Live In* and John Irving's *The World According to Garp.*

A person's notional world provides a window, so to speak, through which he or she acquires a certain perspective on the surrounding reality. One gets a sort of map, by means of which it becomes possible to orient oneself in life. We may, if we have a tenable notional world, achieve knowledge about who we are and what our basic needs and goals in life are. We might even come to discern the means to attain those ends, needs, and goals. We often apprehend who our friends are – and who our enemies are. The notional world sometimes also entails such a wide perspective on reality that it provides a strategy for coping with the problems on planet earth, or dealing with the conflicts of life in our society, in our families, and perhaps also in our most personal, individual lives. Through this framework we also become adept at distinguishing between just and unjust actions, determining what is meaningful and what is not, discerning what is valuable and what is not. Since our notional world usually ential different sorts of expectations, it is reasonable to believe that different notional worlds yield different sorts of experiences. Of course, when we speak about "different" notional worlds, this does not imply that there are distinct lines between them.

But now we must elaborate what it means to say that a notional world represents an order, a system, a structure, among the data and fragments within one's mind. Since the unity of the entire multiplicity of our ideas and beliefs that we hold, cannot be claimed to "correspond" with the unity of the world in itself, and

126

since they cannot be reduced to a single theory that contains *the* truth about reality, and since it cannot be sought in an ambient or neutral 'something' beneath, or above, or behind the world, it has to be found in an overall organization embracing them all.[133] For we need some sort of rational order among our ideas and beliefs which is the presupposition for meaning and orientation in life. Without such an order or structure we would be blind and inoperative. This order or structure is achieved when we *relate the different beliefs and ideas about reality to one or more specific factors, in such a way that we construct a system of relations between them.* (I do not assume that *all* the beliefs and ideas in a person's mind have to be related in this way.) The way in which we organize the data within our notional world has a *hypothetical* character, since many of us share approximately the same life situation and package of knowledge, but disagree as to the correct interpretation of its totality. For there are evidently many ways of organizing or "making" worlds. To achieve such a notional world is comparable with recognizing an emergent pattern in a puzzle. In his book *Ways of Worldmaking* Nelson Goodman says:

> Discovery often amounts, as when I place a piece in a jigsaw puzzle, not to arrival at a proposition for declaration or defence, but to finding a fit. . . Recognizing patterns is very much a matter of inventing or imposing them. Comprehension and creation go on together.[134]

Since there are evidently many ways of creating notional worlds, one way to distinguish between them is to make a distinction between *theistic* and *non-theistic* notional worlds.[135] In the notional world of a theist there is a certain element, which we can refer to as the notion, or the concept, of God. It is this element that gives a specific order to the notional world of the theist. It is this factor to which the theist ultimately relates the various beliefs and ideas in his or her notional world. The notion of God can, therefore, be described as the *ultimate point of reference* within the notional world of a theist.[136]

The hypothesis here is that the notion of God is introduced into the notional world of a theist as the result of a *supplementary process.* 'God' can be understood as a way of filling out the hypothetical structure or pattern of a person's notional world, in analogy with the way one tries to fill out or find a fit in a jigsaw puzzle.[137]

The procedure of filling and weeding out, is common to the construction of *all* notional worlds, including non-theistic ones. This is also what Nelson Goodman affirms.

> The making of one world out of another usually involves some extensive weeding out and filling – actual excision of some old and supply of some new material. Our capacity for overlooking is virtually unlimited, and what we do take in usually consists of significant fragments and clues that need massive supplementation.[138]

In discussing "isomorphism" Goodman goes on to say:

> Insofar as the definitions or derivations are successful, they organize the points and lines, or the four elements, into a system. That there are alternative systems discredits none of them; for there is no alternative but blankness to alternative systems, to organization of one kind or another. To his successors who complained that Thales was *introducing* artificial order and priorities, he might well have rejoined that that is what science and philosophy do, and that complete elimination of the so-called artificial would leave us empty-minded and empty-handed.[139]

This may enable us to argue that we need not assume that the notion of God, or the theistic element in the construction of a notional world, is given independently of the creative powers of human intelligence, as, for instance, Frederick Ferré has pointed out.[140] On the contrary, both the concept of God and of the world are supremely dependent on the conceptual activity of the mind. This was precisely what Kant wanted to highlight in his *transcendental philosophy:*

> God, the World, and I, the thinking being in the World, which links them together. God and the World are the two objects of transcendental philosophy, and (subject, predicate and copula) that is the thinking Man; the subject which binds them together in one proposition.[141]

In accordance with Ferré we may say that the construction of a notional world can be described as a *conceptual synthesis,* and that the theistic element plays a key role within a certain way of ordering the data and the beliefs that a person holds, without which the system would founder. The introduction of this element is necessary for the completion and formation of the entire scheme. To be able to give a coherent and intelligible meaning, or interpretation of the world, which fits with our experience, it might be necessary to introduce a *completely novel kind of entity.* In our effort to *find a livable world,* we look for a form of life-interpretation which renders the most meaning, significance, and coherence to the entire fabric of our beliefs and feelings, values and knowledge, for that which does maximal justice to our experience.

A conclusion we may draw now is that the issue of God's reality cannot be treated separately from the reality – or the truth – of the world to which God is related and in which someone lives. *Religious faith,* then, can be described as a sort of existential and ethical *response* to a religious interpretation of the world, which presupposes the existence of God. Such an interpretation may enable a person, or a group of people, to speak about the nature of the world, and our lives within it, in a certain way, which another interpretation might not. When we earlier discussed Whitehead's theory of value, we argued that the concept of God as Creator may enable someone to speak about the physical or biological nature as intrinsically valuable (not just instrumentally valuable, in relation to us), and, hence, to argue for certain ethical responsibility. In the same manner it also becomes possible to argue, for instance, that all human beings are of the same irreducible value, and that they should be treated in accordance with this value. That such arguments might have both political, social, and existential consequences seems too clear to need elaboration, as does the observation that the "choice" of a notional world will open up the possibility for completely new types of experiences of what life and the world "really" are.

4.8 The Issue of God's Reality and the Concept of Truth Again

The first corollary to establish now is this: to say that God is an inferred or supplemented element in a person's notional world does not mean that God is not something real. For if we mean that only what is observable is real, not much is real. We have already argued, at length, that there are no self-presenting objects and no self-identifying things in the world. Nothing comes to us with a clear-cut label. We must be capable of conceptualizing in order to experience at all. And this is the reason we can say that not only the world and God, but also such entities as "things" and "objects" are partly constructions of our minds, logically speaking. Therefore, we must find a broader criterion of what is to be considered real and true than that which can be verified by means of an empirical examination. For the methods we thereby use, the way we describe our experiences, to a large extent also determine what we experience, i.e., we do not only discover, but also invent empirical objects.

It seems that many people believe it is important to affirm a traditional mode of realism since they think that this conception of reality presupposes the only metaphysics against the background of which it is possible to argue that God is real. What they seem to mean is that our word God corresponds to a reality somewhere out there – extramentally – in what is believed to be the *real* world. Many theologians have also devoted themselves to the project of explaining what sort of entity out there the word God refers to, and numerous philosophers of religion have tried to show how it can make sense to speak *about* God within this conception of what is real, in the face of various attacks on the meaningfulness of God-language. However, it is often argued that many of these efforts have not been altogether successful, at least not convincing, and a reason, then, could be that they presuppose a *theory of reference* which raises insoluble problems. And the reason for this, in turn, could be that this theory rests on a sort of *metaphysical dualism* which is implausible. For in order to answer the question about what the word God refers to, what God is and how we can know anything about God, on this view, it is necessary to answer the following kind of questions: What is reference in the first place? How can that which is in the mind (words, concepts, ideas, beliefs,) reach out and grasp what is outside? What does it mean to say that something mental corresponds to something which is not mental? What is correspondence? In order to answer these questions within the framework of classical realism, it seems impossible to escape a distinction between reality for us and what it is in itself, between what the world appears to be, on the one hand, and what it really is, on the other. And this distinction, we have argued, simply does not make sense to use.

We have instead suggested that the question of God's reality cannot be considered apart from the consideration of the reality, or the truth, of the conception of the world to which it is related. That is to say: the concept of the world and the concept of God are reciprocally dependent (which does not imply that a person cannot have a conception of the world without having a conception of God). This means, therefore, that when one wants to test the truth of religious beliefs, or investigate the question of God's reality, there is no other way than testing the truth value of the conception of the world of which these beliefs are a part. Or, in other words: whether God is real can only be asked meaningfully *within* religion itself. The question of God's reality cannot be *separated* from the question of the validity, the relevance, and the truth of the *whole* religious belief system.

Several corollaries follow, if this suggestion is accepted. The first might perhaps seem trivial. Nevertheless, it is often neglected. Whether a religious belief-system is true, cannot properly be tested until it is made clear what its truth-claims are. This, in turn, presupposes that we must know not only what sort of *ontological* theory, if any, but also what *epistemology* the system is related to. If we do not know the *meaning* of a statement which asserts that God is real, we cannot know whether it is *true,* apart from the fact that it might be inconsistent with respect to the belief-system of which it is a part. Of course, logic must play an important role in the testing of a religious belief-system. A rationally acceptable system, we could suggest, must not be incoherent, or must allow, at least, for a revision of problematic ideas and beliefs, in order to make the system more coherent.

This also leads to the conclusion, in relation to the issue of God's reality, that if one wishes to distinguish between what is to count as 'real' and 'unreal,' the distinction must be sought *within* the language, or the system of description itself. Distinctions between what is real and unreal, true and untrue, cannot simply be imposed on a field of discourse from outside. This point has been summarized, for instance, by Rudolf Carnap, when he discusses ontological issues similar to those which we have considered in our study. He says:

> In order to understand more clearly the nature of these and related problems, it is above all necessary to recognize a fundamental distinction between two kinds of questions concerning the existence or reality of entities. If someone wishes to speak in his language about a new kind of entities, he has to introduce a system of new ways of speaking, subject to new

rules; we shall call this procedure the construction of a linguistic *framework* for the new entities in question. And now we must distinguish between two kinds of questions of existence; first, questions of the existence of certain entities of the new kind *within the framework;* we call them internal questions; and second, questions concerning the existence or reality *of the system of entities as a whole,* called *external questions.* Internal questions and possible answers to them are formulated with the help of the new forms of expressions. The answers may be found either by purely logical methods or by empirical methods, depending upon whether the framework is a logical or a factual one. An external question is of a problematic character, which is in need of closer examination.[142]

To construct such a "system of new ways of speaking" was, by the way, exactly what Whitehead attempted. In order to assert the existence of a completely new kind of entity, he had to create a whole, new language. However, the main point to be illustrated by this quotation from Carnap is that the question about the truth of assertions about the existence of God cannot be *imposed from the outside* of religion, at least not until it is certain what these assertions imply. This was also the point which Nelson Goodman made, arguing that we do not have notions of the existence of things or the truth of statements independent of the "version" of the world which we construct. Therefore it makes no sense for a physicist, for example, to ask a theologian whether God exists, if he expects to receive an answer in the same terms as that of his own language, that is, if he does not allow for the existence of anything but physicalistic entities, such as atoms, molecular kinetic energy, or electromagnetic waves. And if the physicist insists that the theologian *must* explain to him or her in physicalistic language what it means that God exists and what sort of physical entity God is, then the theologian could rejoin that the physicist *must* first prove to him or her that the theory is true which asserts that reality can be exhaustively and comprehensively described in *one* single discourse, namely, physics. But what reason could be given for the belief that a single system, say, physics, is complete, not only for its own purposes (which, for instance, in science very rarely seems to be the case), but for *all* purposes?

In case the theologian, however, actually asserts that God is, ontologically speaking, a physical entity, then he or she is obliged to explain what sort of entity God is, and how we can possibly know this. And if we really want to test such truth-claims, this demands that we look into the ontological and epistemological theories to which they are related, and ultimately also into the metaphysics of such a theological system.

But not only because the meaning of God-language is sometimes uncertain do we have reason to focus more strongly upon ontology and metaphysics. For it seems a plausible assumption that a problem in current theology is that it oc-

131

casionally sounds *as if* the word God refers to a, certainly transcendent but nevertheless, physical reality. Theology, in the sense of statements about God and God's relation to the world, is often a mixture of statements belonging to various systems of description which presuppose different, and perhaps even conflicting, ontological claims. This is not to say that such a mixture could not be warranted, only that this remains an open question until the meaning of theological assertions is clearly formulated.

Sofar we have only discussed what it means to raise internal questions about the truth-claims of religious belief-systems. Such questions, we said, are only answerable provided we know something about the metaphysical theory against the background of which such claims are articulated. Given our theory of religion we also said that the question of God's reality is nothing we can treat separately from the question of the truth, or the reality, of the whole conception of the world, of which the conception of God is a part.

But Carnap also argued that one could raise the question about the truth of a whole system, i.e., the external question. However, when we discussed Descartes' methodological doubt earlier, by means of which he thought that we could acquire certain knowledge about the existence of extramental things, we argued that it made no sense to raise the external question. But then the external question meant that we should try to see whether there is a real world out there which somehow matches the world as we describe it. And the reason this did not work was that no one can tell what reality is in itself. However, this does not mean that there could not be another way of formulating the meaning of the external question, the question about the truth of a whole system.

This means that we can only talk about the world, or reality, in terms of our conceptualization of it, not of what it is totally independently of our representation of it. And conceptualization here means the system, or more correctly, the systems of descriptions – for we use many systems to describe our experiences and beliefs – by means of which we talk and think about reality. But it also implies that when we speak about the *real* world, this does not mean the 'one and only' real world, the ready-made world, but that conceptualization of the world which is *true*. However, since true, or truth, cannot mean the correspondence between our conceptualization of the world, the world for us, and the really real world, this indicates that we must find another formulation of what truth means, if we are to be able to distinguish between real and unreal worlds, or between true and untrue conceptualizations of reality. One such formulation has already been suggested: truth is that which a rational being *would* accept on sufficient reflection and experience of the kind that it is actually possible for a being with our nature to have.[143] This is a formulation, however, which comes close to what John Dewey in his *Logic: The Theory of Inquiry* called "warranted assertability." Of course, such a formulation is very vague, but – as Hilary Putnam puts it – truth "in any other sense is inaccessible to us and inconceivable by us. Truth is the ultimate goodness of fit." If, therefore, we can find it reasonable to accept such a conception of truth, then we could say that a true conceptualization of reality is one which would be assertable as *relevant* and *rationally acceptable*. Or in other words: a true conceptualization of the world is one we have *good reason* to accept. What is meant by "good reason" is what we must now try to unpack.

4.9 Our Values and the Concept of Relevance and Rational Acceptability

As mentioned earlier, Max Weber introduced what came to be one of the most prevalent dichotomies in our culture, namely, that between facts and values. However, it seems as though the original impetus for this dichotomy was present at a much earlier stage in the history of science and philosophy. For the fact – value dichotomy is closely related to the idea that there is a decisive disjunction between what is supposed to be objectively 'there' in nature, and what is only 'there' from our subjective point of view. The real 'things,' or the real 'properties' of the things, are those which can be confirmed to be 'there' independently of the observer, according to this view. Other 'properties' are imposed on the 'things' from the outside. Therefore, they are not really there, they are only within the observer, i.e., in the eye of the beholder. Objectivity here is affirmed to be the character of a description of things and objects in which subjective properties are disregarded – like, for instance, evaluations of what is being described or perceived. As I pointed out before, terms like "good," "bad," "beautiful," and "just" ought to be removed from an objective description of reality, according to the supporters of this view, by which we are allowed to give a true picture of the real world.

We have already noted how Galileo conceived of mass and velocity as the so-called "primary qualities" of nature, the true characteristics of the objective world, independent of the observer. From these qualities he distinguished what were defined as the "secondary qualities," such as color, texture, temperature, and so forth. We also pointed out that this philosophical outlook contributed premises toward the image of the scientist as 'observing' the world and 'reporting' what it is like, and that this image helps to account for the prestige which natural science enjoys in our society. Even our everyday conception of what it is rational to believe about the nature of the world seems often to be construed on this model of science. Values and moral concepts are considered to be highly private and without the hard-cash character which this view lends to the "real" world.

The view, however, that has been defended in this study is akin to the claim that indeed all qualities are secondary and that all facts are soft. The world, we have argued, is what it is in relation to us, not to some metaphysical witness. Now someone might object that although such a view is perhaps defensible

133

from a metaphysical point of view, it nevertheless opens up the door for complete relativism – if not complete nihilism. For nothing is then objectively true anymore. But although the possibility of truth-testing our beliefs by checking with reality in "itself" is taken from us, the correct conclusion is not to surrender all concepts of truth and rationality, but instead to take a closer look at what is asserted, for instance, by the distinction between fact and value, and when it is relevant to use. But to avoid misinterpretations, let us say again that to argue against the assumption that there is a real world standing over, against, and independent of us – as some realist have assumed – is not to argue that there is no world at all, or that everything is just in the head – as some idealists have implied. Nor is it a defence for any form of solipsism, according to which nothing exists except myself, or for a complete relativism in which no world or reality is better, or more true, than any other. Of course, conceptual realism affirms a certain mode of "relativism," namely, that truth or reality is relative to language, to how we describe the world. In fact, that is to say that there *is* a real world, as real as anything can be for us. But of course, it allows for a certain "pluralism," since it resists reductionism. There is no reason to believe that there is only *one* way to tell the truth, the *final* truth, about the world. For there are, rather, many truths about the world. However, that is not to say that there is no distinction between true and false worlds, because it is obvious that many worlds that people live in are false and untrue, and, therefore, not real. They are believed to be real by their countenancer but in fact are not.

The thesis here is that truth, or relevance and rational acceptability, must be conceived in relation to certain values. Otherwise, that which we refer to as "good reason," will only be an empty notion. And after all, values are not just a matter of subjective taste and private preference. The picture of the world we accept both in science and everyday life, that which we find "good" reason to affirm, in a certain sense presupposes our values. The fact that so many people equate "truth" with "scientific truth" depends, if we scrutinize the matter, on our high esteem of science; science represents something utterly valuable in our society. If we take a look at the history of science we shall see that science itself presupposes certain values: the modern scientific outlook on the world originated in an attempt to come to grips with irrationalism and superstition, and to present a "better" conception of reality. This does not imply, of course, that all scientific statements are value judgments and that there are no real facts without values. It is to say, rather, that that we think of the picture of the world which science paints as good, or better, than any other, logically implies some idea of what "good" is. Our 'choice' of picture, of language, of system of description, ultimately of the world, is in part directed by certain values. "Choice" here does not mean choice in the empirical, but in the logical sense. For the world we actually live in is often something we inherit or learn to accept. Of course, within our conceptualization of reality – the system of description by means of which we conceive of the world – we may speak about pure facts, as for instance, that there is a watch on my wrist, or that there are sounds of cars outside my window, and so forth. Also statements about electrons and social classes, for example, may be regarded as "facts." They are not expressions of values in a straightforward sense. However, such statements are no more statements about metaphysical facts, about the absolute or ultimate facts of reality, than the statement of the fact that $2 + 2 = 4$. Facts are always facts relative to the language we use, and it is when such a language as a whole is claimed to be "true" that we can say that it presupposes certain values, certain ideas about the good.

But now we must ask: if facts are somehow relative to language, how can we speak any longer about objectivity or objective knowledge? This is an issue we shall discuss on the basis of examples provided by two philosophers whose names have already been mentioned: Iris Murdoch and Hilary Putnam. In her book *The Sovereignty of Good,* Murdoch gives the following illustration, (which must be cited in its full length if the force of her argument is to be felt).

A mother, whom I shall call M, feels hostility to her daughter-in-law, whom I shall call D. M finds D quite a good-hearted girl, but while not exactly common yet certainly unpolished and lacking in dignity and refinement. D is inclined to be pert and familiar, insufficiently ceremonious, brusque, sometimes positively rude, always tiresomely juvenile. M does not like D's accent or the way D dresses. M feels that her son has married beneath him. Let us assume for purposes of the example that the mother, who is a very 'correct' person, behaves beautifully to the girl throughout, not allowing her real opinion to appear in any way. We might underline this aspect of the example by supposing that the young couple have emigrated or that D is now dead: the point being to ensure that whatever is in question as *happening* happens entirely in M's mind.

Thus much for M's first thoughts about D. Time passes, and it could be that M settles down with a hardened sense of grievance and a fixed picture of D, imprisoned by the cliché: my poor son has married a silly vulgar girl. However, the M of the example is an intelligent and well-intentioned person, capable of self-criticism, capable of giving careful and just *attention* to an object which confronts her. M tells herself: 'I am old-fashioned and conventional. I may be prejudiced and narrow-minded. I may be snobbish. I am certainly jealous. Let me look again.' Here I assume that M observes D or at least reflects deliberately about D, until gradually her vision of D alters. If we take D to be now absent or dead this can make it clear that the change is not in D's behaviour but in M's mind. D is discovered to be not vulgar but refreshingly simple, not undignified but spontaneous, not noisy but gay, not tiresomely juvenile but delightfully youthful, and so on. And as I say, *ex hypothesi,* M's outward behaviour, beautiful from the start, in no way alters.[144]

Now, what happens in this example? It is obvious to us that M has been *active*. She has been doing something which is intrinsically worthwhile. But what? "M has been morally active," claims Murdoch. What M is doing is a purely inward activity, where no observers are involved. What M is attempting to do, Murdoch argues, is not just to see D *accurately* but to see her *justly* and *lovingly*. But is this picture of D a real picture? Is it objective? Is it true? It is certainly not a scientific picture, if by scientific we mean a pure report of so-called 'hard facts,' in terms of an impersonal and exact system of description. And why? For "moral concepts," Murdoch says, "do not move about *within* a hard world set up by science and logic. They set up, for different purposes, a different world." But which world, we may ask? "When M is just and loving she sees D as she *really* is," Murdoch answers. "One is often compelled almost automatically by what one *can* see." As moral agents we try to see "justly," to overcome prejudice, to be open-minded, to be honest and self-critical. We do not simply try to give a bare 'photograph' of the world.

The way in which we create a picture of the world around us is not at all like the way we take pictures. We do not, and actually cannot, copy the world. For one reason, we are often deeply involved in it; for another, there is no ready-made world to copy. What we see, what we experience, is dependent on the way we describe our experiences, which is relative to the system of description, or the conceptual scheme, that we choose to use. One way to describe reality is to do it in terms of the impersonal system of the exact sciences, which presents us with a set of hard facts about the world. And for certain purposes this is the right way to describe the world; this is a picture we need. But there are also other systems, for other purposes, as, for instance, the language by means of which M learns to experience D. And when Murdoch claims that M sees D as she "really" is, when she sees her lovingly and justly, this does not mean that this is the *only* way to see her. But this is one, true picture of D, one objective image of her. The knowledge about reality which M successively acquires represents certain "facts" about D. Or, as Murdoch says:

> Goodness *is* connected with knowledge: not with impersonal quasi-scientific knowledge of the ordinary world, whatever that may be, but with a refined and honest perception of what is really the case, a patient and just discernment and exploration of what confronts one, which is the result not simply of opening one's eyes but of a certainly perfect kind of moral discipline.[145]

The point to be illustrated is not that there are no statements completely devoid of values. It is surely the case that we can abstract, in a formal sense, value judgments from statements about facts. And at certain times this is precisely the kind of objectivity we need. The point, rather, is that there are pieces of true, or objective, knowledge which we cannot acquire unless we subject ourselves to a form of moral discipline that presupposes the affirmation of certain values: what we think it is *good* to do and to be. This, however, is within a given system of description. But also our choice of systems, within which we may perhaps discriminate between facts and values, ultimately presupposes an idea about what a *good* description, or theory, of the world is. It is in this context we must understand what some natural scientists say when they refer to a theory as "beautiful." They also choose to look at reality from a point of view which seems "interesting" or "fruitful." This is what is intended when we say that there are no facts, and consequently no world, where there are no values. For we always choose to perceive, or describe what we perceive, from some point of view, because we cannot tell what the world is apart from all perspectives, i.e., what it is in itself. The world is what it is in relation to us.

Now we shall direct our attention to the next example, provided by Hilary Putnam.[146] He wants us to imagine something similar to Descartes' skeptical device of the evil demon. In Putnam's example all the people in a whole country, say, Australia, believe that there is no real world, and that our senses are deceiving us. "Perhaps," Putnam says, "the Australians believe this because they are all disciples of a Guru, the Guru of Sydney." When we ask these people why they believe this they say: "Oh, if you could only talk to the Guru of Sydney and look into his eyes and see what a good, kind, wise man he is, you, too, would be convinced." And if we ask how the Guru of Sydney can know that we are deceived, if the illusion is as perfect as they claim it to be, they will only reply: "Oh, the Guru of Sydney *just knows.*"

Putnam goes on to say that we may imagine that the Australians in the example are just as good as we at anticipating experiences, at building bridges that stay up (or seem to stay up), etc. They may even be willing to accept our latest scientific discoveries, not as true, but as correct descriptions of what seems to "go on in the image." Putnam wants to have us imagine a case in which a vast number of people have a self-contained belief-system which violently disagrees with ours. There *seems* to be no question of a disagreement in ethical values in the example. The Australians are imagined to have ethics similar to ours.

The first thing that Putnam observes about the hypothetical Australians is this: "Their world-view is crazy." He thinks that we would regard a community of human beings who held such an insane world-view with great sadness. We would understand them as "having sick minds." And, Putnam stresses, "the characterization of their minds as sick is an *ethical* one." But is there any way for us to try to argue with these people, Putnam asks. One thing that may strike us is that we normally try to "give account of how we know our statements to be true." We may argue, for instance, on the ground of a causal theory of perception, about how to distinguish between what is an illusion and what is not.[147] But this is not the case with the Australians. "Judged by our standards of coherence, their belief system is totally incoherent." Putnam also points out that we could

137

list other "methodological virtues" which their system lacks, for instance, the kind of "comprehensiveness" at which we aim, or that it is not "functionally simple," etc. The specific "virtues" are not important for the moment. The important thing to notice is that we price certain virtues which help us to orient ourselves in life, to decide what it is rational to believe and what it is not rational to believe. Or in other words: *we appeal to values when we criticize beliefs we find unacceptable.* And this is especially the case when we look at whole belief-systems from an external point of view. However, we may also appeal to values within belief-systems, or systems of description, when we criticize particular statements or assertions.

Further, Putnam argues for a "picture of science as presupposing a rich system of values." Scientists, he claims, try to "construct a representation of the world which has the characteristics of being instrumentally efficacious, coherent, comprehensive, an functionally simple." But why? Putnam answers that the reason we want this sort of representation and not the "sick" sort of world-view possessed by the Australians, is that "having this sort of representation system is part of our idea of human cognitive flourishing, and hence part of our idea of total human flourishing." In other words: our modern world-view presupposes an idea of the good.

Putnam's example illustrates that facts and values are deeply connected. For it seems as if the Australians only differ from us with respect to certain beliefs about facts of the world, but that we are all completely in line with respects to ethical and moral values. However, a closer look reveals that this is not the case. The Australians do not share our concept of what the good life is, what it is good to do or to be. And precisely for this reason they differ from us in beliefs as to matters of fact. They create a completely different world than ours. They will expect other things; they will act differently because they have other concepts of 'right' and 'wrong', 'good' and 'bad'; they will experience the world differently; and they will believe different things about the world and their fellow creatures on our planet, viz., in the image of the world which they claim we live in. In other words: if we press the fact – value dichotomy too far, confusion will result.

However, to notice that differences in values shape different worlds, we need not refer to an imaginary case like that of the crazy Australians. We can see what pictures of the world people in different communities have. The value structure we partake in, viz., the system of values shared by our culture, influences the way we construct our notional world. The prevalent value-system, the most influential ideas of what 'the good life' is, shapes our picture of the environing world. Compare, for instance, the picture of the world many Americans have with the picture held by people, say, in the Soviet Union. Americans, as any other people of a relatively homogeneous culture, at least with respect to certain values, have their own picture of the good life, which shapes their view of the environment, their society, and other people. But their view of what it is to be a communist or what it means to live in a communist society, is certainly different from the pictures which communists have. And we can easily imagine how different a world Nazis or Fascists live in than do people in democratic countries, where (at least in principle) human rights are respected. Imagine what beliefs they have about facts, friends and enemies, right and wrong, good and evil, and so forth. It is not difficult to realize how 'worlds' depend on our values and ideals. But the fact that there are *many* worlds, i.e., many ways of conceiving the world, does not mean that they are all equally good – or true. That we do not all agree as to what is *good* (to believe or to do), is not to say that there is no 'better' or 'worse' whatsoever. Of course, we must refrain from assuming that *our* idea is the absolute standard of what is to count as true and good. Even within our own culture we live with a variety of descriptions of the world, and many of those are not commensurable.

To argue, however, that our facts are interspersed with our values, is not to argue for pure relativism. To say that the imaginary Australians and the Nazis and the Fascists have "sick minds" is not a *subjective* value judgment. It is a fact; words like 'sick,' 'crazy,' 'insane,' can be used to describe how and what certain states of affairs actually are. This is not to say that we cannot, for certain purposes, isolate some facts from value judgments, or that such words cannot also be used for the purpose of blaming. This is the case with words like 'bad' and 'ugly' as well. It depends on the context in which and the purpose with which we use words like these. It might even be argued that it is false and objectionable not to use so-called value words. For example, imagine that a historian, a psychologist, or a sociologist were to describe racism in South Africa, or the events in Guatemalan prisons or in Nazi concentration camps. Suppose that he or she decided, for the purpose of objectivity, to use some type of physicalistic language, or something similar, in order to 'report' the (alleged) hard facts of what 'really' happened, without any so-called 'value judgments.' Many statements in such a description would be true in a formal sense – but they would be empty. Or would they really be true? Would they actually give a true picture or description of what are (or were) *really* the states of affairs? Would we not consider a discourse with only "value neutral" words as totally irrelevant and inadequate in such a case? Could a description of Fascists or Nazis that did *not* in some way allude to their monstrous mentality be justified? Could it ever be called a true picture. I think not, at least not if truth means relevance and rational acceptability. For we would then regard such a picture as completely distorted and inadequate. We would argue that it is false. Indeed, to say that facts are value-loaded is far from any kind of relativism. We could even augment the argument and say that the really dangerous relativism lurks in an unreflected and uncritical use of the old fact – value dichotomy and in creating a picture of the world based on the model of natural science into the absolute.

The problem of value statements in science is, however, more complicated. For values are not only present in words such as those we have already mentioned, but also in words that *seem* to give valuefree information. Examples of such words are "violence," "exploitation," "health," "elite," "peace," and "democracy." Some Swedish philosophers have attended to this problem, as for instance, Lars Bergström, professor of philosophy at Uppsala, and Lennart Nordenfelt, assistent professor of philosophy at the university of Stockholm. They have pointed out that such words do occur in the social sciences and in the humanities. But they also ask whether such words must be used? Both Bergström and Nordenfelt claim that in order to omit value words, something they think is formally possible, we would have to pay too high a price. One reason is that in the attempt to get rid of such words one is necessarily forced to reconstruct the entire system of description in a way which would make the various assertions of this language more or less inaccessible. Another is that such words, i.e., value words, are sometimes "necessary" and "legitimate." They have also, says Nordenfelt, "the important function of guiding the scientific process in a fruitful direction."[148] Since it is obvious that value words are not always informative but sometimes also expressions of attitudes and more private opinions, we need to know the standards on which such value judgments are based. For not unless we know what standards people use when they speak about reality, do we know whether they tell us the truth or not. Therefore, if such standards are given, a certain possibility of intersubjective testability – or objectivity – is opened up, even for so-called value judgments.

Someone may nevertheless object that such a notion of objectivity is too vague. We need, for instance, standards for distinguishing between subjective and objective values. For the observation that values are intrinsically – though not always directly – related to facts, and not just to subjective preferences, does not mean that there are no purely subjective values. In a later chapter of his book, Hilary Putnam gives an example which might prove useful to us. Here he considers two persons, Smith and Jones, and their preferences for ice cream flavors. Smith likes chocolate ice cream, but dislikes vanilla ice cream. Jones, on the other hand, prefers vanilla ice cream and hates chocolate. Putnam's question is this: "Why do we regard the preference for vanilla ice cream over chocolate as 'subjective' then?" Why does this kind of value judgment not have the sort of objectivity that many value judgments do? Putnam claims that "it isn't just the fact that some people prefer chocolate and some people prefer vanilla that makes the Smith/Jones disagreement in preferences subjective." It does not seem to be the existence of "neutrals," of unimportant preferences, that is decisive, for there are sharp differences between important and unimportant preferences. "Someone who thought it was wonderful to torture small children for the fun of it would be condemned on the basis of that one attitude." But suppose that the matter preferred is not regarded as important in itself, "then whether we make an issue of preferences or take it to be a 'matter of taste' will generally depend on *what, if anything, we think the preference shows.*" The important and decisive issue, in Putnam's opinion, is whether or not the preferences at stake are correlated with *important traits of mind and character.* "The independence of 'I prefer vanilla to chocolate ice cream' from any interesting and significant 'clump' of this kind is just what makes it 'subjective.' " However, it might be mentioned that "subjective" here is not synonymous with 'irrational' or 'arbitrary.' "Jones has a reason – the best possible reason – for liking vanilla, namely the way it tastes to him."

We may now conclude that it is not possible to give a clear-cut definition of objectivity once and for all. For objectivity depends on the language we use. In the language of the exact sciences a special conception of objectivity is required, while in the social sciences, the humanities, and even within common sense language, we may need a different conception of it. This is to say that the conception of objectivity cannot be codified in one form, for all purposes and for all times. Rather, it is in a constant process of development, since our language, our conceptualization of the world, changes and grows. What we can say, nevertheless, is that objectivity becomes important, or even necessary, in cases where *justification* of statements, assertions, and beliefs, is *required on moral grounds.* If we for some purposes can affirm that to be objective is to be *fair* and *respectful,* this is because we think that it is *good* to be fair and respectful. And here good means morally good. This is to say that objectivity in itself has more the character of an *ideal* than of a ready–made criterion which we 'plug into.' And it is interesting to note that many formulations of objectivity reflect something of this ideal. Consider, for instance, the following suggestion: To be objective is to try to consider all the relevant facts involved in an issue; it is to be willing to consider arguments that speak against one's own view as well as to supply reasons for the view or the belief held; it is the effort to minimize incoherencies and inconsistencies within one's own belief-system; it is the attempt at functional simplicity within one's own notional world. In short, to be objective is to try to be impartial, sensitive, receptive, self-critical, honest and open-minded. My concern here, however, is not to unfold the details of the formalization of the concept of objectivity, but to emphasize how profoundly such a conception is related to our values. To claim that a statement, a belief, a view, or a picture of the world is true, is to argue that it could be justified on, for instance, these proposed grounds. That not everyone will share what we think it is good to do or believe, is no reason to think that there is *nothing* objectively good, or that every choice of world – or of version of the world – is completely arbitrary.

4.10 Summary and a Case against Conceptualism

A question at the outset of our study was this: what is the content of theological truth-claims and how can they be tested? Or stated differently: what is the meaning and truth of God-language?

To answer the question concerning the meaning of statements about God, we argued, one must know something about the nature of God; one must have access to an ontological theory which provides the foundation for such statements. On the other hand, to answer the question about the truth of such statements, one must know something about the epistemological theory on which they are based. But since ontological and epistemological theories are logically connected with metaphysical theories, an investigation of theological truth-claims is necessarily an investigation of metaphysics. For theology, we said, presupposes metaphysics.

But what would an appropriate metaphysics look like? We chose to address this problem by a method in which we focused upon one attempt to formulate a complete metaphysical theory, Alfred North Whitehead's philosophy of organism. After having investigated important features of this system we advanced toward a critical assessment of it. We found that it contained several problems, but that only one seemed decisive for the validity of the whole system, namely, Whitehead's conception of realism. The problem with this conception was the kind of metaphysical assumption which it presupposed: that we somehow have access to a position outside reality from which we can know what the world is really like, at the same time as we experience what reality is from within, so to speak. We argued that this epistemological theory was inconsistent with the ontological theory of Whitehead's philosophy, which asserted that nothing in the world, not even God, exists on its own, but that every event in the universe is constituted by its relationships to other events and that nothing exists except by participation.

Since the question of realism is essential to the question about what an appropriate metaphysics for theology might be, we were forced to proceed with a discussion about classical realism as such. By means of a critical discussion of Descartes' methodological doubt we tried to show that such a mode of realism as Whitehead's and many others, namely, the mode which assumes a dualism between what goes on in our minds, and what is outside our minds, i. e., what reality is in itself, could not be affirmed. And our argument was that it makes no sense to speak about what reality is in itself, because we cannot possibly know what the world is independently of our minds.

But an abrogation of this mode of realism also had consequences for our understanding of the nature of truth. For if one cannot speak anymore about what reality is in itself, one cannot speak about truth as a correspondence between statements, assertions, or beliefs, and reality in itself. Instead, we suggested, truth and many others, namely, the mode which assumes a dualism between what goes on in our minds, and what is outside our minds, i. e., what reality is in itself, could not be affirmed. And our argument was that it makes no sense to speak about what reality is in itself, because we cannot possibly know what the world is independently of our minds.

But an abrogation of this mode of realism also had consequences for our understanding of the nature of truth. For if one cannot speak anymore about what reality is in itself, one cannot speak about truth as a correspondence between statements, assertions, or beliefs, and reality in itself. Instead, we suggested, truth must be conceived in terms of coherence.

The rejection of classical realism, however, also had an impact on our understanding of the nature of perception. The core of our argument was that perception – and experience – is partly a form of construction: by means of our conceptualization of the world we organize what we take in via our sense-organs. We point out things, rather than at things. In short, the objects of the world must be understood to 'coexist' with our minds. We called this view *conceptual realism.*

Nevertheless, the idea of perception as a form of ordering the data which we receive through our senses, presupposes something which is not constructed, something which does not depend on our minds, something which is given. For already in experience we are aware of reality as greater than experience. We referred to this as a transcendental dimension in experience. In fact, the belief that reality is not just what is within our minds, and ultimately only in *my* mind, is the metaphysical assumption of something beyond experience. Without this assumption, we argued, one could not believe otherwise than that *everything* is a construction made by us, existing only within our minds. But to try to speak about what this "something" is makes no sense. It represents, rather, a limit to our thinking, as Kant put it.

In relation to the notion of conceptual realism we then tried to elaborate a theory of religion. We argued that not only empirical things, but also entities such as the world and God, represent a sort of construction. What we refer to as the world, is not something out there, ready-made, but something we construct by ordering the various beliefs and ideas we have, in such a way that it forms a whole. One way to construct an image of the world, which we referred to as the *notional world,* is by relating our beliefs and ideas to one or more factors, in such a way that we form a system of relations between our ideas and beliefs. When someone appeals to God as the ultimate point of reference within the notional world, we speak about it as a theistic notional world. We understood the notion of God as a way of filling out the hypothetical structure of a person's notional world, in analogy the way we try to fill out the pattern in a jigsaw puzzle. We then tried to show that speaking about God as an inferred or supplemented element in someone's notional world, does not mean that God is not something real. We suggested, however, that the question of God's reality cannot be considered apart from the consideration of the reality, or the truth, of the conception of the world to which it is related. And since we cannot speak of truth as a corre-spondence between our world, our conceptualization of the world, on the one hand, and the really real world, on the other, truth-testing means determining whether a suggested image of reality is relevant and rationally acceptable. And what this means, we claimed, must be considered as ultimately in relation to certain values, i.e., to our ideas of the good. It is *good*, we would say, to accept a conceptual system which has a sufficient degree of logical consistency, inter-connectedness of ideas, conceptual unity, reduction of arbitrariness and fragmen-tation. This is what we referred to as the coherence of a system. But we also require of an acceptable system that it fits with our experiences, namely, that it should give a meaningful and adequate interpretation of our experiences. However, the crucial question is whether there are any further possibilities for testing a conceptual scheme than those presented here. This is an issue which we shall attend to in the end of this section. However, we must start with a discussion of an attack on conceptual realism and the theory of religion which is related to it.

In recent debate about the validity of God-talk, the view we defended in this study has been criticized by certain philosophers. One of them is Kai Nielsen. He describes the sort of position that we have entertained as "conceptual rel-ativism," which he argues cannot be employed as the basis of a theory in support of theistic claims. A conceptual relativist, according to Nielsen, is one who believes "that what is to count as knowledge, evidence, truth, a fact, observation, making sense and the like, is uniquely determined by the linguistic framework used, and that linguistic frameworks can and do radically vary."[149] On this basis, such persons will, he says, "point out that I have adopted ... a framework in which there can be no direct knowledge of God and in which fundamental religious propositions are not even in principle verifiable. But it is perfectly possible to adopt a linguistic framework in which this is not so."[150] To push this one step further, Nielsen notes that this position denies all talk of any objective reality to which language conforms: "our very idea of reality is given within the particular universe of dis-course we use," and thus "the very distinction between what is real and what is unreal and the conception of what constitutes 'an agreement with' or a 'true link with' reality ... is relative to that universe of discourse."[151] This point is pressed by D. Z. Phillips, Nielsen mentions, who argues that the empiricists make the "mistake of 'speaking as if there were a check on what is real and what is unreal which is *not* found in the actual use of language, but which transcends it,' " instead of recognizing that such talk can be used legitimately only *within particular language-games.*[152] With this in mind, conceptual relativists, in Nielsen's opinion, argue that empiricists treat statements about God

> as if they were pseudo-scientific or empirical hypotheses. But this is the grossest kind of category mistake – a mistake which completely fails to

understand what they do mean, and assimilates in an utterly illegitimate way two very different universes of discourse, with different criteria of reality and intelligibility. What we must recognize is that while religious discourse and scientific discourse are radically different, both are established forms of life with internally coherent linguistic frameworks and distinct but equally legitimate conceptions of reality.[153]

Nielsen says that while this argument undeniably has some force, and while it does save God-talk from the empiricist attack by placing it within its own universe of discourse, this position nevertheless leads to the downfall of religious language, or at least utterly transforms its meaning. His central argument is simple, namely, that conceptual relativism cannot support the "finality" of the Christian claim that Christ is the truth. If Christian God-talk is a conceptually relative language-game, then it can have "no legitimate claim to a superior reality or deeper truth or profounder insight than any other language-game," including "Zande witchcraft-talk, Haitian vodoo-talk, Dobuan talk of sacred yams, Apa Tani talk of the Land of the Dead and the like."[154] Given conceptual relativism, in other words, Christian language can "in no objective sense be a claim to the truth about man or to be the way and the life if man is to gain salvation;" in other words, "there can be no such general statements about the nature of reality, . . . but only about the realities of a particular situation."[155] Consequently, Nielsen argues, the position to which conceptual relativism leads, brings about only skepticism in regard to the traditional claims of Christians; thus, the continuation of belief in the finality of Christian-talk can be maintained only by virtue of *ir-rationalism*. Of course, Nielsen notes, it is possible to argue as does Phillips, that religious language has only subjective truth, or as Norman Malcolm, that, while it is problematic to affirm that "God exists," it is legitimate to confess "belief in" God. Nevertheless, Nielsen comments, in affirming such subjective interpretations, it "begins to appear that they unwittingly have created a new or at least radically altered language-game with Christian terms and an atheistic substance."[156] In summary: Nielsen seems to argue that this approach to theology relentlessly leads to relativism about everything, including religion, which then never supports, but in fact undermines, all talk about God.

This seems to be a hard case against conceptualism. But the question is whether there is not something deceptive about the way Nielsen describes conceptualism. One might suspect that the fact that he speaks about conceptual *relativism* suggests that for him no form of conceptualism can escape complete relativism. But is this so? To argue for conceptualism, or, as we have preferred to say, *conceptual realism,* is not necessarily to hold that "anything goes." If someone wants to choose a "universe of description" in which humans are able to fly like the birds, that person will regret this choice when he or she explores it; that is, if the person survives. Denying that it makes sense to ask whether our concepts 'match' something totally uncontaminated by conceptualization is one thing. To hold that one conceptual system is therefore just as good as any other, would be something quite different. Rather, we have tried to argue that the kind of realism that undergirds the claim that one is able to describe reality as "it is" objectively (independent of the observer), entails the veridical risk of relativism, while conceptualism, as we understand it, can provide us with a much more effective protection against relativism. For conceptual realism can help us realize that any claim to clear-cut reporting of the given reality is downright false.

In order to accept a presented picture of reality, we need to know what *standards* of truth and objectivity the observer employs. Only when we have access to such standards or criteria will we be able to judge whether a given picture is an accurate and just one, and whether we should accept it or not. We can, therefore, calmly resist all descriptions of the world, or of situations in the world, which claim to "copy" reality. There is no ready-made world that one could simply copy. To have objective knowledge of the world is not to try to achieve an image of the world on a quasi-scientific model of truth and objectivity. Objective knowledge, we have suggested, is, rather, related to our values: our ideas of the good.[157] It is, of course, possible to choose to speak about reality in a language within which we discriminate between facts and values. But ultimately, our choice to conceive of the world in this way is connected with an ideal: this is a good way to describe reality, we say.

In a sense, then, it is true that all worlds, or "universes of discourse," as Nielsen would have it, are relative, namely, relative to our languages, and ultimately to our values. But that is certainly not to say that any notion of truth or reality is "as good as" any other. To say that something is "right" or "wrong" relative to something else, is not to say that there is no right or wrong at all. Our choice of worlds, or conceptualizations, or languages, or systems of descriptions, is not completely irrational; if it were, nothing would really matter. Our choice of conceptual scheme, in terms of which we interpret and understand the world, something which also influences our experiences, our acts, our entire life-orientation, *reflects* our values. But our conceptualization actually *depends,* in a certain sense, on our values. When we speak about "choice," we do not use the word in a very sophisticated sense; we mean the kind of choice we are all involved in every day, when we choose to express or describe our various beliefs and experiences, whether these have to do with religion, with politics, or with the social reality which surrounds us. Often, as we have noted before, this choice is not a real choice but something we learn or inherit.[158] The point, however, is that we choose to conceive of the world in the *best* possible way – at least, this is what we would probably all agree one ought to do – and best means best as we understand the word through our view of rationality. We try to justify our descriptions of reality by reference to the fact that the conceptualization we defend really takes account of our theoretical ideas and beliefs, but also our most important values, i.e., our ideas about the good.

Justification, however, does not imply agreement to everyone's satisfaction. For we do not all share the same values, or the same concepts of rationality, or hold the same cognitive virtues in equally high esteem. But justification does not necessarily mean complete agreement. However, this acknowledgement is very different from a relativism where everything goes.

Let us now conclude with a short discussion about some suggestions concerning the issue of the *justification of religious beliefs*. It is one thing to open the door to pluralism, and argue that there might be several interpretations, or conceptualizations, of the world that seem acceptable from a rational point of view. It is another to find ways in which we can justify the choice of a particular belief-system. In the introduction of our study we made a distinction between what is acceptable and what is reasonable, and mentioned that it could be possible to affirm that certain conceptualizations are acceptable, without affirming that they are equally reasonable. We also restricted ourselves to the enterprise of determining what an acceptable metaphysics would look like. Now, however, we may present some brief suggestions as to why we might be justified in choosing or accepting a *religious* belief-system.

Earlier we described religious faith as a special kind of existential and ethical response to a particular interpretation of the world which presupposes the existence of God. We also discussed some criteria for rational acceptability with respect to such conceptualizations of reality, such as adequacy, relevance, comprehensiveness, and so forth. But let us now imagine a case where there are several belief-systems which seem to satisfy a proposed set of criteria equally well. Is there, then, some way in which we could go on to test such systems, and possibly justify the acceptance of one of them? Or is the choice a purely arbitrary one?

Now it seems as though we have a sort of *ethical criterion* available which might apply here. It is rational, we may suggest, to accept as reasonable a conceptual system against the background of which our idea of human flourishing and the good life can be most adequately expressed, if the system is also acceptable with respect to other criteria that we believe to be necessary requirements for rational acceptability. Of course, we are not proposing a clear-cut and decisive method for justification of religious belief-systems. We might still reach a point where we feel indecisive as to whether it is reasonable to accept a particular belief-system.

The point, rather, is that if the sense of *rightness*, or *goodness*, is a part of our lived experience, we may find a way of testing the *whole* system, in order to see whether it does justice to, and fits with, our experience. This is to suggest a kind of *holistic test procedure*. We must discern whether a religious conceptualization – what we have called a theistic notional world – entails the possibility of *doing justice to the sort of value-experiences* – or values – that many people seem to have, for example, of nature, or of human lives, as ultimately valuable beyond human comprehension, in a way which other systems do not have.[159] The existence of such fundamental value-experiences was, by the way, the highlight of Whitehead's system. He said, for instance:

At the base of our existence is the sense of "worth" (MT 109).

It might then be possible that a certain kind of religious interpretation of the world allows a person to speak about, and hence respond to, the nature of the world and of all our lives within it, with a fuller adequacy than some other system. It might be the case, for instance, that the conception of God as Creator of the world may enable a person to speak about nature as intrinsically valuable (in relation to God), far beyond its value for human beings, and, therefore, to argue for a certain ethical responsibility that pertains to this understanding of the world. In the same mode it may be possible for someone to argue that all human beings are equally valuable (in relation to God), and, thus, that they should be treated in accordance with this value, if it is possible to accept such a belief-system. In other words, *if a proposed belief-system can help to articulate our most important values, we might find it justifiable to accept it.* However, this is not to say that a belief-system cannot also be the source of values, in the sense that such a system can help to originate new expressions of a value-experience at the base of our existence.

An author who entertains a similar view is C. J. Ducasse, formerly professor of philosophy at Brown University. He argues that when someone is confronted by a choice between two mutually incompatible, but nevertheless equally rational, hypotheses, where there is no evidence sufficient to prove that one of them is true – or is more probably true – than the other, then it is not only legitimately, but in fact impossible to do otherwise than accept the particular one of the two hypothesis which is most congenial to our values. Ducasse explains that, for instance, questions such as whether the God of Christianity exists, whether humans have immortal souls, whether acceptance of Christ is necessary to salvation, and questions as to the truth or falsity of many others of the beliefs of Christianity or of other religions, constitute options which for many people cannot be decided by them rationally for lack of the knowledge which would be necessary for this. Therefore, if a man or a woman faces a situation where he or she *must* choose between accepting or rejecting a hypothesis that, if true, would offer a way of safeguarding certain values which are considered to be important, and which would otherwise be threatened, *then* it is rational to accept this hypothesis.

No matter how intelligent, educated, vigorous, powerful, and resourceful a man may be, there is always some limit to what he can do to safeguard his values. Hurricanes, earthquakes, floods or fire; disease, accidents, wars, or revolutions; the stupidity, faithlessness, ignorance, or wickedness of others if not himself; and so on; threaten at times, or bring disaster to, either himself or the things or persons he holds most dear, in spite of his best efforts to safeguard them.

When a man (1) faces a situation where there is such a threat; (2) and has already done everything in his power; (3) and yet the values threatened have not thereby been safeguarded; (4) and a hypothesis as to supernatural or extranatural matters presents itself, of the truth or falsity or probability of which he has no sufficent evidence; (5) and it is a hypothesis which, if true, would offer a way, more or less probably effective, of safeguarding those values, or if not, of anesthetizing himself more or less to their loss, *then* two possible courses are open to that man:

a) One is to seek, by acceptance of that hypothesis, the preservation of the threatened values; or the trust or perspective he needs to enable him to bear with some serenity the loss of those values or the prospect of it.

b) The other course is to refuse to accept that hypothesis, and thus remain anxious, worried, fearful, despairing and discouraged.

But evidently, the first of these two courses is the more sensible to take, since *ex hypothesi* it has greater positive value. . .[160]

Not everyone will agree with our choice of values, or with what is important, of course; but values are not for this reason completely arbitrary, subjective, or private. The ideas of justice, peace, love, wisdom, courage, rightness, are not ghosts, or mere conventions. Is it not rather that a sense of *goodness* or *rightness* belongs to our deepest nature. It is not something imposed from the outside. It belongs to the nature of reality itself. Or, as Aristotle expressed this, goodness is one of the transcendental attributes of being, or the common nature shared by everything real. The best way, it seems, to express this it to say that goodness is something *given,* and, therefore, that it represents what is occasionally called "the metaphysical ultimate."[161] For without it there would be no real world. However, when we speak about 'the good' we can only describe our idea of it as this has developed up to a given point in time. But we need to believe in an ideal limit, if our practice of criticizing traditions and trying to improve them is to make any sense at all.

If we are correct here, there will always be a certain personal (though not thereby necessarily subjective or arbitrary) element in assessing religious belief-systems. Perhaps we could even speak about an *experimental* method of justification. The only way, finally, to test a religious belief-system might be to commit oneself to it, in order to see whether it suits or illumines ones personal experience. This can finally be the only possible way to discover whether a system "fits" with experience, ideas, and our values, whether it really has the requisite organizing power. However, it must be emphasized, such an "experimental" method need not be incompatible with a critical attitude toward the system one is testing. Such a testing is not the same thing as surrendering or submitting oneself to the authority of the system.

This, it must be admitted, suggests a different understanding of the relation between religion and experience than is common in more empirically oriented theories of religion. In such theories religion is often regarded as the expression of that deep human experience sometimes called an 'experience of the transcendent;' religion on such a view becomes a distinctive symbolic system, where patterns of thought, feeling, and human conduct are linked together based on the articulation of such experience. In the view we have found plausible, a religion, or religious belief-system, is not so much expression of but rather that which *constitutes* what is at the depth of human experience – our existential and ethical self-understanding. Religion is that which holds together a culture, that with which we hold together our world.[162]

Notes

1. *Myths, Models, and Paradigms; A Comparative Study in Science and Religion*, New York, (1976), 170.

2. Karl Barth also makes a considerable issue of the essential duality of the world in the Christian view, although he explicitly rejects metaphysical or cosmological speculations. Cf. *Church Dogmatics*, Edinburgh, (1936–1962), III/1, 17–22; III/3, 369–531. This note is taken from Gordon D. Kaufman, *God the Problem*, Cambridge, Mass., (1972), 42.

3. "Toward a New Theism," *Process Philosophy and Christian Thought*, Indianapolis, (1977), 178.

4. Op. cit., 179.

5. "The Death of God," in *Christian Scholar*, 48 (1965), 45f.

6. *God the Problem*, Cambridge, Mass., (1972), 42.

7. For a discussion of the debate about metaphysics in Sweden, see Jarl Hemberg, *Religion och metafysik. Axel Hägerströms och Anders Nygrens religionsteorier och dessas inflytande i svensk religionsdebatt* (Religion and Metaphysics. The Religious Theories of Axel Hägerström and Anders Nygren and their Influence on Religious Discussion in Sweden), Stockholm, (1966).

8. "Enquiry," 2; W., II, 283, in Immanuel Kant: *Critique of Practical Reason and Other Writings in Moral Philosophy*, Chicago, (1949).

9. See Frederick Copleston, S. J., *A History of Philosophy*, Vol. 6, Part II, Garden City, New York, (1960), 11.

10. *Metaphysics*, 982 a 26–8. The Oxford translation of the works of Aristotle is published in eleven volumes, and edited by J. A. Smith and W. D. Ross. In this brief discussion of Aristotle's conception of metaphysics, I have kept rather close to Frederick Copleston's *A History of Philosophy*, Vol. 1, Part II, Garden City, New York, (1960), 30–40.

11. Aristotle's concept of "substance" is one of the most complex in his system, which explains why my discourse naturally must be a simplification. Aristotle, for instance, distinguishes between primary substance, which is always the individual concrete thing, and as such the subject of attributes in all the categories, and secondary substance, which is the species and the genera to which the individual things pertain. See for instance Joseph Owen, *The Doctrine of Being in the Aristotelian Metaphysics*, Toronto, (1951).

12. I have received helpful suggestions to the formulation of this definition from both Anders Jeffner and Hans Hof, for which I am grateful.

13. *The Analysis of Sensations*, Chicago and London, (1914), 12.

14. Some theories of perception can be called empirical: concepts, or expectations, arise from what is there in experience. We notice similarities between what we have perceived and what we now perceive, in a way which shapes our expectations. Other theories claim that it is language, the rules of grammar, which forms our expectations. Then concepts would not be formed by experience. A third position would hold that the genesis of concepts is something partly empirical, partly non-empirical. We could describe such a theory as a mixed theory of perception. See Carl-Reinhold Bråkenhielm, *How Philosophy*

Shapes Theories of Religion, Lund, (1975), 130 f. However, it may also be possible to maintain that concepts play different roles in perception, depending on the level of perception. In ordinary sense perception of the objects around us, the contribution of the environment might be pervasive, while on a more sophisticated level of perception, as when we speak about the world, society, or history as a whole, it might be that the way we conceive of reality also shapes what we perceive. I am grateful to Carl-Reinhold Bråkenhielm for having drawn my attention to the distinction between different levels of perception.

15. Roderick M. Chisholm, *Theory of Knowledge,* Englewood Cliffs, New Jersey, (1966), 56.

16. The relation between theological truth-claims and ontology is pressed by Bo Hansson, "Vardag och evighet," *Festskrift till Hampus Lyttkens,* Lund, (1981).

17. An author who also stresses the necessity for metaphysical analysis of the problem of the meaning and truth of theological assertions is David Tracy: "If it be the case that the revisionist model for fundamental theology must validate the cognitive claims for the religious language under investigation, it becomes imperative that the theologian develops criteria for meaning and truth which can validate or invalidate those claims. For that means of validation, in my judgment, the theologian must turn to metaphysics." *Blessed Rage for Order; The New Pluralism in Theology,* New York, (1975), 149. See also Peter R. Baelz, *Christian Theology and Metaphysics,* Philadelphia, (1968), esp. pp. 1–16, 79–135; James A. Martin, *The New Dialogue Between Philosophy and Theology,* New York, (1966), esp. pp. 130–207; James Richmond, *Theology and Metaphysics,* New York, (1971), esp. pp. 1–49, 93–155; Frank B. Dilley, *Metaphysics and Religious Language,* New York, (1964); Dorothy Emmet, *The Nature of Metaphysical Thinking,* London, (1949); Frederick Ferré, *Language, Logic and God,* New York, (1961), esp. pp. 146–165, and *Basic Modern Philosophy of Religion,* New York, (1967).

18. Gordon D. Kaufman, *God the Problem,* Cambridge, Mass., (1972), 44.

19. See Chisholm, *Theory of Knowledge,* Englewood Cliffs, New Jersey, (1966), 41.

20. Gordon D. Kaufman, *Relativism, Knowledge, and Faith,* Chicago, (1960), 102.

21. Frederick Ferré, *Soundings,* Vol. 51, (1968), 341–342.

22. The philosophy of Martin Heidegger might be ranked with Whitehead's. However, Whitehead's metaphysics speaks about God in a way which relates to theology differently than does Heidegger's. Whitehead also deals with scientific issues in a much more inclusive and explicit way than Heidegger. For an interesting critique by Heidegger of Whitehead's metaphysics, see "Whitehead's Metaphysics and Heidegger's critique" by Raymond J. Devettererre, in *Cross Currents,* Vol. 30, No. 3, (1981), 309–322.

23. *A Christian Natural Theology,* Philadelphia, (1965), 17.

24. *Beyond God the Father; Toward a Philosophy of Women's Liberation,* Boston, (1974), 188–189.

25. See William James, *A Pluralistic Universe,* New York, (1971). See also Dorothy Emmet's article on Whitehead in *The Encyclopedia of Philosophy,* Vol. 8, New York, (1972), 294.

26. I owe gratitude to Ivor Leclerc and his *Whitehead's Metaphysics; An Introductory Exposition,* Bloomington, Indiana, (1975). However, my perspective is going to be developed somewhat differently than Leclerc's.

27. Among many of his writings from the period before the Harvard time, we may mention the most famous, *Principia Mathematica,* London, (1910–1913), written together with Bertrand Russell.

28. Aristotle's *Metaphysics,* Z, I, 1028^b 2–8.

29. Ivor Leclerc, *Whitehead's Metaphysics*, Bloomington, Indiana, (1975), 18.

30. Descartes, *Principles of Philosophy*, I 51, in *The Philosophical Work of Descartes*, New York, (1955).

31. Berkeley, (1970), 91, (Copyright 1942).

32. Op. cit., 281.

33. Bernard E. Meland, *Fallible Forms and Symbols; Discourse of Method in a Theology of Culture*, Philadelphia, (1976), 5ff. A helpful discussion, according to Meland, of the new realism that altered the orientation of theological inquiry in recent years, is found in Paul Tillich's *The Protestant Era*, Chicago, (1948), esp. p. 76ff.

34. Meland, op. cit., 9f.

35. Ian Barbour, *Issues in Science and Religion*, New York, (1971), 170f.

36. A clear definition or explanation of the term 'consciousness' is to my best knowledge not given in Whitehead's writings. In Donald W. Sherburne's *A Key to Whitehead's Process and Reality*, New York, (1966), 214, consciousness, as used by Whitehead, is explained as the "holding together in a unity as one datum a feeling of a nexus of actual entities and a feeling of a proposition with its logical subjects members of the nexus." This is an interpretation of what Whitehead says in *Process and Reality:* "Consciousness is how we feel the affirmation-negation contrast" (PR 372). Consciousness is a product of even higher integrations in the process of concrescence. It is "the crown of experience, only occasionally attained, not its necessary base" (PR 408). Consciousness for Whitehead, according to Sherburne, only illuminates the more primitive types of prehensions, so far as these prehensions – or feelings, or experiences – are still elements in the products of integration. It seems as if Whitehead's understanding of consciousness and experience, and their mutual relationship, is a sort of attack on Hume, for Whitehead argues that Hume's whole analysis of causation is irrelevant from the beginning because Hume *started* with conscious perception as his primary fact and argued that "any apprehension of causation was, somehow or other, to be elicited from this primary fact" (PR 263).

37. It may be mentioned here, that Whitehead's view shows a certain resemblance to Bertrand Russell's *neutral monism*, a theory in which both mind and matter are constructions out of particulars that are neither mental nor material, but neutral. Russell's logical constructionism was first employed in his mathematical theory and published in *Principia Mathematica* (3 vols., 1910–1913), a joint-work with Alfred N. Whitehead. Russell's effort is to try to show that the "public physical objects" of the world are constructed as a complex structure of data in immediate experience. The difference between the objects in the world lies in the "grouping" of the constituents in immediate experience. In his *The Analysis of Mind* Russell explains his conversion to neutral monism, following the lead of William James, who earlier formulated the view. The book was first published 1921, a couple of years before Whitehead wrote *Process and Reality*. In *The Analysis of Mind* Russell says for instance: "Electrons and protons, however, are not the stuff of the physical world: they are elaborate logical structures composed by events, and ultimately of particulars ... On the question of the material out of which the physical world is constructed, the view advocated in this volume has, perhaps, more affinity with idealism than with materialism. What are called 'mental' events, if we have been right, are part of the material of the physical world, and what is in our heads is the mind (with additions) rather than what the physiologist sees through his microscope ... On the question of the stuff of the world, the theory of the foregoing pages has certain affinities with idealism – namely, that mental events are part of that stuff, and

that the rest of the stuff resembles them more than it resembles traditional billiard-balls ... (Ch. "Physics and Neutral Monism," in *The Basic Writings of Bertrand Russell*, New York, 1961, 609 ff.). It is interesting to note that Russell seems to conceive of the basic components in reality as some sort of *events*, precisely as does Whitehead. And also like Whitehead he thinks of these events as constituents of both so-called mental and material phenomena.

38. PR 182.

39. Op. cit., 257.

40. It is widely known that through the years Whitehead developed some of his concepts, and that his views are articulated differently in his various books. I have here decided not to focus upon this development, but shall try to come to terms with those ideas which he seemed to retain.

41. *The Basic Writings of Bertrand Russell*, New York, (1961), 241.

42. *Essays in Science and Philosophy*, New York, (1947), 117; quoted from *Process Philosophy and Christian Thought*, ed. by Delwin Brown, Ralph E. James, Jr., and Gene Reeves, Indianapolis, (1971), 8.

43. John B. Cobb, Jr., and David Ray Griffin, *Process Theology; An Introductory Exposition*, Philadelphia, (1976), 15.

44. Although Whitehead, to my knowledge, does not explicitly say so, I think that the term "organism" partly is chosen as a contrast to the metaphysical outlook contained in Newtonian physics, where the picture of separate, self-contained particles, touching externally, resembled a machine more than a living organism.

45. Delwin Brown, *Process Philosophy and Christian Thought*, Indianapolis, (1971), 9.

46. Also William James uses 'experience' to designate the basic 'stuff' that makes up the world. Experience, he claims, does not come in packages marked "subjective" and "objective," "mental" and "physical," "internal" and "external." In *Essays in Radical Empiricism*, New York, (1971) James says: "According to my view, experience as a whole is a process in time" (35), and "I tried to show that thoughts and things are absolutely homogeneous as to their material, and that their opposition is only one of relation and of function. There is no thought-stuff differently from thing-stuff, I said; but the same identical piece of 'pure experience' (which was the name I gave to the *materia prima* of everything) can stand alternately for a 'fact of consciousness' or for a physical reality, according as it is taken in one context or in another" (72).

47. In Whitehead's philosophical terminology there is a difference between "actual entities" and "actual occasions," although he uses the terms more or less synonymously. However, "actual occasions" are finitie, or temporal, kinds of "actual entities," because God is also an actual entity, and God is eternal (PR 135).

48. Eternal objects are not actual, but they are all the same real. However, Whitehead claims that they do not exist apart from an actual entity. In fact, they exist in God's primordial mind.

49. Donald Sherburne makes the remark that the terminology "mental pole" and "physical pole" is not the most happy to introduce in a philosophy that tries to repudiate the Cartesian dualism. However, Sherburne also points out that it was certainly not Whitehead's intention to reintroduce the old concept of mind and matter. See his *A Key to Whitehead's Process and Reality*, New York, (1966), 228f.

50. David Griffin, "Whitehead's contribution to a Theology of Nature", *Bucknell Review*, Vol. 20, No 3, (1972), 14.

154

51. The modern fact-value distinction was introduced by Max Weber, and his argument was that it is not possible to establish the truth of value judgments to the satisfaction of all rational persons. And in this context, rationality meant scientific rationality. See "Max Weber" in *Encyclopedia of Philosophy*, Vol. 8, 282, and *On the Methodology of the Social Sciences*, Glencoe, Ill., (1949).

52. John B. Cobb Jr., and David Ray Griffin, *Process Theology; An Introductory Exposition*, Philadelphia, (1976), 78.

53. Op. cit., 79.

54. John B. Cobb, "Process Theology and Environmental Issues," *The Journal of Religion*, Vol. 60, No. 4, (1980), 449.

55. John B. Cobb, "Ecology, Ethics, and Theology," in *Toward a Steady-State Economy*, San Francisco, (1973), 310.

56. See my forthcoming *An Empirical Study and Analysis of contemporary Life-philosophies among Swedish Environmentalists*, Department of Theology, Uppsala University, (1982).

57. Cobb's article in *Toward a Steady-State Economy*, (1973), 318f.

58. Griffin's article "Whitehead's Contribution" in *Bucknell Review*, (1972), No. 3.

59. Cobb and Griffin, *Process Theology*, Philadelphia, (1976), 65.

60. New Haven, (1948). For a recent Swedish study, see Eberhard Herrmann, *Die logische Stellung des ontologischen Gottesbeweises in Charles Hartshornes Prozeßtheologie und neoklaßischer Metaphysik*, Lund, (1980).

61. See William A. Christian, *An Interpretation of Whitehead's Metaphysics*, New Haven, (1967), 405f.

62. Donald Sherburne, *A Key to Whitehead's Process and Reality*, New York, (1966), 227.

63. *Process Theology; An Introductory Exposition*, Philadelphia, (1976), 67.

64. See p. 45f.

65. Philadelphia, (1976), 82.

66. In his book *God and Other Minds*, Ithaca, N. Y., (1967), pp. 181–183, Alvin Plantinga tries to give account for what it means that God is "logically necessary" for the completion of our interpretation of the world. When we look for an answer "which puts an end to the indefinitely long series of questions and answers where the answer to each question mentions a being or state of affaris about which precisely the same question may be asked," we are looking for what Plantinga calls a *final* answer. A final answer is, therefore, a statement which "puts an end to the series of questions and answers and allows no further question of the same sort." It seems to me as if this notion of "necessity" comes close to the way Scholastic theologians tried to answer the question "If God made the world, then who made God?" by saying that God was self-caused, or *ens necessarium*. However, it might be questioned whether this answer is really intelligible, or whether is explains anything.

67. It may be noticed that Whitehead's notion of God seems to be the solution to the same kind of metaphysical problem as Aristotle's. However, Whitehead seems aware that charges could be brought against him that he had simply introduced a *deus ex machina*, a device which was only an excuse for obscurity and incoherence. Therefore, he maintains that "God is not to be treated as an exception to all metaphysical principles, invoked to save their collapse. He is their chief exemplification" (PR 521).

68. Schubert Ogden, "Present Prospects for Empirical Theology", in *Essays in Divinity, Vol. VII, The Future of Empirical Theology*, Chicago, (1969), 86.

69. For criticisms of Whitehead's concept of God see, for instance, Robert C. Neville's *God The Creator; On the Transcendence and Presence of God,* Chicago, (1968); Stephen L. Ely's *The Religious Availability of Whitehead's God; A Critical Analysis,* Madison, Wisconsin, (1942); Langdon Gilkey's *Maker of Heaven and Earth; A Study of the Christian Doctrine of Creation,* New York, (1959); Edward H. Madden and Peter H. Hare, *Evil and the Concept of God,* Springfield, Ill., (1968); Cornelio Fabro's *God in Exile; Modern Atheism,* Westminster, M. D., (1968).

70. Alvin Plantinga's article "Reply to the Basingers on Divine Omnipotence," in *Process Studies,* Vol. 11, No. 1, (1981), 25.

71. Op. cit., 29.

72. Op. cit., 25. See also Alvin Plantinga, *The Nature of Necessity,* Oxford, (1974), esp. pp. 168–184. Another of his books in this area is *God, Freedom and Evil,* Grand Rapids, Michigan, (1977).

73. *Philosophy of Religion,* Englewood Cliffs, New Jersey, (1963), 41f. For a more extensive discussion, see Hick's *Evil and the God of Love,* London, (1966). See also Antony Flew's "Divine Omnipotence and Human Freedom," in *New Essays in Philosophical Theology,* New York, (1955), and Ninian Smart's critical reply in "Omnipotence, Evil and Supermen," *Philosophy,* April, (1961).

74. See *Against Heresies,* Book IV, Chapter 37 and 38, in tr. by J. Quasten and J. C. Plumpe.

75. New York, (1970), 112.

76. See p. 55.

77. In his *God and the World,* Philadelphia, (1976), 60, 63, John B. Cobb gives an interesting explanation of *why* it is important to envisage God as something independent of our experience of God: "Unless 'God' refers to something whose actuality is *independent* of man's experiencing it, but which nevertheless *affects* man's experience, there can indeed be no reason to deep concern about the use of the word." For, "apart from belief in God, conscious or unconscious, there is little ground for hope," Cobb thinks.

78. "The Incoherence of Whitehead's Theory of Perception," *Process Studies,* Vol. 9, No. 3–4, (1979), 94 ff.

79. Op. cit., 102. In addition to Kimball's argument, we may say that there is no absolutely natural and distinct line in the brain between *sensing* and *thinking,* which Whitehead's theory seems to imply. In the process of seeing, for instance, it is not simply the visual organs that are involved, but the whole brain. The eye is a natural unit at a level of everyday talk, as is a table, or a car, or a tree. But on some other level, say, a scientific, or medical, this is not the case. In fact, the eye *is* a part of the brain. On a level of ordinary language psychology, there is, of course, a significant difference between seeing and thinking, but the line between those two capacities is something *we* draw. It is not a natural distinction in the sense that it is the *only* possible way to draw lines or discriminate between capacities of the brain. I am grateful to Professor Hilary Putnam for having drawn my attention to this observation.

80. The term is borrowed from A. Meinong. See his *Über emotionale Präsentation,* Vienna, (1917). For a more thoroughly developed critical discussion about the concept "directly evident," see Roderick M. Chisholm, *Theory of Knowledge,* Englewood Cliffs, New Jersey, (1966), 24ff.

81. Indianapolis and New York, (1969), 213n. Gilkey also says: "The Whiteheadian must ask himself why he believes, in the first place, in the objective rationality and coherence of process, and the power of speculative thought to reach beyond immediate experience,

and how he might defend those beliefs intelligibly to the modern philosophical mind that finds both almost incredible," 227f. For another criticism of Whitehead's rationalism, see Schilpp's *The Philosophy of Alfred North Whitehead,* Evanston, Ill., (1941).

82. Franz Brentano's theory in his *Wahrheit und Evidenz,* Leipzig, (1930), can be viewed as one example. See also Charles Sanders Peirce's *Collected Papers,* Vol. V, Cambridge, Mass., (1934), 5.408, 5.358n., 5.494, and 5.565.

83. *Theory of Knowledge,* Englewood Cliffs, New Jersey, (1966), 112.

84. Op. cit., 113. To avoid misunderstanding, perhaps we should mention that Chisholm does not claim that we should accept the assumption of the metaphysical witness. He says: "I cannot feel ... that it is reasonable for anyone to accept the theory. But if we reject the theory, we must find some other way of dealing with the problem it was designed to solve."

85. It is a well known fact that the title *Metaphysics* of the fourteen books about "first philosophy" is created by Andronicus in his edition of Aristotle's works. Andronicus gave these books the title in accordance with their localization after the books about physics: $\tau\grave{\alpha}\ \mu\epsilon\tau\grave{\alpha}\ \tau\grave{\alpha}\ \varphi\upsilon\sigma\iota\varkappa\acute{\alpha}$.

86. *Logic and Knowledge,* London, (1956), 182.

87. New York, (1969), 32.

88. See, for instance, Ian Barbour's *Issues in Science and Religion,* New York, (1971), 242. See also G. Bergmann, *The Metaphysics of Logical Positivism,* New York, (1954).

89. See p. 15.

90. See, for instance, *Conjectures and Refutations; The Growth of Scientific Knowledge,* London, (1963). See also G. J. Warnock's review of "The Logic of Scientific Discovery" in *Mind,* Vol. 69, (1960), 99–101. For a discussion about realism in science in general, see J. J. Smart, *Philosophic and Scientific Realism,* London, (1963).

91. London, (1980), Vol. 2, 376.

92. Op. cit., 391.

93. New York, (1971), 135. My italics.

94. London, (1980), Vol. 2, 247. Popper quotes from Whitehead's *Process and Reality,* 20f.

95. Op. cit., 250.

96. Ithaca, N. Y., (1980), 99.

97. Segré, Emilio, *Nuclei and Particles; An Introduction to Nuclear and Subnuclear Physics,* New York, (1964), 197.

98. For a discussion about scientific and non-scientific explanatory hypotheses, see Anders Jeffner's *The Study of Religious Language,* London, (1972), 121ff.

99. *The Open Society and its Enemies,* London, (1980), Vol. 2, 268.

100. See footnote 35.

101. *Rules for the Direction of the Mind,* 3, in Vol. I of *The Philosophical Works of Descartes,* two volumes, New York, (1955). See also *A History of Philosophy* by Frederick Copleston, Vol. 4, New York, (1962), on which my interpretation of Descartes' philosophy is based.

102. *Notes Against a Programme,* 13. Quoted from Copleston, op. cit., 95.

103. *Méditations,* 1. In "Première Méditation" of *Méditation Métaphysiques,* Paris, (1966), 33, the French reading is: "Je supposerai donc qu'il y a, non point un vrai Dieu, qui est la souveraine source de vérité, mais un certain mauvais génie, non moins rusé et trompeur que puissant, qui a employé toute son industrie à me tromper. Je penserai que le ciel,

l'air, la terre, les couleurs, les figures, les sons et toutes les choses extérieures que nous voyons, ne sont que des illusions et tromperies, dont il se sert pour surprendre, ma crédulité. Je me considérerai moi-même comme n'ayant point de mains, point d'yeux, point de chair, point de sang, comme n'ayant aucuns sens, mais croyant faussement avoir toutes ces choses."

104. The translation is taken from Copleston, op. cit., 128. The French text in "Résponses aux quatrièmes objections" in *Méditation Métaphysiques, op. cit.*, 219f, reads: "C'est pourquoi je ne doute point que l'esprit, aussitôt qu'il est infus dans le corps d'un enfant, ne commence à penser, et que dès lors il ne sache qu'il pense, encore qu'il ne se ressouvienne pas par après de ce qu'il a pensé, parce que les espèces de ses pensèes ne demeurent pas empreintes en sa mémoire."

105. Stuart C. Brown, *Do Religious Claims Make Sense?*, New York, (1969), 45.

106. Op. cit., 36f.

107. *Zettle*, Oxford, (1967), sect. 297. Quoted from Brown, op. cit., 46.

108. Brown, op. cit., 47.

109. London, (1970), 19.

110. Brown, op. cit., 34.

111. *Reason, Truth, and History*, forthcoming. Putnam has made a copy of his manuscript available to me, for which I am much obliged. All quotations here are from Ch. 3.

112. Indianapolis, (1978), 19.

113. See Roderick M. Chisholm, *Theory of Knowledge*, Englewood Cliffs, New Jersey, (1966), esp. pp. 24–69, 94–102. Apart from *Reason, Truth, and History*, see also Putnam's *Meaning and the Moral Sciences*, Boston, London, and Henley, (1979). Apart from *Ways of Worldmaking*, see also Goodman's *Fact, Fiction, and Forecast*, Indianapolis, (1979). See W. V. O. Quine's *From a Logical Point of View*, Cambridge, Mass., and London, (1963) and his *Word and Object*, Cambridge, Mass., (1960). For an interesting critique of the correspondence theory of truth, see Michael Dummett's *What is a Theory of Meaning?*, 2 vols., Oxford, (1975, 1976). See also Ludwig Wittgenstein *Philosophical Investigations*, Oxford, (1953).

114. London, (1962), 161.

115. *The Study of Religious Language*, London, (1972), 120n.

116. We have already noted that the idea of "coherence" as a criterion of the truth of a metaphysical system was related to Whitehead's faith in a "cosmic coherence," his belief that reality in itself forms a coherent system. See p. 30.

117. London, (1939), Vol. 2, 316. See also "Coherence Theory of Truth" in *The Encyclopedia of Philosophy*, New York, (1972), Vol. 2, 130, where Blanshard's view is discussed. In my presentation of Blanshard's theory I have kept close to this article.

118. The Danish philosopher Harald Høffding has provided many interesting evidences in support of the theory that there are no individual experiences independently of our frames of reference, i. e., our languages. See his *Religionsfilosofi* (Philosophy of Religion), Copenhagen, (1901), 152ff. The theory that our language determines what we experience is a main thesis in the psychological investigations of the Swedish scholar Hjalmar Sundén. See *Die Religion und die Rollen; Eine Psychologische Untersuchung der Frömmigkeit*, Berlin, (1966). Cf. Ernst Hans Gombrich, *Art and Illusion; A Study in the Psychology of Pictorial Representation*, New York, (1960), and Jerome Seymour Bruner, *Beyond the Information given; Studies in the Psychology of Knowing*, New York, (1973).

119. Blanshard, *The Nature of Thought,* London, (1939), Vol. 2, 228.

120. See p. 107.

121. Cf. the article about the coherence theory of truth in *The Encyclopedia of Philosophy,* Vol. 2, 132.

122. This example is taken from the article referred to in note 121. It has occurred to me, however, that when a person claims that something can be true without anyone's knowing it, he or she might mean, for instance, that one day some scientist will be able to present a solution to the enigmatic problem of cancer, i. e., there is a solution to this problem "waiting to be discovered." I grant that it seems fair to believe that it is a correct prediction that we shall sooner or later find a medical technique or method to deal with cancer, which presupposes a true theory about its nature. However, the reason this is a plausible belief is the fact that medical science *sofar* has been successful in coming to grips with an incredible large number of problems. But I can see no reason to believe that there are somehow true theories or solutions to problems just "waiting" to be discovered. For why should we not assume that there exist problems to which there are no solutions?

123. *Ways of Worldmaking,* Indianapolis, (1978), 6.

124. W. V. O. Quine makes a similar point in his *Word and Object,* Cambridge, Mass., (1960).

125. For a similar view in a more sociologically oriented discourse, see Peter L. Berger's and Thomas Luckmann's *The Social Construction of Reality,* New York, (1967), and Berger's *The Sacred Canopy,* New York, (1969).

126. *Opus Postumum* can be found in Kant's *Gesammelte Schriften,* Berlin, (1902–42), Vol. 21 and 22. This quotation is from Vol. 22, 497. For the translation I depend on Copleston's *A History of Philosophy,* Vol. 6, Part 2, 246.

127. Vol. 1, Chicago, (1955), 228f. My italics. See also his *Frühe Hauptwerke,* Stuttgart, (1959), esp. p. 232.

128. My impression is that we can find an interesting parallel in the Buddhist notion of *emptiness.* Because the highlight of Buddhist emptiness is not that sensory objects are pure phenomena, but that the self-identity of 'things' can only be explained in terms of *form* (laksana). However, their suprasensory and substantial self-identity can be described in terms of *essential nature* (dhaktu). This means that all perceivable things and observational objects in the world can be described in terms of form, but not in terms of what they are in their essential nature, according to Buddhism. To speak about things as "empty," therefore, means that we must not take what things seem to be, for what they really are. For what they *really* are is beyond any human comprehension, or system of description. The ultimate reality, which is nothing, is still something real, in Buddhism, which can be experienced. But in our ordinary dealing with reality, as in sensory experience of everyday life, we cannot get beyond the form of things. Therefore, when people sometimes say: 'Of course, we know that everything is really empty, since that is exactly what physics has taught us. Everything really consists of non-material energy,' the Buddhist would argue that the physical description of reality is also just a way of describing the form of things, and not its essence. Tom me this seems to come close to the warning against reductionism which I have evoked. At the same time it is also a reminder that there is a sort of transcendental dimension in our experience of this world, something which could be expressed as the "emptiness" of things.

I have mentioned this, since there has been an intense and mutual interest among both American process theologians and Buddhist thinkers in the last years concerning their different philosophies, where much effort has been put in the search for a common ground for understanding reality. See for example John B. Cobb's *Christ in a Pluralistic Age,* Philadelphia, (1975), esp. Ch. 13. However, I suspect that there might be a greater affinity between Buddhist thought on this specific point, and the sort of realism that I have tried to argue for in this book, than between Buddhism and Whitehead's realism. Because for Whitehead the ultimate reality is not beyond human comprehension and language, but something we can both understand an speak about, namely creativity. For him, creativity is what all things *are* at their absolute base, and even God, within process philosophy, is distinct from this metaphysical ultimate.

What has been said here, I have learnt from conversation with one of the leading Buddhist scholars in Japan, (now teaching at Claremont, Calif.,) Masao Abe. See also his "Mahāyāna Buddhism and Whitehead – A view by a lay student of Whitehead's philosophy," *Philosophy East and West,* Vol. 25, No. 4, publ. by The University Press of Hawaii. Informative is also his "Buddhist Nirvana: Its Significance in Contemporary Thought and Life," *The Ecumenical Review,* Vol. 25, (1973), and "Buddhism and Christianity as a Problem Today, Part II," *Japanese Religions, Vol. 3, No. 3, (1963).*

129. *Opus Postumum,* Vol. 21, 150 and 22.

130. See p. 119.

131. *Opus Postumum,* Vol. 21, 21.

132. See Dennett's "Beyond Belief" in *Thought and Object,* a forthcoming volume. Dennett has kindly made a copy of his typewritten manuscript available to me, to which I refer here.

133. See Nelson Goodman's *Ways of Worldmaking,* Indianapolis, (1978), 5.

134. Op. cit., 21f.

135. When I speak about "religion" or "religious" I refer to theistic religion, though keeping in mind that there might also be non-theistic religious belief-systems, as Buddhism, for instance, is sometimes claimed to be.

136. See here Gordon Kaufman's *An Essay on Theological Method,* Montana, (1975), 43, for a comparison with a similar view. The concept 'world,' according to Kaufman, is a "limiting idea," while the concept of 'God' functions as a "corrective of, or check on, the over-determination of our thinking which the concept of world permits and even encourages. This is because the concept of God relativizes the concept of world – thus destroying its absoluteness and finality – by holding that the world is in fact dependent upon and grounded upon something beyond itself." Kaufman also speaks about God as "the ultimate point of orientation" for human existence. See p. 51. In fact, there are many similarities between my view and Kaufman's, but also distinct differences. For instance, his language suggests that he is more of a classical realist than I am. Although he affirms that concepts like 'God' and 'world' are 'constructions' in the same sense as I do, he seems to believe that there are things objectively "given" in experience: "God, of course, is not directly perceivable: he cannot be 'pointed out' as can ordinary objects of experience, or easily evoked like feelings or other inner states. Nevertheless, the concept of God has usually been treated as though it referred to a structure or reality that was definitely *there* and *given* (as objects of experience are there and given)." Op. cit., 19.

137. For an example of a similar idea, see Anders Jeffner's *The Study of Religious Language,* London, (1972), 125, where he discusses the process of introducing a new kind of entity into our conception of reality, as a process of supplementation, by which a person might try to find a *Gestalt* in the ambiguous universe in which he lives. Jeffner's view is partly inspired by John Hick's article "Religious Faith as Experiencing – As," in

G. N. A. Vesey's (editor), *Talk of God*, London, (1969). Cf. Langdon Gilkey, *Naming the Whirlwind; The Renewal of God-language*, Indianapolis, (1969), 209.

138. Goodman, op. cit., 14.

139. Op. cit., 100. My italics.

140. *Language, Logic and God*, London, (1962), 161.

141. *Gesammelte Schriften*, Berlin, (1902–42), Vol. 22, 36f.

142. *Meaning and Necessity; A Study in Semantics and Modal Logic*, Chicago and London, (1967), 206.

143. See p. 109.

144. Iris Murdoch, *The Sovereignty of Good*, London, (1970), 17f.

145. Op. cit., 38.

146. Forthcoming under the title *Reason, Truth, and History*. This and subsequent quotations are from Chapter 6. See also footnote 111.

147. By the expression "causal theory of perception" can be meant a theory by means and in terms of which we are able to account for what we take to be the reliability of our perceptual knowledge. However, such an account can be made *within* the theory itself, namely, if it can explain how our perceptions result from the operation of transducing organs upon the so-called external world. In part this can be done by a theory of statistics and experimental design, so that it is possible to show, within the theory, how the procedures that we take to exclude experimental error really do have a tendency in the majority of cases to exclude experimental error. I owe gratitude to Putnam for having pointed this out to me.

148. Lennart Nordenfelt, *Kunskap, Värdering, Förståelse; Introduktion till humanvetenskapernas teori och metod* (Knowledge, Values, Apprehension; Introduction to the Theory and Method of the Humanities), Stockholm, (1979), 110. Lars Bergström, *Objektivitet; En undersökning av innebörden, möjligheten och önskvärdheten av objektivitet i samhällsvetenskapen* (Objectivity; An Investigation into the Meaning, Possibility, and Desirability of Objectivity in the Humanities), Stockholm, (1976), 20–29, and 66–78. My translation.

149. Kai Nielsen, *Contemporary Critique of Religion*, New York, (1971), 96.

150. Op. cit., 97.

151. Op. cit., 98f.

152. Op. cit., 99.

153. Op. cit., 100.

154. Op. cit., 104f.

155. Op. cit., 105.

156. Op. cit., 111.

157. See p. 135, 136f., 140.

158. See p. 134f.

159. The study of this kind of value experiences and their relation to what I call "frameworks for life-orientation," is one of the major tasks of my forthcoming *An Empirical Study and Analysis of Contemporary Life-philosophies among Swedish Environmentalists*, Department of Theology, Uppsala University, (1982).

160. C. J. Ducasse, *A Philosophical Scrutiny of Religion*, New York, (1953), 166.

161. See John B. Cobb's article "Buddhist Emptiness and the Christian God," in *The Journal of the American Academy of Religion*, 45/1, (1977), 17.

162. See C. Geertz's and R. Bellah's article on Religion in *International Encyclopedia of the Social Sciences,* New York, (1968), Vol. 13, 398–413.

Bibliography

Books by Alfred North Whitehead

In this study references to Alfred North Whitehead's books will be by standardized abbreviations, as listed below in the form of capitals within brackets after each title respectively. These abbreviations are introduced parenthetically in the text and are followed only by page numbers, as is common in all literature on Whitehead.

The following bibliography is not a complete list of Whitehead's writings. For such a list see, for instance, William Christian, *An Interpretation to Whitehead's Metaphysics,* New Haven, (1967).

Principia Mathematica (PM), Cambridge: Cambridge University Press, 2nd ed., 1927. (1st ed., published 1910–1913.)

An Enquiry Concerning the Principles of Natural Knowledge (PNK), 2nd ed., Cambridge: Cambridge University Press, 1925. (1st ed. published 1919.)

The Concept of Nature (CN), Cambridge: Cambridge University Press, 1920.

The Principle of Relativity (R), Cambridge: Cambridge University Press, 1922.

Science and the Modern World (SMW), New York: The Free Press, Macmillan Publishing Co., Inc., 1967. (1st ed. published 1925, to which a few references are made.)

Religion in the Making (RM), New York: A Meridian book, New American Library, Inc., 1960. (1st ed. published 1926.)

Symbolism, Its Meaning and Effect (S), New York: Macmillan, 1927.

Process and Reality, An Essay in Cosmology (PR), New York: Macmillan, 1929. References in this study are made to the 1st ed., but I have used the corrected edition published by The Free Press, Macmillan Publishing Co., Inc., New York, 1978.

The Function of Reason (FR), Boston: Beacon Press, 1958. (1st ed. 1929.)

The Aims of Education (AE), New York: Macmillan, 1929.

Adventures of Ideas (AI), New York: The Free Press, Macmillan Publishing Co., Inc., 1967. (1st ed. published 1933, to which some references in this study are made.)

Modes of Thought (MT), New York: The Free Press, Macmillan Publishing Co., Inc., 1968. (1st ed. published 1938.)

Essays in Science and Philosophy (ESP), New York: The Philosophical Library, 1947.

Encyclopedias

Edwards, P. (ed.), *Encyclopedia of Philosophy*, Vol. 1–8, New York: Macmillan Co. and The Free Press, 1972.

Marc-Wogau, K. *Filosofisk Uppslagsbok*, Stockholm: Bokförlaget Liber, 1942.

Runes, D. D. (ed.), *Dictionary of Philosophy*, Totowa, New Jersey: Littlefield, Adams & Co., 1979.

Sills, David L. (ed.), *International Encyclopedia of the Social Sciences*, Vol. 1–18, New York: Macmillan Co. and The Free Press, 1968.

Secondary Literature

Abe, Masao, "Mahāyāna Buddhism and Whitehead – A View by a lay student of Whitehead's Philosophy," *Philosophy East and West*, Vol. 25, No. 4, published by The University Press of Hawaii.

Aristotle, *Metaphysics*. The Oxford translation of Aristotle's work is published in eleven volumes, and edited by J. A. Smith and W. D. Ross, Oxford, 1908–1952.

Aquinas, Thomas, *Summa Theologiæ*, eng. tr., New York: Benziger Bros., 1947.

Baelz, Peter R., *Christian Theology and Metaphysics*, Philadelphia: Fortress Press, 1968.

Barbour, Ian, *Issues in Science and Religion*, New York: Harper & Row, 1971; *Myths, Models, and Paradigms*, New York: Harper & Row, 1976.

Barth, Karl, *Church Dogmatics*, Edinburgh: T. and T. Clark, 1936–1962.

Bellah, Robert, *Beyond Belief*, New York: Harper & Row, 1970.

Berger, Peter L., *The Social Construction of Reality*, (together with Thomas Luckmann,) New York: Anchor Books, Doubleday & Co., Inc., 1967; *The Sacred Canopy*, New York: Anchor Books, Doubleday & Co., Inc., 1969; *The Heretical Imperative*, New York: Anchor Books, Anchor Press/Doubleday & Co., Inc., 1980.

Bergmann, Gustav, *The Metaphysics of Logical Positivism*, New York: Longmans, Green, 1954.

Bergson, Henri, *L'Évolution créatrice*, Paris: Alcan, 1907; *L'Energie Spirituell*, Paris: Alcan, 1920.

Bergström, Lars, *Objektivitet; En undersökning av innebörden, möjligheten och önskvärdheten av objektivitet i samhällsvetenskapen*, Stockholm: Bokförlaget Prisma, 1976.

Blanshard, Brand, *The Nature of Thought*, London: George Allen & Unwin, Ltd., 1939.

Brentano, Franz, *Wahrheit und Evidenz*, Leipzig: F. Meiner, 1930.

Brown, Delwin, *Process Philosophy and Christian Thought,* (ed. together with Ralph E. James, Jr., and Gene Reeves,) Indianapolis: The Bobbs-Merrill Co., Inc., 1971.

Brown, Stuart C., *Do Religious Claims Make Sense?,* New York: Macmillan, 1969.

Bruner, Jerome Seymour, *Beyond the Information Given; Studies in the Psychology of Knowing,* New York: Norton, 1973.

Bråkenhielm, Carl-Reinhold, *How Philosophy Shapes Theories of Religion,* Lund: CWK, Gleerups, 1975.

Carnap, Rudolf, *Meaning and Necessity; A Study in Semantics and Modal Logic,* Chicago and London: The University of Chicago Press, 1967.

Chardin, Pierre Teil hard de, *Le Phénomène humain,* Paris: du Seuil, 1956; *Le Milieu divine,* Paris: du Seuil, 1957; *L'Avenir de l'homme,* Paris: du Seuil, 1959. Tillich, Paul, *The Protestant Era,* Chicago: University of Chicago Press, 1948;

Chisholm, Roderick M., *Theory of Knowledge,* Englewood Cliffs, New Jersey: Prentice-Hall, 1966.

Christian, William A., *An Interpretation of Whitehead's Metaphysics,* New Haven: Yale University Press, 1967.

Cobb, John B. Jr., *A Christian Natural Theology,* Philadelphia: The Westminster Press, 1965; *God and the World,* Philadelphia: The Westminster Press, 1969; *Is it too late?,* Beverly Hills: Bruce Books, 1972; "Ecology, Ethics, and Theology," *Toward a Steady-State Economy,* ed. by Herman E. Daly, San Francisco: W. H. Freeman & Co., 1973; *Christ in a Pluralistic Age,* Philadelphia: The Westminster Press, 1975; *Process Theology; An Introductory Exposition,* (together with David Ray Griffin,) Philadelphia: The Westminster Press, 1976; "Buddhist Emptiness and the Christian God," *Journal of The American Academy of Religion,* 45/1, 1977; *The Structure of Christian Existence,* New York: The Seabury Press, 1979, (first edition 1976); "Christianity and Eastern Wisdom," *Japanese Journal of Religious Studies,* Vol. 5, No. 4, 1978; "Process Theology and Environmental Issues," *The Journal of Religion,* Vol. 60, No. 4, 1980. For a complete list of Cobb's writing before 1977, see John Cobb's Theology in Process, ed. by David Ray Griffin and Thomas J. J. Altizer, Philadelphia: The Westminster Press, 1977.

Copleston, Frederick, *A History of Philosophy,* Vol. 1–8, New York: Image Books, A Division of Doubleday & Co., Inc., 1962.

Daly, Mary, *Beyond God The Father,* Boston: Beacon Press, 1974.

Dennett, Daniel, "Beyond Belief," *Thought and Object,* ed. by Androew Woodfield, Oxford: Oxford University Press, 1981.

Descartes, Renée, *The Philosophical Work of Descartes,* translated by E. S. Haldane and G. R. T. Ross, New York: Dover Publication, 1955; *Méditation Métaphysique,* Paris: Presses Universitaires De France, 1966.

Dewey, John, *Logic: The Theory of Inquiry,* New York: H. Holt & Co., 1938.

Dilley, Frank B., *Metaphysics and Religious Language,* New York: Columbia University Press, 1964.

Ducasse, C. J., *A Philosophical Scrutiny of Religion,* New York; The Ronald Press Company, 1953.

Dummett, Michael, *What is a Theory of Meaning?* 2 vols., Oxford: The Clarendon Press, 1975, 1976.

Ely, Stephen, *The Religious Availability of Whitehead's God; A Critical Analysis,* Madison, Wisconsin: University of Wisconsin Press, 1942.

Emmet, Dorothy, *The Nature of Metaphysical Thinking,* London: Macmillan, 1949.

Fabro, Cornelio, *God in Exile; Modern Atheism,* tr. by A. Gibson, Paulist, Westminster, Md. Newman Press, 1968.

Ferré, Frederick, *Language, Logic and God,* London: Eyre and Spottiswoode, 1962; "Mapping the Logic and Models in Science and Theology," *The Christian Scholar,* Vol. 46, 1963; *Basic Modern Philosophy of Religion,* New York: Charles Scribner's Sons, 1967; "Metaphors, Models and Religion," *Soundings,* Vol. 51, 1968.

Flew, Antony, "Divine Omnipotence and Human Freedom," *New Essays in Philosophical Theology,* New York: The Macmillan Co., 1955.

Frankena, William, *Ethics,* Englewood Cliffs, New Jersey: Prentice-Hall, 1963.

Galilei, Galileo, *Dialogue Concerning the Two Chief World Systems,* eng. tr. by S. Drake, Berkely: University of California Press, 1953.

Geertz, Clifford, "The Interpretation of Cultures," (together with Robert Bellah,) *International Encyclopedia of the Social Sciences,* Vol. 13, pp. 398–413, New York: Macmillan Company & The Free Press, 1968.

Gilkey, Langdon, *Maker of Heaven and Earth; A Study of the Christian Doctrine of Creation,* New York: Doubleday & Co., Inc., 1959; *Naming the Whirlwind: The Renewal of God-language,* New York: The Bobbs-Merrill Co., Inc., 1969.

Gombrich, Ernst Hans, *Art and Illusion; A Study in the Psychology of Pictorial Representation,* New York: Pantheon Books, 1960.

Goodman, Nelson, *The Structure of Appearance,* Indianapolis: The Bobbs-Merrill Co., 1966; *Ways of Worldmaking,* Indianapolis: Hackett Publishing Co., Inc., 1978; *Fact, Fiction, and Forecast,* Indianapolis: Hackett Publishing Co., Inc., 1979.

Griffin, David Ray, "Whitehead's Contribution to a Theology of Nature," *Bucknell Review,* Vol. 20, No. 3, 1972; *Process Theology; An Introductory Exposition,* (together with John Cobb,) Philadelphia: The Westminster Press, 1976; *John Cobb's Theology in Process,* (ed. together with Thomas J. J. Altizer,) Philadelphia: The Westminster Press, 1977.

Hamilton, William, "The Death of God," *Christian Scholar,* Vol. 48, 1965.

Hansson, Bo, "Vardag och evighet," *Festskrift till Hampus Lyttkens,* Lund: Doxa, 1981.

166

Hartshorne, Charles, *The Divine Relativity,* New Haven: Yale University Press, 1948.

Heidegger, Martin, *Sein und Zeit,* Halle: Max Niemeyer Verlag, 1927.

Herrmann, Eberhard, *Die logische Stellung des ontologischen Gottesbeweises in Charles Hartshornes Prozeßtheologie und neoklaßicher Metaphysik,* Lund: CWK Gleerups, 1980.

Hemberg, Jarl, *Religion och Metafysik; Axel Hägerströms och Anders Nygrens religionsteorier och dessas inflytande i svensk religionsdebatt,* Stockholm: Diakonistyrelsens Bokförlag, 1966.

Hick, John, *Faith and Knowledge,* Ithaca, New York: Cornell University Press, 1957; *Philosophy of Religion,* Englewood Cliffs, New Jersey: Prentice-Hall, 1963; *Evil and the God of Love,* London: Macmillan, 1966; "Religious Faith as Experiencing-As," *Talk of God,* ed. by G. N. A. Vesey, London: Macmillan, 1969.

Holmstrand, Ingemar, *Karl Heim on Philosophy, Science and the Transcendence of God,* Uppsala: Acta Universitatis Upsaliensis, Studia Doctrinae Christianae Upsaliensia, 1980.

Husserl, Edmund, *Ideas; General Introduction to Pure Phenomenology,* tr. by W. R. Boyce Gibson, New York: The Macmillan Company, 1931.

Høffding, Harald, *Religionsfilosofi,* København: Det Nordiske forlag, 1901.

Irenaeus, *Against the Heresis,* in *Ancient Christian Writers; The Works of the Fathers in Translation,* ed. by J. Quasten and J. C. Plumpe, Westminster, Maryland, 1946.

James, William, *The Varieties of Religious Experience; A Study in Human Nature,* New York: Longmans, Green and Co., 1952, (1st edition 1903,); *Essays in Radical Empiricism* and *A Pluralistic Universe,* New York: E. P. Dutton & Co., Inc., 1971, (1st edition 1912 and 1909, respectively).

Jeffner, Anders, *The Study of Religious Language,* London: SCM Press, Ltd., 1972.

Kaufman, Gordon D., *Relativism, Knowledge, and Faith,* Chicago: The University of Chicago Press, 1960; *God the Problem,* Cambridge, Mass.: Harvard University Press, 1972; *An Essay on Theological Method,* Missoula, Montana: Scholars Press, 1975.

Kant, Immanuel, *Gesammelte Schriften,* Berlin, 1902–42; *Critique of Practical Reason and Other Writings in Moral Philosophy,* tr. and ed. by L. W. Beck, Chicago, 1949.

Kimball, Robert H., "The Incoherence of Whitehead's Theory of Perception," *Process Studies,* Vol. 9, No. 3–4, 1979.

Kolers, Paul, *Aspects of Motion Perception,* New York: Pergamon Press, 1972.

Leclerc, Ivor, *Whitehead's Metaphysics; An Introductory Exposition,* Bloomington: Indiana University Press, 1975.

Lewis, Clarence Irving, *An Analysis of Knowledge and Valuation:* La Salle, Ill.: The Open Court Publishing Company, 1946.

Mach, Ernst, *The Analysis of Sensations, and the Relation of the Physical to the Psychical*, eng. tr. by C. M. Williams and S. Waterlow, Chicago and London: The Open Court Publishing Company, 1914.

Madden, Edward H., *Evil and the Concept of God*, (together with Peter H. Hare,) Springfield, Ill.: Charles C. Thomas Publishers, 1968.

Martin, James A., *The New Dialogue Between Philosophy and Theology*, New York: The Seabury Press, 1966.

Mays, Wolfe, *The Philosophy of Whitehead*, London: George Allen & Unwin, Ltd., 1959.

Meland, Bernhard E., *The Future of Empirical Theology*, (ed.,) Chicago: The University of Chicago Press, 1969; *Fallible Forms and Symbols; Discourses of Method in a Theology of Culture*, Philadelphia: Fortress Press, 1976.

Midgely, Mary, *Beast and Man*, Ithaca, New York: Cornell University Press, 1980.

Meinong, Alexius, *Über emotionale Präsentation*, Vienna: Alfred Hölder, 1917.

Murdoch, Iris, *The Sovereignty of Good*, London: Routledge & Kegan Paul, 1970.

Neville, Robert C., *God the Creator; On the Transcendence and Presence of God*, Chicago Press, 1968.

Newton, Isaac, *Principia. Mathematical Principles of Natural Philosphy*, eng. tr. by A. Motte and F. Cajori, Berkeley, 1946.

Niebuhr, H. Richard, *Radical Monotheism and Western Culture*, New York: Harper & Row, 1970; *The Meaning of Revelation*, New York: The Macmillan Publishing Co., Inc., 1978.

Nielsen, Kai, "Wittgensteinian Fideism," *Philosophy*, xlii, july, 1967; *Contemporary Critique of Religion*, New York: Herder & Herder, 1971.

Nordenfelt, Lennart, *Kunskap, Värdering, Förståelse; Introduktion till humanvetenskapernas teori och metod*, Stockholm: Liber förlag, 1979.

Ogden, Schubert M., "Present Prospects for Empirical Theology," *The Future of Empirical Theology*, ed. by B. E. Meland, Chicago: The University of Chicago Press, 1969; *The Reality of God*, New York: Harper & Row, 1977; "Toward a New Theism," *Process Philosophy and Christian Thought*, ed. by D. Brown, R. E. James Jr., and G. Reeves, Indianapolis: The Bobbs-Merrill Co., Inc., 1977; *Christ without Myth*, Dallas: SMU Press, 1979.

Owen, Joseph, *The Doctrine of Being in the Aristotelian Metaphysics*, Toronto: Pontifical Institute of Medieval Studies, 1951.

Pierce, Charles Sanders, *Collected Papers*, Cambridge, Mass.: Harvard University Press, 1934.

Pepper, Stephen C., *World Hypotheses*, Berkeley: University of California Press, 1970, (1st edition 1942).

Philipson, Sten M., *En stad där de kunde bo; En bok om kyrkan och storstaden*, (ed.), Stockholm: Verbum, 1975; *Bryta upp; Invit till en teologisk omprövning*, Stockholm: SKEAB förlag, 1979; "Gudstron – ett hållbart argument för människovärdet?," *Årsbok för Kristen Humanism*, 1979; *En empirisk studie och analys av livsåskådningsprofiler i samtida svensk miljörörelse,* Department of Theology, University of Uppsala, forthcoming.

Plantinga, Alvin, *God and Other Minds,* Ithaca, New York: Cornell University Press, 1967; *The Nature of Necessity,* Oxford: Clarendon Press, 1974; *God, Freedom, and Evil,* Grand Rapids: Eerdman's Publishing Company, 1977; "Reply to the Basingers on Divine Omnipotence," *Process Studies,* Vol. 11, No. 1, 1981.

Plato, *The Republic,* eng. tr. by F. M. Cornford, Oxford, 1941; *Theaetetus,* eng. tr. by F. M. Cornford, London, 1935.

Popper, Karl, *Conjectures and Refutations; The Growth of Scientific Knowledge,* London: Routledge & Kegan Paul, 1963; *The Open Society and Its Enemies,* Vol. I and II, London: Routledge & Kegan Paul, 1980, (1st edition 1945).

Putnam, Hilary, *Meaning and the moral Sciences,* Boston, London, and Henley: Routledge & Kegan Paul, 1978; *Reason, Truth, and History,* forthcoming.

Quine, W. V. O., *Word and Object,* Cambridge, Mass.: Technology Press of the MIT 1960; *From a Logical Point of View,* New York: Harper & Row, 1963.

Richmond, James, *Theology and Metaphysics,* New York: Schocken, 1971.

Rorty, Richard, *Philosophy and the Mirror of Nature,* Princeton, New Jersey: Princeton University Press, 1980.

Russell, Bertrand, *Logic and Knowledge,* ed. by R. C. March, London: George Allen & Unwin, 1956; *The Basic Writings of Bertrand Russell,* ed. by Robert E. Egner and Lester E. Denonn, New York: A Touchstone Book, 1961.

Schilpp, Paul Arthur, *The Philosophy of Alfred North Whitehead,* Evanston, Ill.: Northwestern University Press, 1941.

Segrè, Emilio, *Nuclei and Particles; An Introduction to Nuclear and Subnuclear Physics,* New York: W. A. Benjamin, 1964.

Sherburne, Donald W., *A Key to Whitehead's Process and Reality,* New York: The Macmillan Company, 1966.

Smart, J. J., *Philosophy and Scientific Realism,* London: Routledge & Kegan Paul, 1963.

Smart, Ninian, "Omnipotence, Evil and Supermen," *Philosophy,* April, 1961.

Smith, Wilfred Cantwell, *Faith and Belief,* Princeton: Princeton University Press, 1979.

Sundén, Hjalmar, *Die Religion und Die Rollen; Eine Psychologische Untersuchung der Frömmigkeit,* Berlin: Töpelmann, 1966.

Stevenson, Charles L., *Ethics and Language,* New Haven: Yale University Press, 1944.

Tillich, Paul, *The Protestant Era,* Chicago: University of Chicago Press, 1948; *Systematic Theology,* Vol. I and II, Chicago: University of Chicago Press, 1955; *Frühe Hauptwerke,* Vol. I and II, Stuttgart, 1959.

Toulmin, Stephen, *Metaphysical Beliefs,* (together with Ronald W. Hepburn and Alasdair MacIntyre,) London: SCM Press, 1957; *The Philosophy of Science; An*

Introduction, New York: Harper & Row, 1960; *Forsight and Understanding,* London: Hutchinson, 1961.

Tracy, David, *Blessed Rage for Order; The New Pluralism in Theology,* New York: Seabury Press, 1975.

Unger, Johan, *On Religious Experience; A Psychological Study,* Uppsala: Acta Universitatis Upsaliensis, Psychologia Religionum, 1976.

Warnock, G. J., "A review of 'The Logic of Scientific Discovery,'" *Mind,* N. S. Vol. 69, 1960, pp. 99–101.

Weber, Max, *On the Methodology of the Social Sciences,* tr. and ed. by E. A. Shils and H. A. Finch, Glencoe, Ill., 1949.

Whiteley, C. H., "The Cognitive Factor in Religious Experience," *Aristotelian Society Supplementary Volume 29,* 1955.

Wilson, Edward O., *On Human Nature,* Cambridge, Mass.: Harvard University Press, 1979.

Wittgenstein, Ludwig, *Philosophical Investigations,* Oxford: Basil Blackwell, 1953; *Tractatus Logico-Philosophicus,* New York: Humanities Press, 1961; *Zettle,* Oxford: Basil Blackwell, 1967.

Index of Names

Abe, Masao, 160 n.
Agar, W. E., 21.
Andronicus, 157 n.
Aquinas, Thomas, 11, 58, 74.
Aristotle, 11, 13 f., 21, 27f., 63 f., 87, 91 f., 97, 103, 149, 151 n., 152 n., 155 n., 157 n.
Augustine, 11, 74.
Ayer, Alfred A. J., 53, 94.

Bacon, Francis, 94.
Baelz, Peter R., 152 n.
Barbour, Ian, 11, 20, 153 n., 157 n.
Barth, Karl, 11, 13, 151 n.
Bellah, Robert, 162 n.
Berger, Peter L., 159 n.
Bergmann, Gustav, 157 n.
Bergson, Henri, 21, 68.
Bergström, Lars, 140, 161 n.
Berkeley, George, 119 f.
Birch, L. Charles, 21.
Blanshard, Brand, 114 f., 159 n.
Brentano, Franz, 157 n.
Brown, Stuart C., 91, 93, 105–108, 110, 116, 158 n.
Bruner, Jerome Seymour, 120, 158 n.
Bråkenhielm, Carl Reinhold, 151 n., 152 n.
Buddha, 21.

Calderon, 104.
Carnap, Rudolf, 32, 94, 130 f.
Cassirer, Ernst, 120.
Chardin, Pierre Teilhard de, 21.
Chisholm, Roderick M., 88, 113, 152 n., 156 n., 157 n.
Christian, William A., 155 n.
Cobb, John B., 21, 54 f., 57, 61 f., 79, 81, 154 n., 155 n., 156 n., 160 n.
Comte, Auguste, 94.
Copleston, Frederick, 151 n., 157 n., 158 n., 159 n.

Daly, Mary, 22.
Descartes, 24, 27, 33, 38, 41, 48, 50, 52, 74, 91, 94, 102–108, 132, 137, 142, 153 n., 157 n.
Democritus, 98, 104.
Dennett, Daniel, 126, 160 n.
Devettererre, Raymond J., 152 n.
Dewey, John, 16, 132.
Dilley, Frank B., 152 n.
Ducasse, C. J., 148, 161 n.
Dummett, Michael, 158 n.

Ely, Stephen L., 156 n.
Emmet, Dorothy, 152 n.

Fabro, Cornelio, 156 n.
Ferré, Frederick, 113, 128, 152 n.
Flew, Antony, 156 n.

Galilei, Galileo, 38 f., 45, 48, 50, 94, 99, 102, 104, 111, 133.
Gassendi, Pierre, 105.
Geertz, Clifford, 162 n.
Gilkey, Langdon, 87, 156 n., 161 n.
Gombrich, Ernst Hans, 120, 158 n.
Goodman, Nelson, 111, 113, 117, 119 f., 127 f., 158 n., 160 n., 161 n.
Griffin, David Ray, 54–57, 61, 73, 81, 154 n.

Hamilton, William, 12.
Hansson, Bo, 152 n.
Hare, Peter H., 156 n.
Hartshorne, Charles, 21, 58.
Hegel, Friedrich, 21, 97, 119.
Hempel, Carl Gustaf, 94.
Heidegger, Martin, 152 n.
Heisenberg, Werner, 99.
Hemberg, Jarl, 151 n.
Heraclitus, 21.
Herrmann, Eberhard, 155 n.
Hick, John, 76, 160 n.
Hof, Hans, 151 n.
Hume, David, 32, 94, 153 n.
Husserl, Edmund, 126.

172

Hägerström, Axel, 151 n.
Høffding, Harald, 158 n.

Irenaeus, 77 f.
Irving, John, 126.

James, William, 16, 23, 31, 65, 68, 96, 101, 152 n., 153 n., 154 n.
Jeffner, Anders, 113, 151 n., 157 n., 160 n.
Jesus Christ, 72, 77 f.

Kant, Immanuel, 11, 13, 15, 21, 32, 91, 97, 103, 109, 120, 123–125, 128, 143, 151 n., 159 n.
Kaufman, Gordon D., 12, 151 n., 152 n., 160 n.
Keller, Helen, 126.
Kimball, Robert H., 85 f., 156 n.

La Mettrie, Julien Offray de, 105.
Leclerc, Ivor, 153 n.
Leibniz, Gottfried Wilhelm, 74.
Locke, John, 32.
Luckmann, Thomas, 159 n.

Mach, Ernst, 15, 94.
Madden, Edvard H., 156 n.
Malcolm, Norman, 145.
Martin, James A., 152 n.
Maxwell, James Clerk, 110.
Meinong, A., 156 n.
Meland, Bernard E., 21, 153 n.
Midgley, Mary, 98.
Mill, John Stuart, 94.
Montague, William P., 31.
Moore, G. E., 31.
Murdoch, Iris, 41, 88, 108, 135 f.

Neville, Robert C., 156 n.
Newton, Isaac, 24, 39, 45, 48, 56, 91, 94 f., 98 f., 104 f., 111.
Niebuhr, Reinhold and H. Richard, 31, 81.
Nielsen, Kai, 144–146, 161 n.
Nordenfelt, Lennart, 140, 161 n.
Nunn, T. P., 31.
Nygren, Anders, 151 n.

24